Contents at a Glance

Table of Contents

About the Authors

Craig James Johnston has been involved with technology since his high school days at Glenwood High in Durban, South Africa, when his school was given some Apple][Europluses. From that moment, technology captivated him, and he has owned, supported, evangelized, and written about it.

Craig has been involved in designing and supporting large-scale enterprise networks with integrated email and directory services since 1989. He has held many different IT-related positions in his career, ranging from sales support engineer to mobile architect for a 40,000-smartphone infrastructure at a large bank.

You can see Craig's previously published work in his books *Professional BlackBerry*, *My iMovie*, and many other *My* series books that cover devices by BlackBerry, Palm, HTC, Motorola, Samsung, and Google.

Craig also enjoys high-horsepower, high-speed vehicles and tries very hard to keep to the speed limit while driving them.

Originally from Durban, South Africa, Craig has lived in the United Kingdom, the San Francisco Bay Area, and New Jersey, where he now lives with his wife, Karen, and a couple of cats.

Craig would love to hear from you. Feel free to contact Craig about your experiences with *My Samsung Galaxy S6* at http://www.CraigsBooks.info.

All comments, suggestions, and feedback—both positive and negative—are welcome.

Eric Butow began writing books in 2000 when he wrote *Master Visually Windows 2000 Server*. Since then, Eric has authored or coauthored 26 other books. Those books include Addison-Wesley's *User Interface Design for Mere Mortals*, Amacom's *How to Succeed in Business Using LinkedIn*, Wiley Publishing's *Droid Companion*, Wiley Publishing's *Google Glass For Dummies*, Que Publishing's *Blogging to Drive Business,* Second Edition, and Que Publishing's *My Samsung Galaxy Tab S*.

Eric lives in Jackson, California. He has a master's degree in communication from California State University, Fresno, and is the owner of Butow Communications Group (BCG), an online marketing ROI improvement firm.

Website: http://butow.net

LinkedIn: http://linkedin.com/in/ebutow

Dedication

"I love deadlines. I like the whooshing sound they make as they fly by."
—Douglas Adams

To everyone who never gave up on me.
—Eric Butow

Acknowledgments

We would like to express our deepest gratitude to the following people on the *My Samsung Galaxy S6* team who all worked extremely hard on this book:

- Michelle Newcomb, our acquisitions editor, who worked with us to give this project an edge

- Christian Kenyeres, our technical editor, who double-checked our writing to ensure the technical accuracy of this book

- Charlotte Kughen, who edited the manuscript skillfully

- Betsy Gratner, who kept the book project on schedule

- Gloria Schurick, who combined the text and art into colorful pages.

We Want to Hear from You!

As the reader of this book, *you* are our most important critic and commentator. We value your opinion and want to know what we're doing right, what we could do better, what areas you'd like to see us publish in, and any other words of wisdom you're willing to pass our way.

We welcome your comments. You can email or write to let us know what you did or didn't like about this book—as well as what we can do to make our books better.

Please note that we cannot help you with technical problems related to the topic of this book.

When you write, please be sure to include this book's title and author as well as your name and email address. We will carefully review your comments and share them with the authors and editors who worked on the book.

Email: feedback@quepublishing.com

Mail: Que Publishing
ATTN: Reader Feedback
800 East 96th Street
Indianapolis, IN 46240 USA

Reader Services

Visit our website and register this book at quepublishing.com/register for convenient access to any updates, downloads, or errata that might be available for this book.

Samsung Galaxy S6

Samsung Galaxy S6 edge

In this chapter, you become familiar with the external features of the Galaxy S6 and the basics of getting started with the Android operating system. Topics include the following:

→ Getting to know your Galaxy S6's external features
→ Learning the fundamentals of Android 5.0 (Lollipop) and TouchWiz
→ Setting up your Galaxy S6 for the first time
→ Installing desktop synchronization software

Getting to Know Your Galaxy S6

Before you start customizing your Galaxy S6 and working with apps, you should examine the external features, device features, and the Android 5.0 operating system.

In addition to Android 5.0 (Lollipop), this chapter covers the Samsung TouchWiz interface, which is overlaid on top of Android to adjust the way things look and function.

Your Galaxy S6's External Features

Becoming familiar with the external features of your Galaxy S6 is a good place to start because you will be using them often. This section covers some of the technical specifications of your Galaxy S6, including the touchscreen and camera. There are two versions of the Samsung Galaxy S6: the S6 and the S6 edge. With the exception of a few extra features provided by the curved screen on the S6 edge, the functionality and look and feel of the interface on the two phones are exactly the same.

Front

- **Proximity/gesture sensor**—Detects when you place your Galaxy S6 against your head to talk, which causes it to turn off the screen so that your ear doesn't inadvertently activate any onscreen items. This sensor also allows you to use gestures (in conjunction with the accelerometer). Gestures are covered later in the chapter.
- **Light sensor**—Adjusts the brightness of your Galaxy S6's screen based on the brightness of the ambient light.
- **Earpiece**—The part you hold against your ear while on a call.
- **Indicator light**—Indicates new events (such as missed calls, new Facebook messages, and new emails).
- **Front camera**—A 5.0-megapixel front-facing camera that you use for video chat, taking self-portraits, and even unlocking your Galaxy S6 using your face.

- **Touchscreen**—The Galaxy S6 has a 5.1" 1440×2560 pixel Quad HD Super AMOLED (Super Active-Matrix Organic Light-Emitting Diode) screen that incorporates capacitive touch. The Galaxy S6 edge has a 5.1" 1440×2560 pixel Quad HD Super AMOLED (Super Active-Matrix Organic Light-Emitting Diode), dual-edge screen that incorporates capacitive touch.
- **Back button**—Tap to go back one screen when using an application or menu. This is a touch-sensitive button.
- **Recent Apps button**—Tap to see a list of apps you recently used. You can then touch to jump to them or swipe them off the screen to close them. Touch and hold to see additional options for the current screen. The Recent Apps button replaces the Menu button on previous Galaxy S series phones.
- **Home button/fingerprint reader**—A physical button that you press to go to the Home screen. The application that you are using continues to run in the background. Press twice to launch the Camera app. Press and hold to launch Google Now. A fingerprint reader is built in to the Home button; you can read more about it in Chapter 1, "Making the S6 Your Own."

Back

Noise-canceling microphone

Infrared port

SIM card tray (S6 edge)

Rear camera

LED camera flash

Volume up/down buttons

Power button

Heart rate sensor

SIM card tray (S6)

- **Volume up/down buttons**—Enable you to control the audio volume on calls and while playing audio and video.
- **Power button**—Allows you to wake up your Galaxy S6 by pressing once. Press and hold for one second to reveal a menu of choices. The choices enable you to power off your S6, put it into Airplane mode (all radios turned off), restart your S6, or put it into Emergency mode. In Emergency mode, your S6 greatly reduces battery usage and starts reporting its location to a chosen contact.
- **Rear camera**—A 16-megapixel camera with autofocus and Optical Image Stabilization (OIS) that takes clear pictures close up or far away.
- **LED (light-emitting diode) camera flash**—Helps to illuminate the surroundings when you're taking pictures in low light.
- **Heart rate sensor**—While using the S Health app, place your finger over the heart rate sensor to allow S Health to detect your heart rate.
- **SIM card tray**—Use the SIM card tray ejection tool provided in the box to eject the SIM card tray and insert a new or replacement SIM card. On the S6, the SIM card tray is on the right side under the Power button, but because of the S6 edge's curved screen, the tray is located on the top of the device on that model.
- **Infrared port**—Allows you to control your television from your S6 using an infrared signal.
- **Noise-canceling microphone**—Use in conjunction with the regular microphone to reduce background noise during phone calls. This microphone is also used when you record videos.

Bottom

3.5mm
headphone jack

MHL 3.0–compliant
Micro USB 2 port

Speaker

Microphone

- **MHL 3.0–compliant Micro USB 2 port**—You can use the Micro USB 2 port to synchronize your Galaxy S6 to your desktop computer and charge it, but because it is Mobile High-definition Link (MHL) compliant, you can use it to play movies on your TV via high-definition multimedia interface (HDMI) using a special cable or dock. Read more about MHL 3.0 at http://en.wikipedia.org/wiki/Mobile_High-Definition_Link#MHL_3.0_features.
- **Microphone**—You use the microphone when you are on a call and holding your Galaxy S6 to your ear.
- **Speaker**—The speaker is used when you use the speakerphone function while on a phone call, and it is also used to play all audio, including notifications, music, and audio from videos.
- **3.5mm headphone jack**—Plug in your Galaxy S6 or third-party headset to enjoy music and talk on the phone.

Gestures and Motions

Gestures and motions allow you to quickly use certain functions or features by making hand gestures or moving the S6 in a specific way.

- **Direct Call**—While you are looking at a missed call, reading an SMS (text message) from someone, or viewing someone's contact information, if you lift your S6 to your ear and hold it there, the phone number being viewed will be dialed.

- **Smart Alert**—If you have missed calls or messages, when you pick up your S6 from a flat surface, it vibrates.

- **Mute**—To mute incoming calls and alarms, either place your hand over the screen or turn your S6 over.

- **Palm Swipe to Capture**—You can capture a screenshot by holding your palm perpendicular to the screen, touching it on the screen, and swiping it from left to right or right to left. The captured screenshot goes to the Screenshots album, which you can view using the Gallery or Photos app.

First-time Setup

Before setting up your new Samsung Galaxy S6, you should have a Google account because your Galaxy S6 running Android is tightly integrated with Google. When you have a Google account, you can store your content—including any books and music you buy or movies you rent—in the Google cloud. If you do not already have a Google account, go to https://accounts.google.com on your desktop computer and sign up for one.

1. Press and hold the Power button until you see the animation start playing.

2. Tap to change your language if needed.

3. Tap the right arrow to continue.

4. Tap a Wi-Fi network you want to connect to during setup. If you'd rather not connect to a Wi-Fi network, tap Next and continue at Step 8.

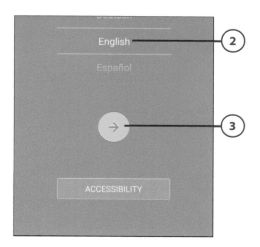

Why Use Wi-Fi During Setup

As you go through the first-time setup of your S6, you may choose to restore a backup of a previous device to your S6, and at the end of the device setup, a number of apps may need to be updated. Both of these activities can use a lot of data. Using Wi-Fi speeds up these activities as well as saves you the cost of the cellular data charges. Therefore, although you do not have to connect to a Wi-Fi network for device setup, it is advisable.

Tap to turn Wi-Fi on

Tap to skip and use cellular data

5. Enter the password for the Wi-Fi network using the onscreen keyboard.

6. Tap Connect. Your Galaxy S6 connects to the Wi-Fi network.

7. Tap Next.

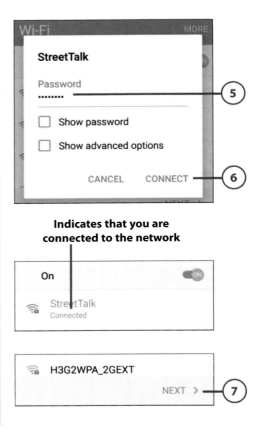

Indicates that you are connected to the network

>>>Go Further
SMART NETWORK SWITCH

Smart network switch is a feature that, once enabled, allows your S6 to seamlessly switch between the two Wi-Fi bands (2.4GHz and 5GHz) and cellular data to maintain a stable Internet connection. Your S6 constantly analyzes its connection to the Internet and switches between Wi-Fi networks operating on 2.4GHz and 5GHz to provide the best connection, and if the Wi-Fi connectivity becomes poor, it switches to the cellular data network. Bear in mind that with this option enabled you might start seeing higher cellular data usage, especially in areas where Wi-Fi is unstable, slow, or overcrowded. To enable Smart Network Switch, after your device is set up, tap Settings, Wi-Fi, More, Smart Network Switch.

8. Check the box to allow Samsung to collect diagnostic and usage data from your S6.

9. Tap Next.

10. Tap Agree after you have read and understood the End User License Agreement (EULA).

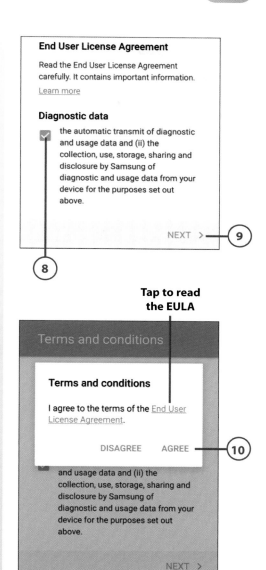

End User License Agreement

Read the End User License Agreement carefully. It contains important information.

Learn more

Diagnostic data

☑ the automatic transmit of diagnostic and usage data and (ii) the collection, use, storage, sharing and disclosure by Samsung of diagnostic and usage data from your device for the purposes set out above.

NEXT >

Tap to read the EULA

Terms and conditions

Terms and conditions

I agree to the terms of the End User License Agreement.

DISAGREE   AGREE

and usage data and (ii) the collection, use, storage, sharing and disclosure by Samsung of diagnostic and usage data from your device for the purposes set out above.

NEXT >

11. If you have another Android device (tablet or smartphone) running Android 5.0 (Lollipop) and you want to transfer the data from it to your new phone, follow the instructions on this screen, or tap Skip to continue.

12. Enter your Google account email address (your Gmail address).

13. Tap Next.

14. Enter your Google account password.

15. Tap Next to continue.

16. Tap Accept to continue.

17. Tap to select a backup from a previous device, or select Setup as New Device to skip restoring an old backup and set your S6 up as a new device.

18. Tap to select which apps to restore from the backup you selected in Step 17. This option is not visible if you chose to set up a new device in Step 17.

19. Tap Next to continue.

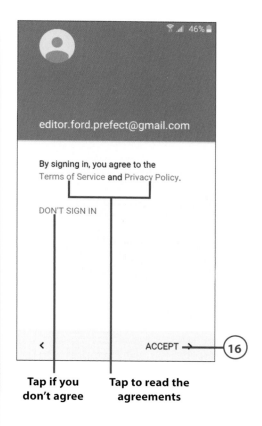

Tap if you don't agree   **Tap to read the agreements**

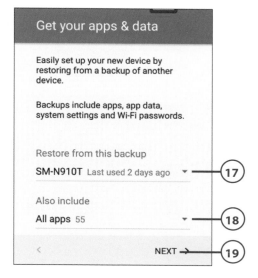

20. Check this box if you want to back up your phone's data so that it can be restored to a new Android phone or smartphone in the future.

21. Check this box if you are okay with Google collecting information about your geographic location at any time. Although Google keeps this information safe, if you are concerned about privacy rights, you should uncheck this box.

22. Check this box if you are okay with your phone scanning for Wi-Fi networks even if you have the Wi-Fi radio turned off. This helps improve location accuracy.

23. Check this box if you are okay letting Google collect diagnostic information about your phone and the apps running on it.

24. Tap Next to continue.

25. Tap to sign in to your Samsung account if you have one, or tap Skip and jump to Step 33.

Create a Samsung account using your Google account ID

Create a Samsung account

>>>*Go Further*

DO I NEED A SAMSUNG ACCOUNT?

Android was designed to be used with a Google account. That Google account enables you to access the Google ecosystem of Android apps, music, movies, and books; plus, your phone's settings are backed up to the Google cloud. If you change devices, your new device reverts to the way you had your old device set up. A Samsung account does a similar thing, but it uses the Samsung ecosystem. If you would like to take advantage of the extra Samsung services on your S6, such as the Galaxy app store, the ability to locate your lost device, or to keep track of your S Health diet and health information, you should sign up for a Samsung account.

26. Enter the email address you used for your Samsung account.

27. Enter your Samsung account password.

28. Tap Sign In.

29. Check the box to agree to all of Samsung's terms and conditions.

30. Tap Agree.

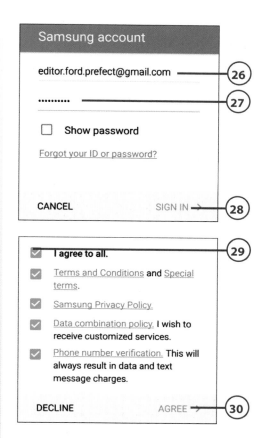

31. Check the box to enable automatically backing up your data to your Samsung account.

32. Tap Later.

33. Tap Set to set your wake-up command for Samsung's S Voice. When this is set, you can say your wake-up phrase (like "Hi Galaxy") plus a command such as "Call Charlie mobile," and your S6 performs that task for you. You can also tap Later and skip to Step 37.

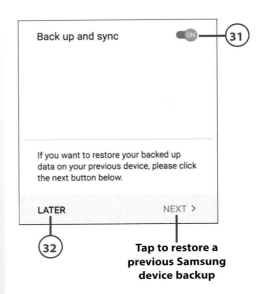

If you want to restore your backed up data on your previous device, please click the next button below.

LATER   NEXT >

Tap to restore a previous Samsung device backup

Set wake-up command

S Voice helps you control your device with your voice. Use your voice to easily wake up your device, open apps, make calls, and more.

LATER   SET →

Tap to do this later

34. Hold your S6 about 8–12 inches (20–30 cm) from your mouth and tap Start.

35. Follow the on-screen prompts to say your wake-up command four times. The screen automatically advances after four successful attempts.

20 - 30 cm
(8 - 12 inches)

START→ (34)

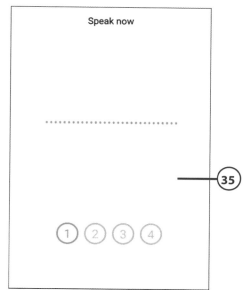

Speak now

(35)

(1) (2) (3) (4)

36. Tap Done.

37. Tap Add to add one or more fingerprints via the fingerprint reader in the Home button, which enables you to use your fingerprint to unlock your S6, sign in to certain services, and activate Samsung Pay. Tap Later to add your fingerprints later, and skip to Step 43.

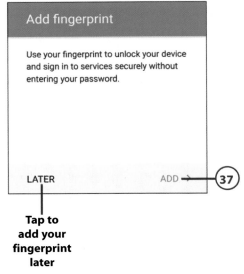

Tap to add your fingerprint later

38. Follow the on-screen instructions to add your fingerprint. This involves placing your finger on the Home button lightly (so as not to press it) and then lifting your finger when you feel the vibration. You repeat this action multiple times until your S6 has added your entire fingerprint.

39. Enter a backup password that you can use if your S6 is having trouble recognizing your fingerprint. The password must be at least six characters long and must contain at least one letter and one number.

40. Tap Continue.

41. Retype your backup password.

42. Tap OK.

43. Tap to turn the switch on if you want your S6 to use Easy mode. Easy mode uses a simplified Home screen layout, plus enlarges the text and size of the app icons. You can always disable Easy mode later if you decide it's not for you.

44. Tap Finish to complete your S6's setup. Depending on the wireless provider you are using, after you finish the device setup, you may see some extra screens that are specific to your wireless provider.

Fundamentals of Android 5.0 and TouchWiz

Your Galaxy S6 is run by an operating system called Android. Android was created by Google to run on any smartphone, and your Galaxy S6 uses a version called Android 5.0 (or Lollipop). Samsung has made many changes to this version of Android by adding extra components and modifying many standard Android features. They call this customization TouchWiz.

The Lock Screen

If you haven't used your Galaxy S6 for a while, the screen goes blank to conserve battery power. This task explains how to interact with the Lock screen.

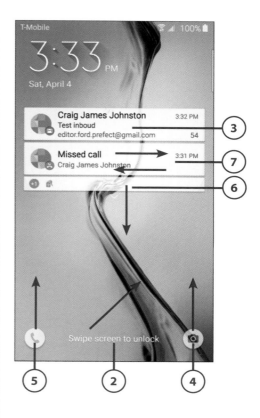

1. Press the Power button or Home button to wake up your Galaxy S6. It is better to press the Home button, especially if you are making use of the fingerprint reader to unlock your S6.

2. Slide your finger across the screen in any direction to unlock your Galaxy S6.

3. Tap a notification, such as a missed call or new email notification, and then swipe the screen to unlock and go directly to the call log or email message.

4. Swipe up from the Camera icon to launch the Camera.

5. Swipe up from the Phone icon to launch the Phone.

6. Swipe the notifications down if you want to see more of them.

7. Swipe the notifications left or right to dismiss them.

Working with Settings on the Lock Screen

You can work with settings right on the Lock screen. Swipe down from the top of the screen to show the Quick Settings. You see the Quick Settings plus any notifications. Tap Clear to clear all notifications.

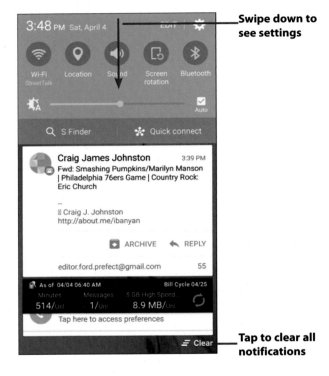

Swipe down to see settings

Tap to clear all notifications

Answering a Call from the Lock Screen

If your Galaxy S6 is locked when a call comes in, you have three choices: Drag the green icon to the right to answer the incoming call; drag the red icon to the left to reject the incoming call and send it straight to voicemail; or drag up from the bottom of the screen to reject the call and send a preset text message (SMS) to the caller.

Drag to answer

Drag to reject

Slide up to reject and send a text message

The Home Screen

After you unlock your Galaxy S6, you are presented with the Home screen. Your Galaxy S6 has four Home screen panes (although you can create more). The Home screen panes contain application shortcuts, a Launcher icon, Notification Panel, Shortcuts, Favorites Tray, and widgets.

Notification icons

Notification Panel

Widgets

App shortcut

App folder

Swipe left and right to see all Home screen panes

Favorites Tray

Launcher icon

- **Notification Panel**—The Notification Panel shows information about Bluetooth, Wi-Fi, and cellular coverage, as well as the battery level and time. The Notification Panel also serves as a place where apps can alert or notify you using notification icons.

- **Notification icons**—Notification icons appear in the Notification Panel when an app needs to alert or notify you of something. For example, the Phone app can show the Missed Calls icon, indicating that you missed a call.

- **Widgets**—Widgets are applications that run directly on the Home screens. They are specially designed to provide functionality and real-time information. An example of a widget is one that shows the current weather or provides a search capability. Widgets can be moved and sometimes resized.

- **App shortcut**—When you tap an app shortcut, the associated app launches.

- **App folders**—You can group apps together in a folder as a way to organize your apps and declutter your screen.

- **Favorites Tray**—The Favorites Tray is visible on all Home screen panes. You can drag apps to the Favorites Tray so that they are available no matter which Home screen pane you are looking at. You can rearrange or remove apps in the Favorites Tray.

- **Launcher icon**—Tap to show application icons for all applications that you have installed on your Galaxy S6.

The Special Home Screen Pane: Briefing

If you swipe all the way to the left-most Home screen pane, you will see the Briefing app. The Briefing app is a portal for news including business, technology, celebrity, science, entertainment, style, food, and travel. Scroll up and down to see all news feeds. Tap the Menu icon to customize each news topic, and rearrange the topic layout. Swipe left to return to the first Home screen pane.

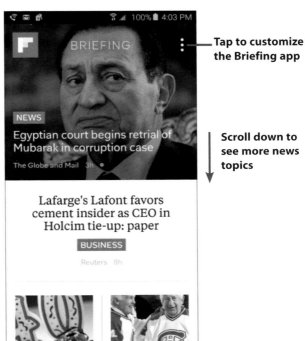

Tap to customize the Briefing app

Scroll down to see more news topics

Work with Notifications

To interact with notifications that appear in the Notification Panel, place your finger above the top of the screen and drag to pull down the Notification Panel and reveal the notifications. Swipe individual notifications off the screen to the left or right to clear them one by one, or tap Clear to clear all of them at once. The Notification Panel also includes Quick Settings, such as the ability to turn on or off Wi-Fi or Bluetooth.

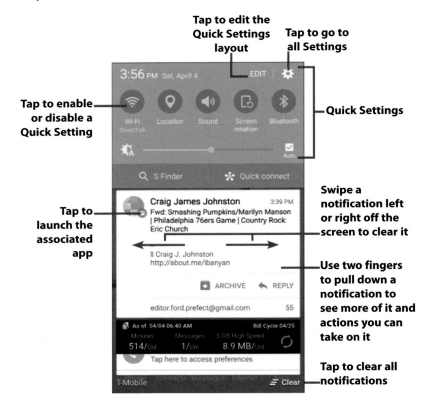

Tap to edit the Quick Settings layout

Tap to go to all Settings

Tap to enable or disable a Quick Setting

Quick Settings

Tap to launch the associated app

Swipe a notification left or right off the screen to clear it

Use two fingers to pull down a notification to see more of it and actions you can take on it

Tap to clear all notifications

What Are Quick Settings?

Quick Settings are icons that allow quick on/off actions. Examples are turning Wi-Fi on or off and turning Bluetooth on or off. You cannot change the settings for items; you can only turn them on or off. To change the settings for these items, you need to tap the cog icon to go to the full Settings screen. Tapping Edit enables you to rearrange the Quick Setting icon positions and choose which ones are visible.

Create App Shortcuts

Tap the Launcher icon to see all of your apps. Touch and hold on the app you want to make a shortcut for. After the Home screen appears, drag the app shortcut to the location you want the shortcut to be on the Home screen, drag it to an app folder, or drag it left or right off the screen to move between Home screen panes. Release the icon to place it.

Touch and hold an app icon

Drag to where you want the icon and release it

Drag the icon to the right-most pane to create a new Home screen pane and place the icon on it

Drag between Home screen panes

Create App Folders

To create a new app folder, touch and hold the first app shortcut you want in your folder and drag it on top of the second app shortcut you want in your folder. After you give your app folder a name, tap outside the folder to see the folder on your Home screen. Now you can drag other app shortcuts into that folder. To open the folder, tap it to reveal the shortcuts in that folder.

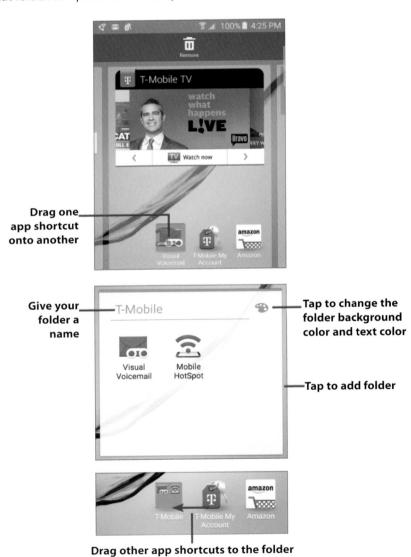

Drag one app shortcut onto another

Give your folder a name

Tap to change the folder background color and text color

Tap to add folder

Drag other app shortcuts to the folder

Create a New Home Screen Pane and Remove an App Shortcut

If you want to create a new Home screen pane, touch and hold an app shortcut icon. Drag your app shortcut icon to the Create Page icon (the plus symbol), and the shortcut is placed on a brand-new Home screen pane. To remove an app shortcut icon, drag it to the Remove icon.

Drag an app shortcut icon to the Remove icon to delete it from the Home screen pane

Drag an app shortcut icon to the right-most pane to put it on a new Home screen pane

Use the Touchscreen

You interact with your Galaxy S6 mostly by touching the screen, which is known as making gestures on the screen. You can tap, swipe, pinch, touch and hold, double-tap, and type.

- **Tap**—To start an application, tap its icon. Tap a menu item to select it. Tap the letters of the onscreen keyboard to type.

- **Touch and hold**—Touch and hold to interact with an object. For example, if you touch and hold a blank area of the Home screen, a menu pops up. If you touch and hold an icon, you can reposition it with your finger.

- **Drag**—Dragging always starts with a touch and hold. For example, if you touch the Notification Panel, you can drag it down to read all of the notification messages.

- **Swipe or slide**—Swipe or slide the screen to scroll quickly. To swipe or slide, move your finger across the screen quickly. Be careful not to touch and hold before you swipe or you will reposition something. You can also swipe to clear notifications or close apps when viewing the recent apps.

- **Double-tap**—Double-tapping is like double-clicking a mouse on a desktop computer. Tap the screen twice in quick succession. For example, you can double-tap a web page to zoom in to part of that page.

- **Pinch**—To zoom in and out of images and pages, place your thumb and forefinger on the screen. Pinch them together to zoom out or spread them apart to zoom in (unpinching). Applications such as Browser, Gallery, and Maps support pinching.

- **Rotate the screen**—If you rotate your Galaxy S6 from an upright position to being on its left or right side, the screen switches from portrait view to landscape view. Most applications honor the screen orientation. The Home screens and Launcher do not.

Use the Keyboard

Your Galaxy S6 has a virtual or onscreen keyboard for those times when you need to enter text. You might be a little wary of a keyboard that has no physical keys, but you will be pleasantly surprised at how well it works.

Most applications automatically show the keyboard when you need to enter text. If the keyboard does not appear, tap the area where you want to type and the keyboard slides up, ready for use.

Tap to capitalize the next character

Double-tap to engage CAPS Lock

Tap for numbers and symbols

Tap to speak the text

As you type, your Galaxy S6 makes word suggestions. Think of this as similar to the spell checker you would see in a word processor. Your Galaxy S6 uses a dictionary of words to guess what you are typing. If the word you were going to type is the middle option in the list of suggestions, tap space or period to select it. If you can see the word in the list but it is not the middle word, tap the word to select it.

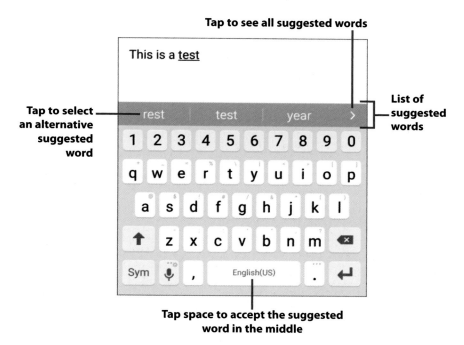

Tap to see all suggested words

Tap to select an alternative suggested word

List of suggested words

Tap space to accept the suggested word in the middle

>>>Go Further
NEXT WORD SUGGESTION

When you are between typing words, the keyboard tries to predict the next word you want to type. (In this example I typed "This is a test"; the keyboard is suggesting that the most obvious word I want to type next is "drive," but it is also showing that I might want to type "of" or end the sentence with a period.) All you need to do is tap the correct word, and the keyboard types it for you. If the keyboard is not showing a word that you want to use, simply continue typing. The more you type, the more the keyboard learns how you write and the better it will become at suggesting the next words you are likely to type.

This is a test |

List of suggested next words

Tap a suggested next word to use it

Tap to see all suggested next words

To make the next letter you type a capital letter, tap the Shift key. To make all letters capitals (or CAPS), double-tap the Shift key to engage CAPS Lock. Tap Shift again to disengage CAPS Lock.

To type numbers or symbols, tap the Symbols key. When on the Numbers and Symbols screen, tap the Symbols key to see extra symbols. There are two screens of symbols. Tap the ABC key to return to the regular keyboard.

Tap to see more symbols

Tap to return to letters

Quick Access to Symbols

If you want to type commonly used symbols, touch and hold the period key. A small window opens with those common symbols. Tap a symbol to type it or tap the Sym icon to see all symbols.

Touch and hold to see common symbols

To enter an accented character, touch and hold any vowel or the C, N, or S key. A small window opens enabling you to select an accented or alternative character. Slide your finger over the accented character and lift your finger to type it.

Touch and hold for accented characters

To reveal other alternative characters, touch and hold any other letter, number, or symbol.

Want a Larger Keyboard?

Turn your Galaxy S6 sideways to switch to a landscape keyboard. The landscape keyboard has larger keys and is easier to type on.

Landscape keyboard

Swipe to Type

Instead of typing on the keyboard in the traditional way by tapping each letter individually, you can swipe over the letters in one continuous movement. This is called Swiftkey Flow. It is enabled by default; to use it, just start swiping your finger over the letters of the word you want to type. Lift your finger after each word. No need to worry about spaces because your Galaxy S6 adds them for you. To type a double letter (as in the word *pool*), loop around that letter on the keyboard. As you swipe, a blue line trails your finger.

Dictation—Speak Instead of Type

Your Galaxy S6 can turn your voice into text. It uses Google's speech recognition service, which means you must have a connection to the cellular network or a Wi-Fi network to use it.

1. Tap the microphone key.

2. Wait until you see the green microphone icon and start speaking what you want to be typed. You can speak the punctuation by saying "comma," "question mark," "exclamation mark," or "exclamation point."

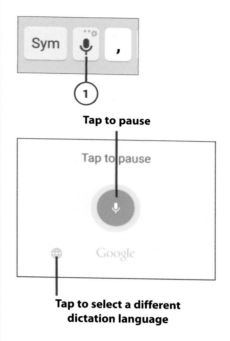

Tap to pause

Tap to select a different dictation language

Edit Text

After you enter text, you can edit it by cutting, copying, or pasting the text. This task describes how to select and cut text so you can paste over a word with the cut text.

1. While you are typing, touch and hold a word you want to copy.

2. Slide the blue end markers until you have selected all of the text you want to copy.

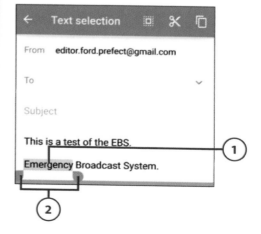

3. Tap to cut the text. Cutting text places it in the Clipboard, just like a Copy action would do.

4. Touch and hold the word you want to paste over.

5. Tap to paste what you cut earlier.

Tap to copy the selected text

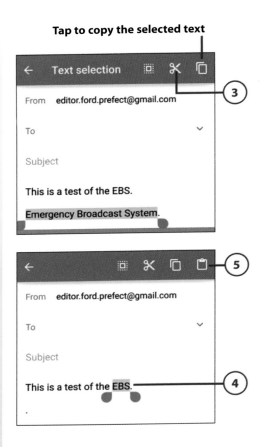

Placing a Cursor

You can also simply place a cursor on the screen and move it around to do manual text editing, such as backspace to delete letters or manually insert a new word. To do this, tap the screen in the text area. A single blue marker displays; drag that marker to the point in the text where you want to make changes. Start typing or tap backspace, and the action occurs at the cursor position.

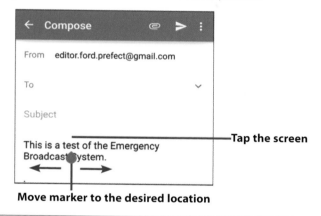

Tap the screen

Move marker to the desired location

Keyboard Tricks

You can write instead of typing, use emoticons (smiley faces), and enable a one-handed keyboard.

1. Touch and hold the microphone key (to the right of the Sym key).

2. Tap to use dictation.

3. Tap to see everything you have previously copied to the clipboard. If there is text, you can touch it to paste it at the cursor position.

4. Tap to type emoticons (smiley faces).

5. Tap to choose a one-handed keyboard.

6. Tap to change keyboard settings, including choosing a new keyboard.

>>>*Go Further*

ONE-HANDED TYPING

If you would prefer to have the ability to type with one hand, you can choose the one-handed keyboard mode. This mode squashes the keyboard so that you can type with one thumb. To enable one-handed mode, follow Steps 1 and 5 in the "Keyboard Tricks" task. Drag the shrunken keyboard anywhere on the screen where it is comfortable for you to type with one hand. Repeat Steps 1 and 5 in the "Keyboard Tricks" task to revert to the normal keyboard.

Drag the keyboard

Menus

Your Galaxy S6 has two types of menus: app menus and context menus. All applications use an app menu. To see the app menu, tap the Menu icon, which is normally on the top-right of the screen. As an alternative (but slower) method, you can touch and hold the Recent Apps button to see the app menu.

>>>*Go Further*

OLDER APPS AND THE MENU BUTTON

Some older Android apps that have not been updated to handle newer model Samsung devices may not display the regular Menu icon (three vertical dots) because they think that the Samsung phone has a physical Menu button.

Because newer Samsung phones (including your Galaxy S6) now no longer have a physical Menu button, if you suspect that the app you are using should have a Menu icon, touch and hold the Recent Apps button to trigger the app menu.

Touch and hold for the menu

Tap to see the app menu

A context menu applies to an item on the screen. If you touch and hold something on the screen (in this example, a link on a web page), a context menu appears. The items on the context menu are based on the type of object you touched.

Touch and hold a link to reveal the link context menu

Switch Between Apps

You can switch between running apps as well as close apps using the multitasking feature.

1. Tap the Recent Apps button (to the left of the Home button).

2. Scroll up and down the list of running apps.

3. Tap an app to switch to it.

4. Touch and hold an app icon to see memory and processor usage for each active app.

5. Tap to open the app in split-screen mode. This opens the app so that it only takes up the top half of the screen. See more about running multiple apps at the same time in the next section.

6. Swipe an app left or right off the screen to close it or tap the X on the top right of the app.

Tap to close all apps

Run Multiple Apps on the Screen at the Same Time

Your Galaxy S6 has a feature called Multi Window that allows certain apps to run on the same screen at the same time. They can either run in a split-screen configuration, in multiple separate small windows, or a combination of both.

Two Apps Together on a Split Screen

This section explains how to run two apps at the same time in a split-screen configuration.

1. Touch and hold the Recent Apps button while on the Home screen, to see apps that support Multi Window.

2. Tap an app you want to run. The
   app launches in the top half of
   the screen.

Scroll left and right to see all apps

Choose Apps That Are Already Running

When choosing which apps to start in Multi Window mode, if you keep scrolling right so that you see the left-most screen, it looks very much like the Recent Apps screen. Tap an app that is already running to switch it to Multi Window mode.

Tap to choose a running app

It's Not All Good

Not All Apps Support Multi Window

Apps must be specially written to take advantage of Samsung's Multi Window mode because Multi Window mode is not part of the Android operating system. This means that you might not see the apps you are looking for until the developer updates the app to support Samsung's Multi Window mode.

3. Tap a second app icon to launch it in the bottom half of the screen.

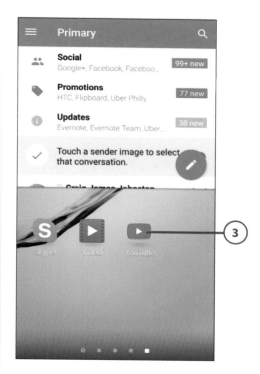

4. Drag the circle up or down to give more or less room to each app.

5. Tap the circle to reveal extra Multi Window features.

6. Tap to swap the position of the apps on the screen.

7. Tap to enable dragging content (such as text or an image) between windows.

8. Tap to minimize the selected app to a small draggable circle on the screen. A blue box indicates which is the selected app.

9. Tap to maximize the selected app to full screen. A blue box indicates which is the selected app.

10. Tap to close the app in the selected window. The selected app has a blue box around its perimeter.

>>>Go Further

MINIMIZED APPS

When you choose to minimize an app as shown in Step 8, the app shrinks to a small circle on the screen. You can drag the minimized app anywhere on the screen. If you touch and hold the app, a trash can icon appears; drag the app to the trash can to close the app. If you tap the minimized app, it enlarges to a pop-up window instead of maximizing back to its original window in the split screen. You can then continue working on the app in its small window. When an app is in a pop-up window, you can resize it by dragging the blue border around the app. Minimized and pop-up apps continue to be shown no matter what screen you are on and what app you are running.

Minimized apps

App in a pop-up window

Quicker Way of Running Multi Window

If you only want to use apps that are already running in Multi Window, you can do this more quickly. Tap the Recent Apps button. Tap the Multi Window icon on any running app. That app switches to Multi Window mode and displays in the top-half of the screen. Next, tap a second app to run in the bottom half of the screen. Remember that not all apps support Multi Window so some apps may not have the Multi Window icon.

Tap to select app for Multi Window

Choose a second app

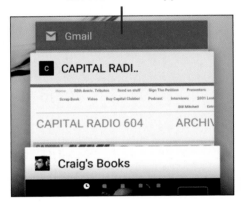

Installing Synchronization Software

Because your Galaxy S6 is tightly integrated with Google and its services, all media that you purchase from the Google Play Store on your phone is stored in the Google cloud and accessible anywhere, anytime. However, you might have a lot of music on your computer and need to copy that to your Google cloud. To do that, you need to install the Google Music Manager software or the Android File Transfer app for your Mac to copy any files back and forth.

Install Android File Transfer (Apple Mac OS X)

You only need the Android File Transfer app when using a Samsung Android phone (such as your Galaxy S6) on an Apple Mac running OS X.

1. From your Mac, browse to http://www.android.com/filetransfer/ and download the Android File Transfer app.

2. Click the Downloads icon.

3. Double-click the app in your Safari Downloads.

4. Drag the green Android to the Applications shortcut to install the app.

Install Google Music Manager (Apple Mac)

Don't install Google Music Manager unless you plan to upload files from your computer to the Google cloud.

1. Visit https://music.google.com/music/listen#manager_pl from your desktop web browser and log in to your Google account if you're prompted.

2. Click to download Music Manager.

3. Click the Downloads icon.

4. Double-click the app in your Safari Downloads.

5. Drag the Music Manager icon to the Applications shortcut to install the app.

6. Double-click the Music Manager icon in the Applications folder.

7. Skip to the "Configure Music Manager (Windows and Apple Mac)" section to complete the installation.

Install Google Music Manager (Windows)

Don't install Google Music Manager unless you plan to upload files from your computer to the Google cloud.

1. Visit https://music.google.com/music/listen#manager_pl from your desktop web browser and log in to your Google account if you're prompted.

2. Click to download Music Manager.

3. Double-click the app in your Downloads folder.

4. Skip to the "Configure Music Manager (Windows and Apple Mac)" section to complete the installation.

Configure Music Manager (Windows and Apple Mac)

1. Click Continue.

2. Enter your Google (Gmail) email address.

3. Enter your Google (Gmail) password.

4. Click Continue.

5. Choose where you keep your music.

6. Click Continue.

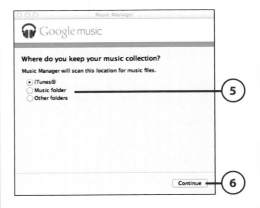

7. Choose whether to upload all of your music or just some of your playlists. Remember that you can only upload 20,000 songs for free. Skip to Step 12 if you chose to upload all music.

8. Check if you also want to upload podcasts.

9. Click Continue.

10. Select one or more playlists of music.

11. Click Continue.

12. Choose whether you want to automatically upload any new music that is added to your computer.

13. Click Continue.

14. Click Close.

Samsung Kies

Samsung has its own synchronization software called Kies. You can find it at http://www.samsung.com/us/kies/ or just Google *Samsung Kies*. After you install Kies, you can synchronize media files between your computer and your S6, plus you can back up your S6 and update its firmware.

Device media ——
Browse device
Computer media ——

- **Device media**—The music, photos, and video that are on your Galaxy S6 or S6 edge.

- **Computer media**—The music, photos, and videos that you have added to the Kies library from your computer.

- **Browse device**—Clicking here allows you to browse the file system on your Galaxy S6 or S6 edge. This enables you to browse to any file on your device, and you are not limited to only media files.

Choose what to synchronize
Click to synchronize

- **Choose what to synchronize**—On the Sync tab, choose whether you want to synchronize your Galaxy S6 or S6 edge with your computer's contacts or calendar.

- **Click to synchronize**—Click the Sync button to manually synchronize the selected items between your Galaxy S6 or S6 edge and your computer.

Click to back up **Choose what to back up**

Click to restore

- **Click to back up**—On the Backup/Restore tab, click Backup and choose what you would like to back up from your Galaxy S6 or S6 edge to your computer.

- **Click to restore**—On the Backup/Restore tab, click restore and choose from a previous backup on your computer to restore to your Galaxy S6 or S6 edge.

Import from iTunes

If you have all of your music in iTunes, you can use Kies to import music that is part of an iTunes playlist. First you need to create a new playlist in iTunes that contains all the music you want on your Galaxy S6 or S6 edge. In Kies, click File, Import iTunes Playlist to Library to import all songs in the chosen iTunes playlist into the Kies music library. After the songs are imported, you can synchronize them to your Galaxy S6 or S6 edge.

Import music from iTunes

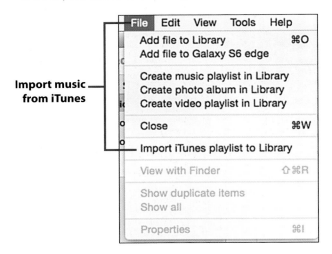

Tap to choose where to use the wallpaper

Tap to choose a new wallpaper

In this chapter, you find out how to customize your Galaxy S6 to suit your needs and lifestyle. Topics include the following:

→ Using wallpapers and live wallpapers
→ Replacing the keyboard
→ Adjusting sound and display settings
→ Setting the region and language
→ Using the fingerprint scanner
→ Managing the edge features

Making the S6 Your Own

Your Galaxy S6 arrives preconfigured to appeal to most buyers; however, you might want to change the way some of the features work, or even personalize it to fit your mood or lifestyle. Luckily, your Galaxy S6 is customizable.

Changing Your Wallpaper

Your Galaxy S6 comes preloaded with a cool wallpaper. You can install other wallpapers, use live wallpapers that animate, and even use pictures in the Gallery application as your wallpaper.

1. Touch and hold in an open area on one of the Home screen panes.

2. Tap Wallpapers.

3. Tap to select where you want to change the wallpaper. You can choose a new wallpaper for the Home screen only or the Lock screen only, or you can use the same new wallpaper for both the Home and Lock screens.

4. Use the steps in one of the following three sections to choose the type of wallpaper to use, as well as to select your new wallpaper.

Set Up Wallpaper from Gallery Pictures

You can use any picture in your Gallery as a wallpaper.

1. Swipe from left to right over the wallpaper thumbnails until you see one labeled From Gallery.

2. Tap From Gallery.

3. Navigate your photo albums and tap a photo you want to use for your wallpaper.

4. Zoom in and out of the picture using the pinch gesture. Sometimes if the photo you have chosen is very large, you will not be able to zoom in or out.

5. Move the photo by dragging it so that the part of it you want to use is visible.

6. Tap Done.

Set Up Live Wallpaper

Live wallpaper is wallpaper with some intelligence behind it. It can be a cool animation or even an animation that keys off things such as the music you are playing on your Galaxy S6, or it can be something simple such as the time. There are some very cool live wallpapers in the Google Play Store that you can install and use.

1. Swipe from left to right over the wallpaper thumbnails until you see the thumbnails with titles. Live wallpapers are kept on the right side of the wallpaper thumbnails.

2. Tap the live wallpaper you want to use.

3. Tap Settings to change the way the live wallpaper works (not all live wallpapers have settings that you can adjust).

4. Tap Set as Wallpaper to use the live wallpaper.

Finding More Wallpaper

You can find wallpaper or live wallpaper in the Google Play Store. Tap the Play Store icon to open the Google Play Store app and search for "wallpaper" or "live wallpaper." Read more on how to use the Google Play Store in Chapter 12, "Working with Android Applications."

Set Up Wallpaper

Choose a static wallpaper that is pre-loaded and sized correctly for your screen.

1. Swipe left and right over the wallpaper thumbnails to see static wallpaper options. Static wallpapers are in between the From Gallery option and the live wallpapers.

2. Tap a wallpaper to preview it. This example uses the Star Trek: Red Alert live wallpaper.

3. Tap Set as Wallpaper to use the wallpaper.

Changing Your Keyboard

If you find it hard to type on the standard Galaxy S6 keyboard, or you just want to make it look better, you can install replacement keyboards. You can download free or purchase replacement keyboards from the Google Play Store. Most, if not all, keyboards come with their own installation wizard that walks you through adding and activating a keyboard, but if the one you installed does not have a wizard, or you want to manually switch keyboards in the future, these steps will be useful.

1. Pull down the Notification Panel and tap the Settings icon.

2. Tap Language and Input under the System section.

3. Tap Default Keyboard.

4. Tap Set Up Input Methods.

Doing Your Research

When you choose a different keyboard in Step 5, the Galaxy S6 gives you a warning telling you that nonstandard keyboards have the potential for capturing everything you type. Do your research on any keyboards before you download and install them.

5. Tap the On/Off switch to the right of the keyboard you want to enable. In this example the keyboard is called SwiftKey Keyboard.

What Can You Do with Your New Keyboard?

Keyboards you buy in the Google Play Store can do many things. They can change the key layout, change the color and style of the keys, offer different methods of text input, and even enable you to use an old T9 predictive input keyboard that you might have become used to when using an old "dumb phone" that had only a numeric keypad.

6. Tap OK to confirm that you want to enable and use this keyboard.

7. Tap the back icon to return to the previous screen.

8. Tap Default Keyboard one more time.

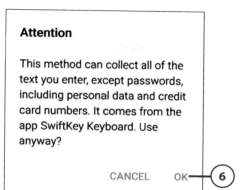

Attention

This method can collect all of the text you enter, except passwords, including personal data and credit card numbers. It comes from the app SwiftKey Keyboard. Use anyway?

CANCEL   OK — 6

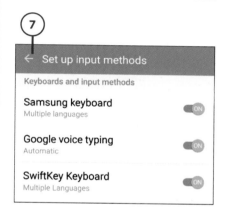

7

← Set up input methods

Keyboards and input methods

Samsung keyboard
Multiple languages   ON

Google voice typing
Automatic   ON

SwiftKey Keyboard
Multiple Languages   ON

← Language and input

Language
English

Default keyboard ——————————— 8
Samsung keyboard

Keyboards and input methods

Samsung keyboard
Multiple languages

Google voice typing
Automatic

SwiftKey Keyboard
Multiple Languages

Tap to configure your new keyboard

9. Tap the keyboard you enabled in Step 5. In this example it is the SwiftKey Keyboard.

Adding Widgets to Your Home Screens

Some applications that you install come with widgets that you can place on your Home screen panes. These widgets normally display real-time information, such as stocks, weather, time, and Facebook feeds. Your Galaxy S6 also comes preinstalled with some widgets.

Add a Widget

Your Galaxy S6 should come preinstalled with some widgets, but you might also have some extra ones that have been added when you installed applications.

1. Touch and hold an open area on the Home screen.

2. Tap Widgets.

3. Touch and hold a widget to move it to a Home screen pane. Keep holding the widget as you move to Step 4. This example uses the Alarm widget.

2

3

Widget's size

Tap to see all widgets in a group

Swipe left and right to see all widgets

4. Position the widget where you want it on the Home screen pane.

5. Drag the widget to different Home screen panes if you want to place it on a different pane, or drag it to the right-most pane to create a new Home screen pane and place the widget on the new pane.

6. Release your finger to place the widget. Some widgets may prompt you with a few setup questions after they are positioned.

How Many Widgets Can I Fit?

By default, each Home screen pane is divided into a grid of four blocks across and four blocks down (4×4). In the figure for Step 3, the widgets show their size in blocks across and down (such as 2×1). From that, you can judge whether a widget is going to fit on the Home screen pane you want it to be on, but it also helps you position it in Step 4. You can increase the number of blocks available in the grid pattern by touching and holding an open area on the Home screen and tapping Screen Grid. On the Screen Grid screen, choose between a screen grid of 4×4, 4×5, or 5×5. Notice that app shortcuts and widgets shift closer together when you've chosen more grid rows and columns. Tap Apply when you are satisfied with your new Screen Grid choice.

Adjust Screen Grid

Choose new grid size

Resizing Widgets

Some (not all) widgets can be resized. To resize a widget, touch and hold the widget until you see an outline and then release it. If the widget can be resized, you see the resizing borders. Drag them to resize the widget. Tap anywhere on the screen to stop resizing.

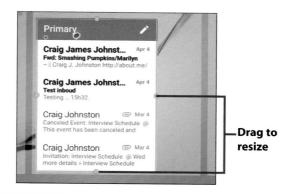

Drag to resize

Remove and Move a Widget

Sometimes you want to remove a widget or move it around.

1. Touch and hold the widget until the widget zooms out, but continue to hold it.

2. Drag the widget to the word Remove to remove it.

3. Drag the widget around the screen or drag it to one of the Home screen panes to reposition it.

4. Release the widget.

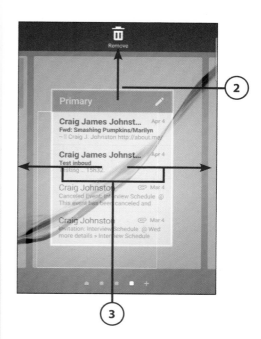

Setting the Language

If you move to another country or want to change the language used by your Galaxy S6, you can do so with a few taps.

1. Pull down the Notification Panel and tap the Settings icon.

2. Tap Language and Input under the System section.

3. Tap Language.

What Obeys the Language Setting?

When you switch your Galaxy S6 to use a different language, you immediately notice that all standard applications and the Galaxy S6 menus switch to the new language. Even some third-party applications honor the language switch. However, many third-party applications ignore the language setting on the Galaxy S6. Therefore, you might open a third-party application and find that all its menus are still in English.

4. Tap the language you want
to switch to. The language is
changed, and you are returned to
the previous screen automatically.
The choice of available languages
is based on your wireless carrier
and where in the world you
purchased your Galaxy S6 or
S6 edge.

Changing Accessibility Settings

Your Galaxy S6 includes built-in settings to assist people who might
otherwise have difficulty using some features of the device. The Galaxy S6
has the ability to provide alternative feedback, such as vibration and sound.
It can even read menu items aloud to you.

1. Pull down the Notification Panel
and tap the Settings icon.

2. Tap Accessibility under the Personal section.

3. Tap one of the categories on the Accessibility screen and use the following sections to change the settings in the different categories.

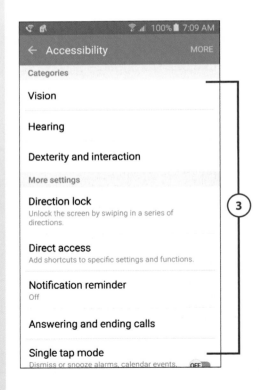

Vision

1. Tap to enable or disable TalkBack and change the TalkBack settings. When enabled, TalkBack speaks everything, including menus, but it also has other features, such as requiring that you double-tap something to select it instead of single tapping. When TalkBack is turned on, the options in Steps 2–4 become available.

2. Tap to enable the Dark Screen feature. After this feature is enabled, you double-press the Power key to enable and disable the Dark Screen functionality. When you have it enabled, your screen remains off for privacy.

3. Tap to enable the Rapid Key Input feature. When enabled, it overrides the TalkBack requirement of having to double-tap each key while typing.

4. Tap to enable Speak Passwords. When this feature is enabled, TalkBack speaks each character of your password as you type it.

5. Tap to record voice labels and write them to Near Field Communication (NFC) tags.

6. Tap to set the font size used on your Galaxy S6. You can choose sizes ranging from tiny to huge.

7. Scroll down for more settings.

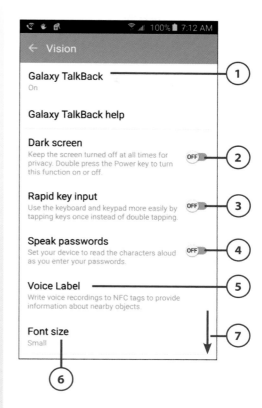

What Is a Voice Label?

Imagine if you could hold your S6 or S6 edge near an NFC tag that was close to an object in the room, and a voice played back telling you about the object. Voice labels allow you to do just that. When you tap Voice Label in Step 5, you can record your voice saying the name of the object, or something relevant about the object (for example, a refrigerator). After you have recorded what you want to say, you are prompted to hold a new NFC tag against the back of your S6 or S6 edge and your recording is written to the NFC tag. You can then stick the NFC tag near the object. When your S6 or S6 edge comes close to the NFC tag in the future, what you recorded is automatically played back.

8. Tap to enable or disable magnification gestures, which include the ability to magnify any screen by triple-tapping it. When a screen is magnified, you can pan around it.

9. Tap to enable or disable a Magnifier Window that can magnify whatever is under it. You can change the size of the Magnify Window and how much magnification is applied.

10. Tap to enable or disable the Grayscale feature, which makes everything on the screen grayscale instead of full color.

11. Tap to enable or disable the Negative Colors feature, which makes all colors displayed on your Galaxy S6 reversed. (For example, black text on a white background instead appears as white text on a black background.)

12. Tap to enable the Color Adjustment Wizard, which helps you adjust the screen colors if you have difficulty reading the screen with the default colors.

13. Tap to enable or disable the Accessibility Shortcut feature. When it's enabled, you can access accessibility features by performing certain gestures.

14. Tap to change the settings for the Text-to-Speech service provided by Samsung or to switch to the Google Text-to-Speech service.

15. Tap to save your changes and return to the previous screen.

Hearing

1. Tap to enable or disable an option that makes your S6 vibrate when it detects a baby crying or a doorbell ringing.

2. Tap to enable or disable making your S6 light up the camera flash when you have a new notification.

3. Tap to turn off all sounds.

4. Tap to enable or disable improving the sound quality if you use a hearing aid.

5. Tap to enable video subtitles provided by Samsung, and adjust how the subtitles appear on the screen.

6. Tap to enable or disable video subtitles provided by Google, and adjust how the subtitles appear on the screen.

7. Tap to adjust the balance of audio played when wearing earphones.

8. Scroll down for more settings.

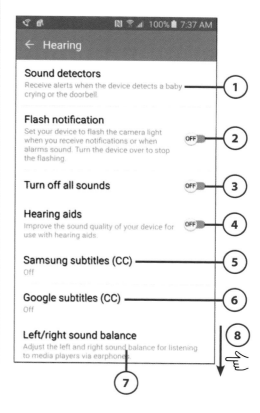

9. Tap to use mono audio when wearing one earphone.

10. Tap to enable or disable a feature that causes your S6 to vibrate in time to music being played, a video being watched, or a game being played.

11. Tap to save your changes and return to the previous screen.

More About Text-to-Speech

By default, your Galaxy S6 uses the Samsung Text-to-Speech service with an option to use the Samsung service to speak any text you need to read. You can install other text-to-speech software by searching for them in the Google Play Store. After you've installed the software, you'll have multiple choices.

Dexterity and Interaction

1. Tap to manage using universal switches to control your Galaxy S6. Switches can include tapping on the screen; detecting movement of your head, eyes, or mouth; and pressing buttons on an externally connected accessory.

2. Tap to enable or disable the Assistant menu. When it is enabled, you can set your dominant hand, reorder the menu items, and adjust the level of zoom. The Assistant menu appears as a small gray box on your screen at all times. When you tap it, it provides quick access to common device functions.

3. Tap to enable or disable the Gesture Wake Up feature. When this feature is enabled, you can wave your hand over the front of the device while it lies on a flat surface to wake it up.

4. Tap to adjust the press and hold delay (also known as touch and hold).

5. Tap to enable or disable interaction control, which includes blocking areas of the screen so they do not respond to taps.

6. Tap to save your changes and return to the previous screen.

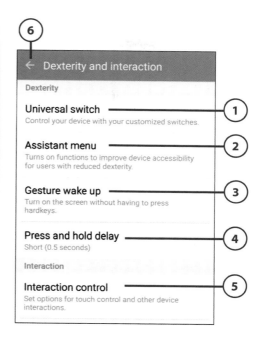

Direction Lock

1. Tap to enable Direction Lock. When you enable it, you are asked to draw a series of directions on the screen (consisting of up, down, left, and right) that can be used as an unlock pattern.

2. Tap to change the screen security from Direction Lock to something else.

3. Tap to receive vibration feedback each time you successfully draw a direction on the screen.

4. Tap to hear a sound played each time you successfully draw a direction on the screen.

5. Tap to see an arrow showing the direction you just drew on the screen.

6. Tap to hear a voice speaking the direction you just drew on the screen.

7. Tap to save your changes and return to the previous screen.

Direct Access

1. Tap to enable or disable direct access to certain accessibility settings. When this feature is enabled, press the Home button three times in quick succession to see the Direct Access menu.

2. Choose which accessibility settings you want direct access to.

3. Tap to save your changes and return to the previous screen.

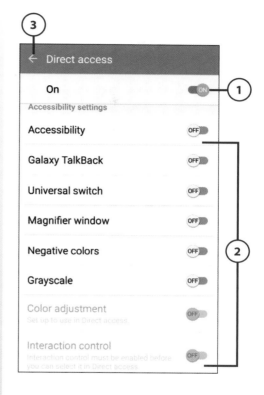

Notification Reminder

1. Tap to enable or disable extra notifications for certain apps.

2. Choose whether to vibrate when one of your chosen apps sends a notification.

3. Choose whether to turn on the blue indicator light when one of your chosen apps sends a notification.

4. Choose the reminder interval if you have not responded to the notification.

5. Choose which apps should give you this extra notification.

6. Tap to save your changes and return to the previous screen.

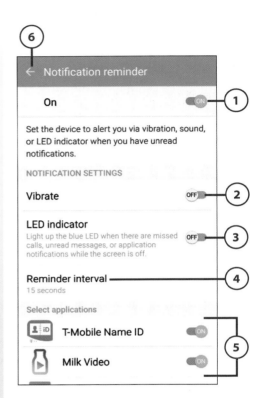

Answering/Ending Calls

1. Tap to enable or disable answering a call by pressing the Home button.

2. Tap to enable or disable using voice commands to answer or reject calls. When enabled, just say "Answer" or "Reject."

3. Tap to enable or disable ending a call by pressing the Power button.

4. Tap to save your changes and return to the previous screen.

Manage Accessibility

1. Tap to import accessibility settings that someone has shared with you or to export your settings.

2. Tap to share your accessibility settings with friends. You must first export your settings as mentioned in Step 1.

3. Tap to return to the previous screen.

Adjusting Sound and Notifications Settings

You can change the volume for games, ringtones, and alarms, change the default ringtone and notification sound, plus control what system sounds are used.

Adjust Sound Settings

1. Pull down the Notification Panel and tap the Settings icon.

2. Tap Sound and Notifications in the Device section.

3. Tap to change the sound mode between Sound (play all sounds), Vibrate (vibrate instead of playing sounds), or Mute (silence all sounds and vibrations).

4. Tap to change the volume for ringtones, music, video games, and other media, notifications, and system alerts.

5. Tap to change the ringtones and sounds for notifications from Messages, Calendar, and Email, as well as adjust system sounds.

6. Tap to choose the intensity of vibrations for incoming calls, notifications, and haptic feedback. This screen also allows you to create custom vibration patterns.

7. Tap to choose whether you want to go through a wizard so that your S6 can adapt its audio output to your ears, and choose whether you want to enable SoundAlive+ or TubeAmp. See the "Sound Quality and Effects" task later in this chapter for more information.

8. Tap to choose whether you want to enable Do Not Disturb, and choose any exceptions.

9. Tap to choose whether you want notifications to be displayed on the Lock screen, and if so which ones.

10. Tap to choose which apps you want to see notifications for, and also which ones you want to see as priority notifications.

11. Scroll down for more settings.

12. Tap to enable or disable having the LED indicator light up when charging, recording a voice memo, or when you receive a new notification.

13. Tap to save your changes and return to the previous screen.

Ringtones and Sounds

This task picks up after you have tapped Ringtones and Sounds in Step 5 of the "Adjust Sound Settings" task.

1. Tap to choose which ringtone plays when you receive an incoming phone call. While choosing the ringtone, you can add any audio file on your Galaxy S6 as your ringtone.

2. Tap to choose the default notification sound that plays when a new notification is displayed.

3. Tap to choose whether you want to be notified when you receive a new SMS or MMS message, what ringtone plays when the notification is shown, and whether your Galaxy S6 must also vibrate.

4. Tap to choose whether you want to be notified when you receive a new calendar notification (such as an event reminder), what ringtone plays when the notification is shown, and whether your Galaxy S6 must also vibrate.

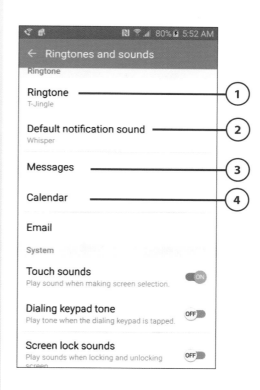

5. Tap to choose whether you want to be notified when you receive a new email, what ringtone plays when the notification is shown, and whether your Galaxy S6 must also vibrate. This alert does not change the Gmail notification setting.

6. Tap to enable or disable playing a sound when you interact with the touchscreen, such as when you tap a menu item.

7. Tap to enable or disable playing touch tone sounds when typing a phone number on the dialpad.

8. Tap to enable or disable playing a sound when you lock or unlock your Galaxy S6.

9. Scroll down for more settings.

10. Tap to enable or disable playing a sound for each key that you tap on the on-screen keyboard.

11. Tap to save your changes and return to the previous screen.

Vibrations

This task picks up after you have tapped Vibrations in Step 6 of the "Adjust Sound Settings" task.

1. Tap to choose the vibration intensity for incoming calls, notifications, and vibration feedback.

2. Tap to choose a default vibration pattern for notifications. You can also create your own custom vibration pattern that can later be assigned to contacts.

3. Tap to choose whether you want your Galaxy S6 to also vibrate when receiving an incoming call.

4. Tap to choose whether you want vibration feedback when you tap the Recent Apps and Back buttons.

5. Tap to choose whether you want to feel a vibration as you type on the on-screen keyboard.

6. Tap to save your changes and return to the previous screen.

Creating Your Own Vibration Patterns

In Step 2, you can choose the vibration pattern to be used when you are notified, but you can also create your own. Tap Create. On the next screen, tap in the area where it reads Tap to Create, and then tap out your vibration pattern on the screen using short taps for short vibrations and long taps for longer vibrations. The example in the figure uses Morse Code for Save Our Souls (SOS). You can create any vibration pattern you want. You can create more than one custom vibration pattern and can then use those custom patterns to distinguish between incoming calls from certain people in your Contacts. To do that, open the Contacts app, tap a contact, tap Edit, tap Add Another Field, and choose Vibration Pattern. You can then change the Vibration Pattern from Default to one of your custom patterns.

Tap to play back your vibration pattern

Tap to save it

Sound Quality and Effects

This task picks up after you have tapped Sound Quality and Effects in Step 7 of the "Adjust Sound Settings" task.

1. Tap to run through an audio test to determine your exact auditory range. You can customize the sound to best suit your hearing abilities.

2. Tap to enable or disable the SoundAlive+ feature that simulates surround sound. You can only enable this feature if you have a wired or Bluetooth headset connected.

3. Tap to enable or disable the Tube Amp feature that simulates a tube amplifier. You can only enable this feature if you have a wired or Bluetooth headset connected.

4. Tap to save your changes and return to the previous screen.

Do Not Disturb

This task picks up after you have tapped Do Not Disturb in Step 8 of the "Adjust Sound Settings" task.

1. Tap to enable or disable Do Not Disturb. When enabled, you will receive no notifications unless you specify exceptions.

2. Tap to allow exceptions to the Do Not Disturb rule. For example you probably want to allow the alarm to still wake you up in the morning, and maybe allow incoming calls from certain people.

3. Tap to set a schedule when Do Not Disturb is automatically enabled and disabled. For example you may want to set it to be enabled when you go to sleep, and disabled when you wake up.

4. Set the Do Not Disturb schedule.

5. Tap to save your changes and return to the previous screen.

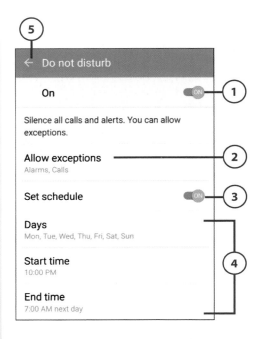

Modifying Display Settings

You can change many display settings, the screen mode, the wait time before your Galaxy S6 goes to sleep, the size of the font used, and the pulse notification light settings.

1. Pull down the Notification Panel and tap the Settings icon.

2. Tap Display in the Device section.

3. Tap to change the screen brightness manually or set it to automatic. When on automatic, your Galaxy S6 uses the built-in light sensor to adjust the brightness based on the light level where you are.

4. Tap to change the system font and how large the font style is. The system font is used for all menus, notifications, alerts, and warnings on your Galaxy S6.

5. Tap to choose how many minutes of inactivity must pass before your Galaxy S6 puts the screen to sleep.

6. Tap to enable Smart Stay. When this feature is enabled, your Galaxy S6 uses the front-facing camera to look for your eyes. It keeps the screen on as long as it detects that you are looking at the screen.

7. Tap to choose the Screen mode, which is how the screen represents colors. You can manually choose AMOLED Cinema, AMOLED Photo, and Basic, or leave it set to Adapt Display, which means your Galaxy S6 chooses the best settings based on usage.

8. Tap to enable or disable Daydream mode, decide what must be displayed when daydreaming, and when to daydream. Daydream mode is essentially a screensaver.

9. Tap to save your changes and return to the previous screen.

Is Adaptive Display Mode Good?

If you leave your screen mode set to Adaptive Display, you should know that your Galaxy S6 adjusts the color range, saturation, and sharpness of the screen for the Gallery, Camera, Internet Web Browser, Samsung Video, Samsung Smart Remote, and Google Play Books apps only. All other system apps and apps that you install are not optimized. With this in mind, you might prefer to manually select an appropriate Screen mode in Step 7.

Aren't Screensavers Obsolete?

In Step 8 you can enable and manage the Daydream mode, which is essentially a screensaver like those used on desktop computers. For many years now, screensavers have not been needed because we no longer use Cathode Ray Tube (CRT) monitors and screens. In the days when we used CRTs, if an image remained in one spot for a long time, it would be burned into the front of the screen. Having a screensaver on a CRT monitor made sense because the images were moving and changing constantly. Screensavers continued to be used because people liked seeing the patterns and images in the screensavers. This is why Daydream mode is on your Galaxy S6. Once activated, it can display your photos or cool color patterns after a period of inactivity, when you plug your Galaxy S6 into a dock, or when it is charging.

Adjusting the S6 Edge Settings

If you own a Galaxy S6 edge, there are some additional features that make use of the curved edges of the screen. The steps below do not work on a regular S6; they're only for the S6 edge.

1. Pull down the Notification Panel and tap the Settings icon.

2. Tap Edge Screen.

3. Use the following sections to manage your S6 edge features.

Edge Lighting

Edge Lighting, when enabled, lights up the curved edge of the screen when you receive an incoming call, and your Galaxy S6 edge is lying upside down on its screen. If you also have People Edge enabled, the color of the light used will match the color you have chosen for the caller.

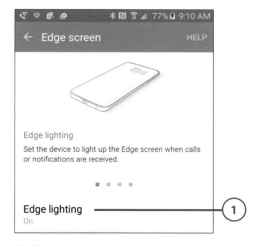

1. Tap Edge Lighting.

2. Tap to enable or disable Edge Lighting.

3. Tap to enable or disable the ability to send a quick reply to the caller and manage the text of the message.

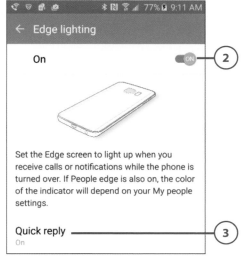

4. Tap to enable or disable Quick Reply.

5. Tap to change the Quick Reply message that is sent.

How Does Quick Reply Work?

To start, make sure that you have Edge Lighting enabled, you have enabled Quick Reply, and have set a Quick Reply message. Then make a habit of placing your Galaxy S6 edge upside down on its screen when you are not using it. When someone calls, emails, or sends you a text message, you see the curved edge of the screen start pulsating with white light. If you are also using the People Edge feature, the color of the pulsating light will change to indicate who is calling or sending a message. If it is an incoming call and you would like to send the caller a Quick Reply message, place your finger over the heart rate sensor for two seconds. Your Galaxy S6 edge sends the Quick Reply message to the caller as an SMS (text message).

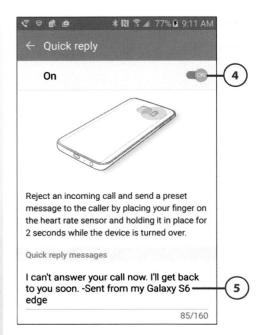

People Edge

People Edge works in conjunction with the Edge Lighting feature to enable you to assign a color to up to five contacts. This then allows you to identify who is calling by the color of the light.

1. Tap People Edge.

2. Tap to enable People Edge.

3. Tap to manage which contacts you want to assign a color to.

4. Tap to enable a feature that vibrates and dimly lights the screen to show you any alerts (such as missed calls) from the people you choose in Step 3, when you pick up your Galaxy S6 edge.

How Does People Edge Work?

To start, make sure that you have Edge Lighting enabled. Then make a habit of placing your Galaxy S6 edge upside down on its screen when you are not using it. When someone calls, emails, or sends you a text message, you see the curved edge of the screen start pulsating with light. The color of the pulsating light indicates who is calling, texting, or emailing. If the pulsating light is white, it means that the caller or sender is not one of the five people you have chosen. If it is an incoming call and you would like to send the caller a Quick Reply message, place your finger over the heart rate sensor for two seconds. Your Galaxy S6 edge sends the Quick Reply message to the caller as an SMS (text message). If you recognize who is calling because of the color of the light, pick up your Galaxy S6 edge and answer the call as you normally would. If you miss the call, when you later look at your phone, you see a block of color on the curved edge of your screen indicating that one of your People Edge contacts called. Swipe the block of color inward and choose a method of contacting them back. You can call them, send them an SMS (text message), or send them an email.

Swipe to contact the missed caller

Dismiss the missed call

Contact the caller

Quicker Way to Manage People Edge and Reach Your Chosen Contacts

When People Edge is enabled, you see a white transparent block on the curved edge of your screen. This block is always there while People Edge is enabled. Swipe the block of color inward. Tap the settings icon to manage People Edge. If you tap a contact to which you have already assigned a color, you can call that contact, send an SMS (text message), or send an email. Tap the plus symbol of a specific color to quickly assign a contact to that color.

Swipe to manage People Edge or contact people

Manage People Edge

Contact this person

Add a new contact

Select Notifications

When using Edge Lighting, you can choose what type of notifications the curved edge of the screen will light up for.

1. Tap Select Notifications.

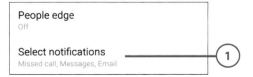

People edge
Off

Select notifications
Missed call, Messages, Email

2. Choose which notifications you want to be notified of by showing a pulsating light on the curved edge of the screen.

3. Tap to save your changes and return to the previous screen.

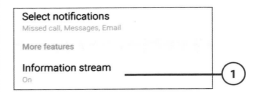

Information Stream

When Information Stream is enabled, you can use a swiping gesture along the curved edge of your screen to see information feeds such as weather, notifications, sports scores, financial information, and more. The Information Stream gesture is a little tricky to master. To see the Information Stream, while your phone's screen is off, swipe your finger across the curved edge of the screen in one direction, and in the same motion, swipe it back.

1. Tap Information Stream.

2. Tap to enable or disable Information Stream.

3. Tap to manage what feeds you want to see in the Information Stream.

4. Tap to choose the number of seconds that the Information Stream will remain visible.

5. Tap to choose whether you want the weather to be included in the Information Stream, and adjust the unit of measure, how often the weather information is refreshed, and whether your current location is used.

Managing Information Stream Feeds

When you choose to manage your feeds in Step 3, you have the ability to rearrange the feeds, choose which feeds to include in the Information Stream, download new feed types from Samsung, and change the settings for some feeds.

Reorder feeds

Tap to include or exclude feed

Download new feeds

Change feed settings

Night Clock

Night Clock shows the time and date along the curved edge of the screen during specific times of the night.

1. Tap Night Clock.

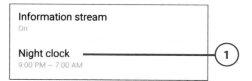

2. Tap to enable or disable Night Clock.

3. Choose the start and end time for Night Clock.

4. Tap to save your changes and return to the previous screen.

Edge Screen Position

Only one side of your S6 edge's screen can be used for all of the edge features. By default, it is set to use the right side curved edge, but you can change it.

1. Tap Edge Screen Position.

2. Choose which side of your screen you want the edge features to be on.

3. Tap to save your changes and return to the previous screen.

Easy Home Screen Mode

Home Screen mode changes which widgets are placed on your Home screen and how many you have on the Home screen. When Easy mode is enabled, a lot of widgets that have shortcuts to many apps are placed on the Home screen, and their icons are larger.

1. Tap Easy Mode in the Personal section of the Settings.

2. Tap to enable Easy Mode.

3. Scroll down to select which apps you want to have shortcuts to on your Home screen.

4. Tap Done to save your changes. You return to the Easy Mode Home screen.

Privacy and Safety

Privacy and Safety allows you to set whether you want to allow your geographic location to be available to Google and apps running on your phone, manage Private mode, and set up a feature that allows your phone to send information to people when you are in an emergency situation.

1. Tap Privacy and Safety in the Personal section.

2. Tap to manage whether Google or apps running on your phone have access to your geographic location.

3. Tap to manage Private Mode.

4. Tap to enable or disable allowing your phone to report diagnostic information to Google.

5. Tap to manage how SOS messages are handled.

Private Mode

Private mode is a bit confusing at first, but while it is enabled, you can move content from certain apps to a secret area on your Galaxy S6 or S6 edge. When Private mode is disabled, the content is invisible unless you come back into Settings and enable it again.

1. After performing Step 3 of the "Privacy and Safety" section, choose a method for securing Private mode. The method you use here is in addition to the method you already use for unlocking your Galaxy S6 or S6 edge. You only need to do this the first time you want to enable Private mode.

2. Tap to enable or disable Private mode.

3. Tap to change the method for securing Private mode.

4. Tap to enable or disable automatically disabling Private mode when the screen turns off. This is recommended.

5. Tap to save your changes and return to the previous screen.

>>>Go Further
USING PRIVATE MODE

Private mode is a confusing feature. Essentially when Private mode is enabled, you can move content from certain apps to a secret, hidden area on your Galaxy S6 or S6 edge. You are also able to see content that you previously moved to this secret area. When you disable Private mode, anything in the secret area becomes unavailable and invisible. To re-enable Private mode, you have to use a password, PIN, pattern, or your fingerprint. Private mode only works with the following apps (that Samsung has heavily modified): Gallery, Video, Music, Voice Recorder, My Files, and Internet (not the Chrome browser). When Private mode is enabled, you can tap the Menu icon to reveal a new menu item called Move to Private.

Move selected items to the Private area

Send SOS Messages

When you have this feature enabled, if you find yourself in an emergency situation where you need help, you can press the Power button on your Galaxy S6 or S6 edge three times in quick succession, and your phone starts taking note of your geographic location, recording audio and taking pictures, and sending it all to one or more contacts that you have previously set up.

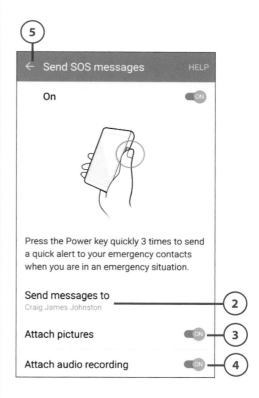

1. Tap to enable the Send SOS messages feature. This first time you enable it, you are asked to choose at least one person from your contacts or to enter a new mobile phone number to be used by the feature.

2. Tap to manage which contacts will be sent your location, audio, and pictures when you trigger this feature. You can use more than one contact.

3. Tap to enable or disable including pictures with the SOS messages.

4. Tap to enable or disable including audio recordings with the SOS messages.

5. Tap to save your changes and return to the previous screen.

>>>Go Further

USING THE SEND SOS MESSAGES FEATURE

If you find yourself in an emergency situation, press the Power button on your Galaxy S6 or S6 edge three times in quick succession. Your phone immediately starts sending SOS text messages to the people you have set up to receive them. If you have turned on the Attach Pictures feature, your phone starts taking pictures and sending them to the designated contact. Finally, if you have turned on the Attach Audio Recording feature, your phone starts recording audio and sending it to your chosen contacts. The SOS behavior continues until you stop it. To stop sending SOS messages, press the Power button on your phone three times in quick succession.

Themes

Themes are packaged settings that change the look and feel of your Galaxy S6 and S6 edge. Themes affect the system sounds, wallpaper, icons, fonts used, and colors used in phone menus, including the Notification Panel. The themes can also modify the look and feel of some core Samsung apps such as the Phone app.

1. Pull down the Notification Panel and tap the Settings icon.

2. Tap Themes in the Personal section or in the Quick Settings section.

3. Tap a theme to download it and make it active.

4. Tap Download to download and install the theme. If the theme was previously downloaded and installed, skip to Step 5.

Find more themes

Applied theme **Downloaded but not applied**

Scroll left and right to see all screenshots of the theme

5. Tap Apply.

6. Tap Apply to acknowledge that you understand that any unsaved work in your open apps will be lost when you apply the theme.

Tap to delete the theme

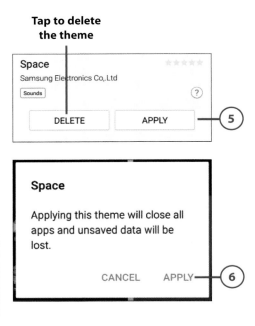

Lock Screen and Security

With the settings screens in the Lock Screen and Security section you can control what is shown on the Lock screen, how your device is unlocked, whether you want non-Google Play apps to be installed, and many other security-related options.

1. Pull down the Notification Panel and tap the Settings icon.

2. Tap Lock Screen and Security.

3. Tap to change what you must do to unlock your phone's screen. You can choose to do nothing, require a swipe across the screen, or use a security method (a numeric PIN, a pattern, a password, or your fingerprint).

4. Tap to choose what information is shown on the Lock screen. You can choose to show the clock, weather, and even your name.

5. Tap to choose the animation effect used when you swipe to unlock your phone.

6. Tap to manage your fingerprints. This includes adding or removing fingerprints, choosing when to use your fingerprint, and changing the backup password that you use when your fingerprint cannot be detected.

7. Tap to choose whether you want to enable Samsung's KNOX Active Protection (KAP) or install and use Samsung's My KNOX, which is a secure container for your company apps and data.

8. Tap to enable and manage Samsung's Find My Mobile service. After it's enabled, you can log in to the Find My Mobile website to track your stolen phone and send a remote wipe command to it. Read more about Find My Mobile in the sidebar at the end of this chapter.

9. Scroll down for more settings.

10. Tap to allow you to install Android apps that are not found in the Google Play Store. This is not recommended because apps not found in the official app store may contain viruses and malware; proceed with caution if you choose to enable this option. If you have enrolled your device in your company's Mobile Device Management (MDM) system, you may be required to enable this option.

11. Tap to see other security settings.

12. Tap to encrypt your phone's file system. When your file system is encrypted and you power off your phone, when you power it back on again you need to enter a numeric PIN to unencrypt your device before it will start up.

13. Tap to set and manage a PIN to unlock your SIM card. If you use a PIN to lock your SIM card, you need to enter it in addition to entering any security measures you set for your phone.

14. Tap to enable or disable briefly showing each character of a password as you type it.

15. Tap to manage how your phone gets security policy updates from Samsung. You can choose to have them automatically downloaded and installed, and you can choose to only have them download over Wi-Fi. Think of Samsung's security policy updates like virus definition updates on a Windows computer.

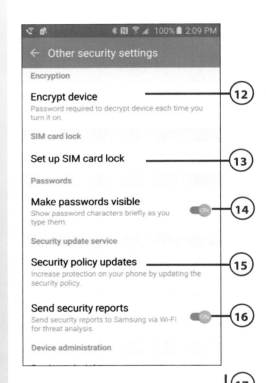

16. Tap to enable or disable automatically sending security reports to Samsung.

17. Scroll down for more settings.

18. Tap to manage Device Administrators.

19. Tap to view storage type information. Here you can see whether your phone supports storing your private encryption keys in the hardware (hardware-backed) or whether it is stored only in software.

20. Tap to view and select or de-select trusted certificates that the Android system uses and certificates you may be using.

21. Tap to install certificates from your phone's storage. You can use this feature only if you have previously saved the certificate to storage.

22. Tap to remove all trusted user certificates (if you are using any).

23. Scroll down for more settings.

More About Device Administrators

Device Administrators are apps that you have given permission to administer your phone. One of the Device Administrators is the Android Device Manager. This enables you to log in to www.google.com/android/devicemanager on a desktop computer and reset your device password or erase all your device's data if it has been stolen. If you enroll your phone in your company Enterprise Mobile Management (EMM) system, like those made by AirWatch or MobileIron, those systems also add a Device Administrator.

24. Tap to enable or disable Screen Pinning, which allows you to "pin" an app so that the person using it cannot exit the app.

25. Tap to manage which apps running on your phone are allowed to collect app usage information about all apps you have installed. This usage information includes how often each app is run, how long it sits in the foreground (active on your screen), and how long it sits in the background (still running but not visible).

26. Tap to manage which apps have access to notifications that appear on your phone. Typically if you use an Android Wear smartwatch, the Android Wear app is listed in this screen.

27. Tap to save your changes and return to the previous screen.

More About Pinning an App

When you enable Screen Pinning in Step 24, you are enabling a feature that allows you to "pin" an app to the screen. When an app is pinned to the screen, you cannot exit the app, go back to the Home screen, pull down the Notification Panel or Quick Settings bar, or do anything other than interact with the app. You can pin only the last app you ran, not any app. To pin an app to the screen, first run the app so that it is the most recently used app. Tap the Recent Apps button, slide the app up so that you can see the pin icon. Tap the pin icon to pin the app to the screen. To exit pinned mode, touch and hold the Back and Recent Apps buttons at the same time. Pinning an app to the screen is a quick way to allow someone to use your phone without letting them access anything else other than the app they should be using.

Tap to pin
an app

More About Fingerprints

You can store one or more thumb- or fingerprints on your Galaxy S6 or S6 edge. You can choose to use the prints to unlock your phone, but you can also use them to sign in to websites and verify your Samsung account. To manage your fingerprints, tap Settings, Lock Screen and Security, Fingerprints. Use this screen to add fingerprints. As you add a new fingerprint, your phone walks you through the process of capturing your fingerprint via the fingerprint sensor in the Home button. You can also choose or change your backup password. Your backup password can be used if the fingerprint sensor cannot detect your fingerprint.

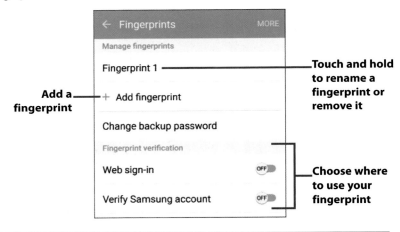

>>>Go Further

MORE ABOUT FIND MY MOBILE

If you have a Samsung account, and you have enabled Find My Mobile in Step 8, you can locate and remotely wipe your phone if it ever gets lost. To do this, open a web browser on a computer, browse to https://findmymobile.samsung.com, and log in with your Samsung account. When you're logged in, click Registered Device to select the device you want to work with (if you have more than one device registered). You can then locate your device, make the device play a ringtone (if you lost it in the couch and need to find it), enable emergency mode, and enable ultra power saving mode to conserve the battery. You can also remotely lock your device's screen or send a wipe command that will wipe your device and set it back to factory condition. You would use this last in a situation where your device has been stolen and you want to make sure that the thief doesn't get to your data.

Choose device if you have more than one

Turn your current call into a conference call

In this chapter, you find out how to make and receive phone calls (including conference calls) using your Galaxy S6. Topics include the following:

→ Making phone calls
→ Receiving phone calls
→ Making conference calls

2

Making and Receiving Calls

As a cellular phone, your Galaxy S6 includes powerful features that enable you to make phone calls swiftly and easily.

Getting to Know the Phone App

With the Phone app, you can quickly make and receive calls across the cellular network. This section introduces you to some of the features you might frequently use.

Open and Navigate the Phone App

The Phone app contains three tabs that enable you to make calls in various ways and to track the calls you receive.

Phone

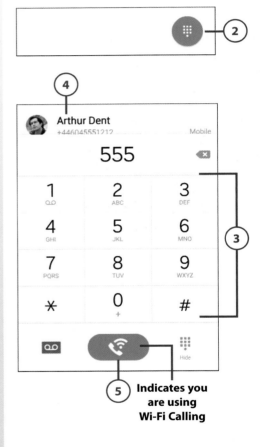

1. On the Home screen, tap Phone.

2. Tap the dialpad icon to display the dialpad. The dialpad icon is always visible on the bottom right of the screen while you are in the Phone app.

3. Tap the keys to dial a number.

4. If the Phone app displays a suggested contact with a matching number, you can tap the contact if it is the one you want.

5. Tap the green phone icon to place the call.

Indicates you are using Wi-Fi Calling

What Is Wi-Fi Calling?

The technical name for Wi-Fi Calling is Universal Media Access (UMA). This technology is provided by some carriers around the world and enables your Galaxy S6 to roam between the cellular network and Wi-Fi networks. Typically when you are connected to a Wi-Fi network, any calls you make are free and of higher audio quality because of the faster speeds. As you move out of Wi-Fi coverage, your S6 hands the call off to the cellular network—and vice versa—allowing your call to continue without interruption. The Phone app indicates when you are using Wi-Fi Calling by placing a Wi-Fi symbol next to the phone icon. If you want to read more about UMA or Wi-Fi Calling, read this online article: http://crackberry.com/saving-call-charges-recession-your-blackberry. The article is on a BlackBerry blog, but the descriptions of the technology still apply.

Call Log

The Call Log tab shows all activity in the Phone app, including incoming calls, missed calls, and placed calls.

1. Tap Log to see a list of the calls you have missed, placed, and received.

2. Tap a log entry to see more information about the caller.

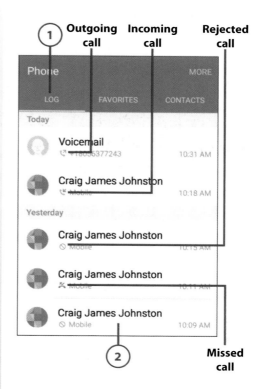

3. Tap the phone icon to place a call to the caller.

4. Tap the envelope icon to send an SMS (text message) to the caller.

5. Tap Edit to delete one or more call log entries for this caller.

6. Tap More to view the full contact record for this caller, or add the caller to your Auto Reject List.

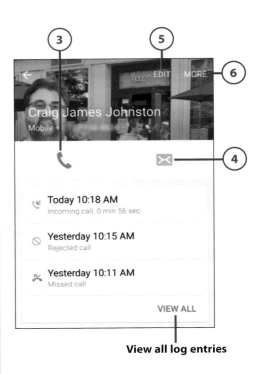

View all log entries

Favorites

The Favorites tab shows contacts you have marked as favorite and contacts you call often.

1. Tap Favorites to see your favorite and frequently called contacts.

2. Tap the contact image of a favorite contact to place a call to him or her.

3. Tap the information icon to the right of a favorite contact's name to see all of the information about the contact.

4. Tap Add to add additional favorite contacts from your Contacts list.

5. Tap More to remove favorite contacts, or to reorder their positions on the Favorites tab.

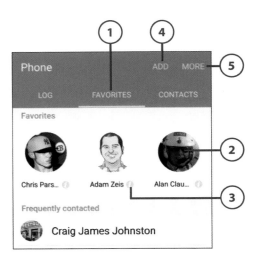

Contacts

The Contacts tab shows all of the contacts that you have added to the Contacts app.

1. Tap Contacts to see all of your contacts.

2. Tap a contact to see all information about that contact.

3. Tap to search for a contact.

4. Tap Create to add a new contact.

5. Tap More to remove contacts or see your Speed Dial screen.

Search by voice

>>>Go Further

SPEED DIAL

Speed dialing is a bit of a holdover from the 1980s and '90s when phones weren't as sophisticated as they are today. However, you might still find it useful to touch and hold one key to call a number. To add or edit your Speed Dial numbers, tap the Menu icon and tap Speed Dial. (Voicemail is already assigned to speed dial 1.) Tap the plus symbol for a numbered entry to add a contact for that Speed Dial number. To use Speed Dial, while the keypad is visible, touch and hold a number associated with a Speed Dial contact. That number will be dialed.

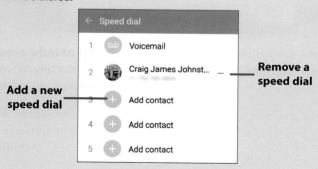

Add a new speed dial

Remove a speed dial

Receiving a Call

When someone phones your Galaxy S6, you can accept the call, reject it, or reject it and send a text message.

Accept a Call

1. When the phone rings, look at the contact name (if it is available) or the phone number (if the name is not) and decide whether to take the call.

2. Swipe the green phone icon to the right to accept the call.

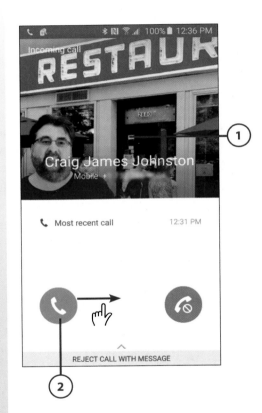

3. Tap to switch the call audio to the speaker.

4. Tap to switch the call audio to a Bluetooth device you have previously paired, such as a headset, your smartwatch, or your vehicle's built-in Bluetooth.

5. Tap to mute the call. Tap again to turn off muting.

6. Tap to show the keypad if you need to type extra numbers after the call is connected.

7. Tap to boost the call volume if the caller is very soft.

8. Tap to put the call on hold.

9. Swipe to the right to see more options, such as the ability to write a memo that is associated with the caller.

10. Tap to write a memo that is associated with the caller while you're on the call.

11. Tap to open the Calendar app, view the calendar, and create a new appointment if needed.

12. Tap to open the Internet browser and use it while on the call.

13. Tap to send an SMS (text message) to the caller.

14. Tap to send an email to the caller.

15. Tap to show the caller's information in the Contacts app.

16. Swipe to the left to return to the main call screen.

17. Tap to end the call.

Reject a Call

If you do not want to accept the call, you can reject it so that it goes to your voicemail.

1. When the phone rings, swipe the red phone icon to the left to reject the call.

   The call goes to voicemail, and your Galaxy S6 displays the screen you were using before the call came in.

Reject a Call and Send a Text Message

Instead of simply declining a call and sending it to your voicemail, you can send an SMS (text message) straight back to the caller. Your Galaxy S6 provides a selection of canned messages for general needs. You can also create your own messages or type custom messages for particular calls.

1. When the phone rings, swipe up to display the Reject Call with Message shade.

2. Tap to send one of the canned messages.

Tap to create and send a custom message

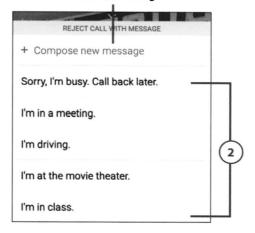

Creating Your Own Reject Messages

To create and save your own reject messages, open the Phone app and tap More. On the More menu, tap Settings. On the Call Settings screen, tap Call Rejection and then tap Rejection Messages. On the Rejection Messages screen, type a new rejection message and tap the plus symbol to create a new rejection message, or tap an existing message to open it for editing. Tap the red minus symbol to delete a rejection message.

Handle Missed Calls

If you miss a phone call, you can quickly locate it in the Phone app's logs so that you can return it, but you can also take actions on missed calls from the Lock screen or any other screen.

1. Tap to see the missed call from the Lock screen. If you use a Lock screen password or other method of locking your S6, you are required to use that method to unlock your S6 before you can continue.

2. Swipe from left to right across the missed call log entry to call the number back.

3. Swipe from right to left across the missed call log entry to send an SMS (text message) to the caller.

4. Tap the missed call log entry to see its details.

5. Tap to call the person back.

6. Tap to send an SMS (text message) to the caller.

7. Tap to delete one or more call log entries from this caller.

8. Tap to view the caller's full contact information (if you already have the person in your Contacts), or add the number to your Auto Reject list. When someone's number is on the Auto Reject list, your S6 automatically rejects calls from that number.

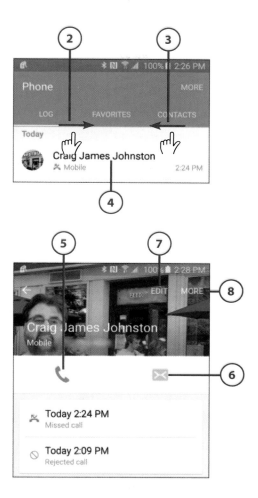

Making Calls

Aside from making a call the traditional way—by using the dialpad to punch in the numbers—you voice-dial a call on your Galaxy S6, or you can make a conference call.

Starting a Call from the Contacts App

Instead of launching the Phone app and then tapping the Contacts tab to go to the Contacts app, you can start a call directly from the Contacts app. Tap Contacts on the Home screen or the Apps screen to launch the Contacts app, tap the contact to display his or her details, and then tap the green phone icon to the right of the number you want to call.

Dial Using Your Voice

With the S Voice feature, your Galaxy S6 enables you to dial calls using your voice.

1. Say "Hi Galaxy" or whatever you set your S Voice Wake-up command to. A blue bar appears on the bottom of your screen indicating that S Voice is listening for a command. Please refer to the Prologue in the section "First-time Setup" to read more about the wake-up command.

2. Say "Call," followed by the contact's name; if the contact has multiple phone numbers, say the type of number as well. For example, say "Call Dana Smith mobile" or "Call Craig at Home."

3. Wait while S Voice dials the number. The Dialing screen appears.

Using Other Apps During a Call

During a call, you can use most other apps freely, but you cannot play music or video. You can take photos with the Camera app, but you cannot shoot videos. To switch to another app, either use the Recent Apps list or press the Home button and use the Apps screen as usual. While you are using another app, your Galaxy S6 displays a green bar at the top of the screen to remind you that you are on a call. Pull down the Notification Panel to control the call or return to it or take actions such as switch to speakerphone, mute, and hang up.

**Green bar indicates
call is in progress**

**Tap to return
to your call**

Make Conference Calls

You can quickly turn your current call into a conference call by adding other participants.

1. With a call in progress, tap Add Call on the call screen.

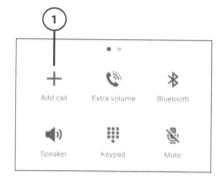

2. Dial the call in the most convenient way. For example, either type out the phone number or dial from the call log, Favorites, or Contacts.

3. Tap to swap between the original call and the one you just added, if you need to.

4. Tap Merge to merge the calls and complete the conference call setup.

5. Repeat Steps 1–4 to add additional callers. The exact number of callers you can have on a conference call is governed by your wireless carrier.

6. Tap Manage if you need to hang up on only one of the conference call parties, or if you need to split one of the parties off the conference call while still keeping them connected and on hold.

7. Tap the red phone icon to the right of a conference party you want to hang up on and remove from the conference call.

8. Tap Split if you want to remove the party from the conference call, but need to keep them connected to your phone and on hold.

Configuring the Phone App

To make the Phone app work your way, you can configure its settings.

1. Tap More.

2. Tap Settings.

3. Tap to enable or disable the feature that allows you to swipe over a call log entry to either place a call to that number, or send a text message to it.

4. Tap to choose certain numbers for which calls will be automatically rejected. Tapping here also lets you edit your canned call rejection messages.

5. Tap to choose whether you want to use Voice over LTE (VoLTE) when it is available.

6. Tap to choose how you want to answer and end calls. You can choose to use your voice (saying "answer" or "reject"), press the Home button, or press the Power button.

7. Tap to enable or disable a feature that automatically answers an incoming call if you have your S6 connected to a Bluetooth device or your vehicle's built-in Bluetooth.

8. Tap to choose options for vibrations, call status tones, and alerts during calls. You can choose whether your Galaxy S6 vibrates or plays a tone when someone answers your call and when they hang up. You can also choose to receive or suppress notifications during calls.

9. Tap to choose the ringtone that plays when you receive an incoming call. You can also choose whether you want your phone to vibrate when you receive an incoming call, and what vibration pattern to use.

10. Scroll down for more settings.

11. Tap to enable or disable Wi-Fi Calling, and choose how you want your S6 to utilize Wi-Fi Calling. You can choose to have your S6 prefer Wi-Fi but use cellular if Wi-Fi is unstable; prefer the cellular network, and only use Wi-Fi if cellular service is unavailable; or only use Wi-Fi for all calls.

12. Tap to see additional settings, including how Caller ID is handled, call forwarding, call waiting, and Fixed Dialing Numbers (FDN). When you tap, the settings are loaded over the wireless network, so you might need to wait a few seconds before they appear.

13. Tap to choose which voicemail service to use (if you have more than one option). If you use Google Voice, it is common to use the Google Voice voicemail system as opposed to the one provided by your wireless carrier.

14. Tap to adjust voicemail settings (if options are available).

15. Tap to choose your ringtone for announcing voicemail.

16. Tap to choose to also vibrate when you are notified of a new voicemail.

17. Tap to save your changes and return to the main phone screen.

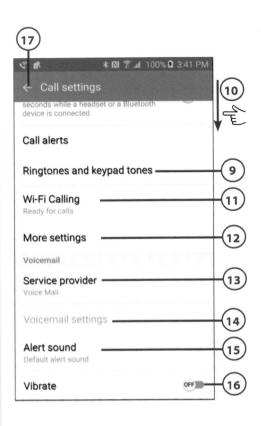

What Does Call Rejection Do?

Your Galaxy S6's call rejection feature allows you to specify certain numbers to automatically reject, or to reject incoming calls that have no number or show as Unknown. Automatically rejecting specific numbers enables you to avoid calls from people you do not want to talk to.

What Is VoLTE?

LTE (or Long-Term Evolution) is the fourth generation of cellular data technology (not to be confused with the slightly faster version of 3G technology that has been incorrectly called 4G for years). VoLTE stands for Voice over LTE. Effectively, your voice call is sent as regular data over the LTE data channel as opposed to over the cellular voice channel. Voice quality is much better due to the higher rate at which the data is transmitted and received, and if the person you are calling also uses VoLTE, you can speak at the same time. Most wireless carriers treat VoLTE as regular voice minutes and don't let it count against your data plan. However, you should verify the situation with your local wireless carrier; otherwise, your data plan might take an unexpected hit.

Store, manage, and use all your contacts

Search for contacts on your Galaxy S6

In this chapter, you find out how to add and search contacts and calendar events. Topics in this chapter include the following:

→ Setting up contacts accounts
→ Managing contacts
→ Searching for contacts
→ Linking contacts to social network website accounts
→ Using contacts

Managing Contacts

Your Galaxy S6 is highly capable of helping you organize your busy life. The preinstalled Contacts app helps you improve your daily efficiency by enabling you to manage personal contacts. This chapter takes a close look at what you can do with the Contacts app.

Configuring Contacts

The Contacts app enables you to manage all the important information you receive from colleagues, friends, and prospective business associates. Think of your Galaxy S6 as a virtual filing cabinet or Rolodex where you can store contact information such as names, addresses, emails, and notes. If you collect contacts with other social networking services, you can also configure Contacts to sync information between accounts.

Set Up Contacts Accounts

The Galaxy S6 can synchronize its contacts information with multiple accounts, such as Google, Corporate Exchange, other email providers, and sites such as Facebook and Google+. Information on your Galaxy S6 is updated when you make changes to information in your accounts.

1. Tap the Apps icon on the Home screen.

2. Tap the Settings icon.

Where's the Settings Icon?

The default location for the Settings icon is on the second page of the Apps screen, but if you reorganize your app icons, it might eventually end up in a different location. The first time you're looking for it, though, swipe from left to right to find it on the second page.

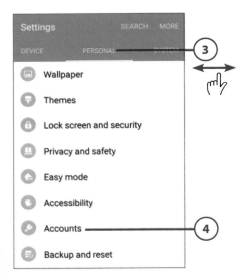

3. Swipe from right to left in the Settings screen until you open the Personal tab in the menu bar.

4. Tap Accounts.

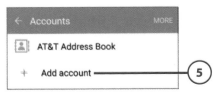

5. Tap Add Account.

6. Tap an account that you would like to set up. This example uses a Google account.

7. Follow the prompts to set up each account that you would like to add. The accounts you add appear in the Accounts area within the Settings list.

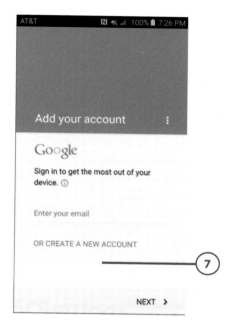

Add Contacts

Using the Contacts app, you can store contact information for family, friends, and colleagues for quick access and to send messages.

1. Tap Contacts on the Home screen.

Why Do I See a Data Backup Setup Screen?

After you tap the Contacts on the Home screen, you might see a screen asking you if you want to back up your contacts and other phone data to your data carrier's online file storage service. You can choose to set up your backup service or skip setup to continue with Step 2 in these instructions.

2. A list of all contacts appears.

3. Tap the Add icon to open the Save Contact To window.

4. Tap Device to choose whether to save the contact on your phone SIM card, on another account, or to Device so you save the contact on your Galaxy S6. Device is the default storage location.

Why Can't I Sync Contacts I Add to the Galaxy S6?

The Galaxy S6 can't sync contacts you add to the device itself to any other device to which you connect the Galaxy S6. If you want to sync to other devices, you can add the contact to your online contact database stored in your Samsung, Google, or Microsoft Exchange ActiveSync account.

5. Tap the photo icon to add a contact photo by either selecting a photo stored on your Galaxy S6 or taking a photo with the Galaxy S6 camera. After you select or take the photo, the photo appears to the left of the contact name.

6. Type the first and last name in the Name field.

7. If you want to add the first and last name in different fields, tap the arrow icon located to the right of the Name field to add a Name Prefix, First Name, Middle Name, Last Name, and Name Suffix to the contact. There is no need to use the Shift key on the keyboard to capitalize the name because the Galaxy S6 does this automatically.

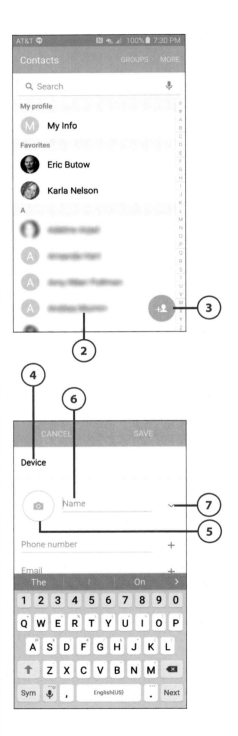

8. Tap the plus icon to the right of the Phone section text to add a phone number.

9. Type the phone number in the Phone field starting with the area code.

Don't Worry About Formatting

You don't need to type parentheses or dashes for the phone numbers you enter. The Galaxy S6 formats the number for you.

10. Specify the type of phone number you entered, such as the contact's home phone number, by tapping Mobile to the right of the phone number.

11. Tap the phone number type in the Select Phone Number Type window. After you tap the phone number type, the new type appears to the right of the phone number in the contact screen.

12. Return to the contact screen without making any changes by tapping the Back icon in the menu bar.

13. Tap the plus icon to the right of the Phone header text to add an additional field, or tap the minus icon to remove a field.

14. Close the keyboard by tapping the Back touch button.

15. Tap the plus icon to the right of the Email section text to add an email address.

16. Type the email address in the Email field.

17. Specify the type of email address you entered, such as the contact's work email address, by tapping Home to the right of the email address.

18. Tap the email address type on the Select Email Address Type screen. After you tap the email address type, the new type appears to the right of the email address in the contact screen.

19. Return to the contact screen without making any changes by tapping the Back icon in the menu bar.

20. Tap the plus icon to the right of the Email header text to add an additional field, or tap the minus icon to remove a field.

21. Close the keyboard by tapping the Back touch button.

22. Tap Groups to select a group in the Select Group screen.

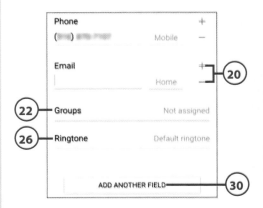

23. Tap one or more check boxes for the groups to which you want to assign a contact. You can select as many as eight groups: Favorites, ICE-Emergency Contacts, Business, Co-Workers, Family, Friends, My Contacts, or Starred in Android.

24. If you select one or more groups and then change your mind, you can undo assignment to one or more groups by tapping the Not Assigned check box.

25. Return to the contact screen by tapping the Back icon in the menu bar.

26. Tap Ringtone to specify a unique ringtone that sounds when this contact calls you.

27. In the Ringtones screen, swipe up and down the screen to view all available ringtones. The default ringtone is Default Ringtone.

28. Listen to the ringtone by tapping the ringtone name in the list.

29. Select the ringtone and stop the ringtone from playing by tapping the Back icon in the menu bar.

30. Tap Add Another Field to add more contact information.

31. In the Add Another Field window, swipe up and down the list to view all the fields you can add.

32. Tap Event to add events related to the contact, such as the person's birthday, and then tap Add.

33. Tap the Birthday label to choose the type of event you want to add, such as a birthday or anniversary.

34. Select the date by tapping Date and then selecting the date in the Date window.

35. Add another field to the form by swiping down the screen, repeating Steps 30 and 31, tapping the field you want to add, and then tapping Add.

36. Tap Save to complete the new contact.

>>>*Go Further*
UPDATING A CONTACT AND DISPLAYING CONTACTS

You can update a contact by first tapping an existing contact in the Contacts list and then tapping the Edit button located at the upper right of the screen. The contact screen opens so that you can edit or add information.

Tap to update a contact

You can control how your contacts are listed by setting sorting and display preferences. After you launch the Contacts app, you can tap the More button located at the upper-right corner of the screen, tap Settings, and then tap Sort By. The Display Contacts By menu enables you to list by First Name (which is the default setting) or by Last Name.

Tap to sort display order

Search for Contacts

Your list of contacts is sure to grow the longer you have your Galaxy S6. So how do you search your large list of contacts for a specific contact?

1. Tap Contacts on the Home screen.

2. Tap the Search field and use the keyboard to type the name of the contact you are looking for. As soon as you begin to type, the screen displays the contact that most closely reflects what you've typed into the field. Continue typing until you have narrowed the search.

3. View the contact in its entirety by tapping the contact in the list.

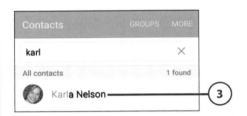

Link Contacts

When you synchronize the contacts on your Galaxy S6 with multiple accounts, such as the contact information you have on your Google account, you can have varying numbers and address information for a single contact. You can combine all the contacts' numbers and addresses in a single contact entry by linking contacts.

1. Tap Contacts on the Home screen. Your contact information appears on the screen.

2. Scroll down the contact list if necessary until you find the contact to which you want to join another contact. Tap the contact name in the list.

3. Tap the More option.

4. Tap Link Contacts in the menu.

5. Swipe down the list if necessary until you see the name of the contact you want to link to the contact you selected in Step 2.

6. Tap the name in the list; a green check box with a white check mark appears to the left of the contact name.

7. Tap Link.

How Many Contacts Can I Link?

You can link as many as nine contacts at one time. As you tap each name in the list, you see the number of contacts you've linked out of the maximum nine you selected in the orange menu bar at the top of the screen. For example, if you see 3/9 in the menu bar, you know you've selected three of the maximum nine contacts you can link.

8. The contacts are now linked and the information for both entries in each account has merged.

9. Add another contact by tapping More and then repeating Steps 4 through 7.

10. Close the Contact window by tapping the Back icon in the menu bar.

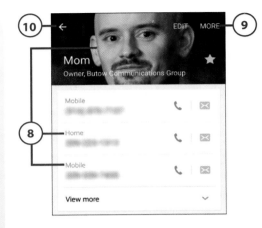

Use Contacts

After you have entered a contact in your Galaxy S6, you can utilize a few functions and displays directly from the Contacts page. Start by opening a contact's record.

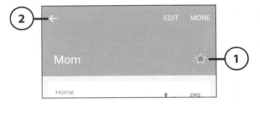

1. Tap the star icon to the right of the contact name to set that contact as a favorite. The star color changes from gray to gold, which signifies the contact is a favorite.

2. Return to the contact list by tapping the Back icon in the menu bar.

3. Tap Groups to view the list of contacts you have assigned to a group.

4. Press and hold your finger on a contact's name in the contact list. After a second, a green check box with a white check mark appears to the left of the contact name.

5. Tap Share to open the Share Namecard With/Via window.

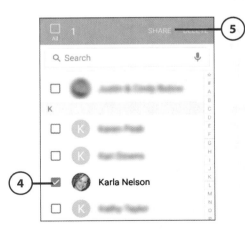

6. Select how to share the contact's name card. (Think of a name card as an electronic business card.) Choices are Android Beam, your carrier mail service (in this example, AT&T Mail), Bluetooth, Google Drive, or in an email message sent using the Email or Gmail apps.

7. Tap the page icon to view more sharing options on the second page within the window.

8. Share the contact's name card in an email message using the Messages app, OneNote, Samsung Quick Connect, or Wi-Fi Direct.

9. Close the window without sharing your selected contact by tapping the Back touch button.

How Do I Unlink Contacts?

Unlink contacts by tapping the linked contact name in the contact list. Next, tap More in the upper right corner of the screen and then tap Unlink Contacts in the menu. In the Linked Contact window, tap the red minus icon to the right of the contact name you want to unlink. The contact name you unlinked no longer appears in the Linked Contact window. Tap the Back touch button to view the newly unlinked contact's information screen.

Track your appointments and events

Add events and tasks to your calendar

In this chapter, you find out how to organize your daily schedule and add calendar events within the preinstalled Calendar app. Topics in this chapter include the following:

→ Checking and adding events to your personal schedule
→ Creating calendar events
→ Using calendar views
→ Adding and managing tasks

Using the Calendar

The preinstalled Calendar app on the Galaxy S6 helps you improve your daily efficiency by enabling you to schedule and stay apprised of important appointments. This chapter takes a close look at how you can use the Calendar app to help keep your daily life on track.

Managing Your Busy Schedule

The Calendar app enables you to manage all your appointments and events from one convenient location. Calendar enables you to view a busy schedule in multiple views such as Day, Week, Month, Year, and Agenda. You can also instruct Calendar to send you a reminder, in the form of an alert, before an event to help ensure that you never miss a meeting and are always on time.

Create Calendar Events

Your Galaxy S6 was designed for you to be mobile while still enabling you to manage the important stuff, such as doctor appointments, business meetings, and anniversaries. The Calendar app enables you to add important event dates to calendars to help ensure that you do not over-look them.

1. Tap the Apps icon on the Home screen.

2. Tap Calendar.

3. By default, the calendar opens to the Month and Agenda view. The current date is indicated by a green circle around the date.

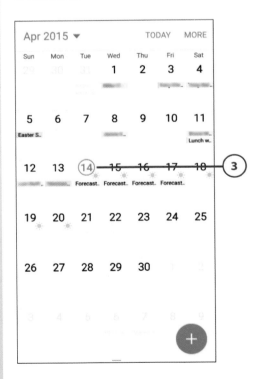

4. Tap the date for which you want to add an event. A green circle appears around the date.

5. If the date has one or more events associated with it, such as the day's weather forecast, the information appears in the Agenda window below the date. Close the window by tapping the Close icon.

6. Tap the + button in the lower-right corner of the screen to open the Appointment screen.

7. The Title field is selected by default. Type a title for the event in the field.

8. Tap the palette icon to select an event color in the Select Event Color window.

9. Slide the All Day slider from left (Off) to right (On) if the event will happen all day.

10. Tap the date and time in the Start field to enter the start date and time of the event. You can also use the controls in the Set Date and Time window to designate an event for a future date and not just the date you specified in Step 4. When you tap the date and time in the Start field, the Calendar window appears so you can select a future date and time.

11. The current month appears in the calendar, and the date you set for the event in Step 4 is highlighted in the calendar. Change the event date by swiping left and right within the calendar to view months and dates and then tap the date for the event within the calendar.

12. Tap the up and down arrows in the hour and minute tiles to enter the start time for the event.

13. Tap the time of day tile to change the time between AM and PM.

14. Tap Done.

15. Tap the date and time in the End field to bring up the controls and set the date and time for the event as you did when you set the date in the Start field.

Can I Set the Start and End Times Within the Calendar Window?

When you set the start or end times for an appointment, the Start or End buttons are highlighted in green at the top of the Calendar window depending on the time you're editing. If you want to change the start or end time without exiting the window, tap the white Start or End button at the top of the window to change the start or end time, respectively.

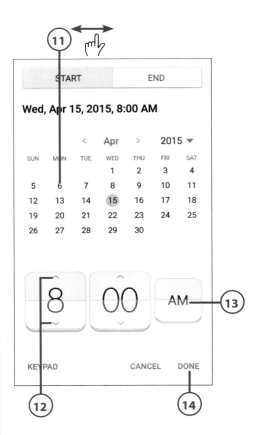

16. Tap the email address to change the account that contains the calendar to which you want to add the event.

17. Tap the account in the Calendar window. You can choose from My Calendars, which is the calendar stored on the Galaxy S6, or another calendar, such as the one stored in your Google account.

18. Tap the Reminder button to choose an alarm time for the event.

19. Tap Notification to have the event reminder appear as a notification, or you can send the notification to your email account.

20. Tap the time you want the alarm to appear. You can select from five options from On Time (the time the event starts) to one day before the start time. You can also customize the alarm time by tapping Customize and then setting the time in the Reminder window.

21. Remove the alarm by tapping the red minus icon.

22. Tap the plus icon at the right of the Reminder field to add another notification that will appear at a different time and/or be delivered in a different manner.

23. Tap the Location field to add a location for the event.

24. If you want to find the location in the Maps app, tap Map to the right of the field. You find out more about using the Maps app in Chapter 7, "Google Now and Navigation Using Google Maps."

25. Tap Repeat if you need to set a repeating cycle for the event.

26. Tap Invitees to add names from your contacts.

27. Tap Notes to type a description for the event.

28. Make the event private (that is, viewable only by you) by tapping Privacy. Otherwise, the event is public, so anyone who sees your calendar can view the event.

29. Tap Time Zone to change the time zone for the event.

30. Tap Save to complete the event and save it to your calendar.

How Do I View the Reminder in the Status Bar?

When you receive a reminder, you get an audio reminder and also see a reminder icon at the left side of the Status bar. Tap and hold your finger on the top edge of the screen and swipe down to open the Quick Settings and Notification Panel. The reminder displays at the bottom of the Notifications area.

Use Calendar Views

The four views in which you can see the contents of your calendar are Year, Month and Agenda, Week, and Day. This section examines each view.

Year View

The Year view shows the entire calendar year. Open the Year view by tapping the calendar view, such as the month, at the left side of the menu bar and then tapping Year in the list.

The current year appears above the calendar. Swipe from left to right to view the calendar for the previous year, or swipe from right to left to view a calendar for the following year. When you change the year, your selected year appears at the left side of the menu bar. Tap Today in the menu bar to highlight the current date in the calendar.

Current year — 2015 ▼   TODAY — **Jump to today's calendar**

January	February	March
S M T W T F S	S M T W T F S	S M T W T F S
1 2 3	1 2 3 4 5 6 7	1 2 3 4 5 6 7
4 5 6 7 8 9 10	8 9 10 11 12 13 14	8 9 10 11 12 13 14
11 12 13 14 15 16 17	15 16 17 18 19 20 21	15 16 17 18 19 20 21
18 19 20 21 22 23 24	22 23 24 25 26 27 28	22 23 24 25 26 27 28
25 26 27 28 29 30 31		29 30 31

April	May	June
S M T W T F S	S M T W T F S	S M T W T F S
1 2 3 4	1 2	1 2 3 4 5 6
5 6 7 8 9 10 11	3 4 5 6 7 8 9	7 8 9 10 11 12 13
12 13 14 15 16 17 18	10 11 12 13 14 15 16	14 15 16 17 18 19 20
19 20 21 22 23 24 25	17 18 19 20 21 22 23	21 22 23 24 25 26 27
26 27 28 29 30	24 25 26 27 28 29 30	28 29 30
	31	

July	August	September
S M T W T F S	S M T W T F S	S M T W T F S
1 2 3 4	1	1 2 3 4 5
5 6 7 8 9 10 11	2 3 4 5 6 7 8	6 7 8 9 10 11 12
12 13 14 15 16 17 18	9 10 11 12 13 14 15	13 14 15 16 17 18 19
19 20 21 22 23 24 25	16 17 18 19 20 21 22	20 21 22 23 24 25 26
26 27 28 29 30 31	23 24 25 26 27 28 29	27 28 29 30
	30 31	

October	November	December
S M T W T F S	S M T W T F S	S M T W T F S
1 2 3	1 2 3 4 5 6 7	1 2 3 4 5
4 5 6 7 8 9 10	8 9 10 11 12 13 14	6 7 8 9 10 11 12
11 12 13 14 15 16 17	15 16 17 18 19 20 21	13 14 15 16 17 18 19
18 19 20 21 22 23 24	22 23 24 25 26 27 28	20 21 22 23 24 25 26
25 26 27 28 29 30 31	29 30	27 28 29 30 31

Day View

The Day view is composed of a list of events over the current day. These events are blocked for each hour. Open the Day view by tapping the calendar view, such as the year or the current month, at the left side of the menu bar. Then tap Day in the menu.

Previous day

Current date — May 1, 2015 ▼   TODAY — MORE — Jump to today's calendar

Sun   Mon   Tue   Wed   Thu   Fri   Sat

26   27   28   29   30   ①   2 — Next day

📍 Jackson   59°F ☀

All-day event — Book events in Bay area — Current day

Forecast for Jackson, CA (85° | 57°)

8 AM

9

10

11

12 PM

1

⊕ — Add event

You can press your finger to the list and flick up or down to scroll through the list of events. All events scheduled with a duration of All Day are located at the very top of the list.

Tap Today in the menu bar to open the calendar for the current date. The timeline located just under the menu bar enables you to tap specific days three days before and three days after the current day. Swipe to the left or right within the timeline to move to the previous or following week, respectively. Tap Today in the menu bar to return to the current day's schedule no matter where you are in the calendar.

You can tap an event in the window to view notes, edit the entry, delete the event, or share it as a VCS or text file using your phone carrier's mail service (if any), Android Beam, Bluetooth, OneNote, in a memo, on the clipboard, the Google Drive online file storage service, the Email or Gmail apps, Facebook or Google+, the Memo app, the Messages or Hangouts instant messaging apps, Samsung Quick Connect, or Wi-Fi.

Week View

The Week view is arranged into seven-day parts. Open the Week view by tapping the calendar view, such as the year or the current day, at the left side of the menu bar. Then tap Week in the menu.

Tap the left arrow to the left of the current week or the right arrow to the right of the current week to view the previous and following week, respectively. Tap Today in the menu bar to highlight the current date.

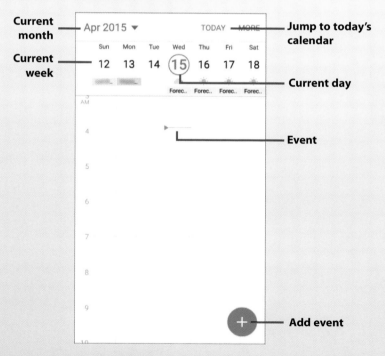

Each event for that week is found in its respective scheduled day block. You can tap an event in the window to view notes, edit the entry, delete the event, or share it as a VCS or text file using your phone carrier's mail service (if any), Android Beam, Bluetooth, OneNote, in a memo, on the clipboard, the Google Drive online file storage service, the

Email or Gmail apps, Facebook or Google+, the Memo app, the Messages or Hangouts instant messaging apps, Samsung Quick Connect, or Wi-Fi.

Month and Agenda View

The Month and Agenda view provides a broad view of events for a given month. Month and Agenda view contains a monthly calendar with an agenda of events and tasks listed within each calendar date box. Open the Month and Agenda view by tapping the calendar view, such as the year or the current week, at the left side of the menu bar. Then tap Month and Agenda View in the menu.

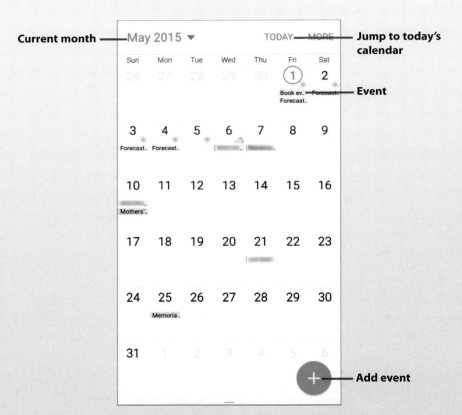

Each section lists the events scheduled for that particular month. The current day block
you are viewing is highlighted within the calendar section. Any event designated as an All
Day Event is highlighted in the day block of the Calendar view.

Tap Today in the menu bar to highlight the current date in the calendar. The current
month appears above the calendar. Swipe from left to right to view the calendar for the
previous month, or swipe from right to left to view a calendar for the following month.
When you change the year, your selected month appears in the upper-left corner of the
screen.

Tap the date to view the agenda for the day in the Agenda window. You can close the
window by tapping the Close icon in the upper right corner of the window.

The Close icon

An all-day event and
the weather forecast in
the Agenda window

You can tap an event in the window to view notes, edit the entry, delete the event, or
share it as a VCS or text file using your phone carrier's mail service (if any), Android Beam,
Bluetooth, OneNote, in a memo, on the clipboard, the Google Drive online file storage
service, the Email or Gmail apps, Facebook or Google+, the Memo app, the Messages or
Hangouts instant messaging apps, Samsung Quick Connect, or Wi-Fi.

View More Event Options

Within the Month and Agenda, Week, and Day views you can access more options for finding events and tasks, managing your calendars, and changing settings.

1. Tap More in the menu bar.

2. Tap Search to open the Search screen and search for one or more events.

3. Tap Manage Calendars to open the Manage Calendars screen so you can add an account with a calendar to create a combined calendar view across all accounts. You can also determine what information appears in your agenda for each day, such as the day's weather forecast.

4. Tap Settings to change app setting information including showing or hiding declined event information.

Add a Task to Your Calendar

It's easy to add a task to your calendar so you can be reminded about deadlines for getting something important done.

1. Tap the current view information, such as the year or the current month, at the left side of the menu bar.

2. Tap Tasks in the menu to open the Tasks screen.

3. In the window, tap in the Enter New Task field.

4. Type a title for the task in the Enter New Task field. When you start typing you see buttons and options appear around the field.

5. Tap Today to set the current day as the due date.

6. Tap Tomorrow to set the next day as the due date.

7. Save the task by tapping Save. If you don't specify a due date, you'll see the task in the task list under the No New Date section. The last two sections in this chapter explain more about the task list.

8. Tap the Expand icon to view and change all details within the task.

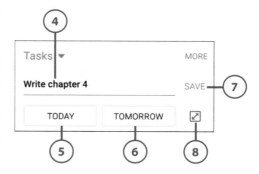

Do I Have to Retype a Recurring Task Title Every Time I Add a New Task?

If you entered a task title previously, when you start typing you'll see a list of previously entered task titles underneath the Today and Tomorrow icons. You can tap the title in the list to save yourself time and effort.

9. Slide the Due Date slider from left (Off) to right (On).

10. Tap the date in the Due Date button to enter the due date for the task.

11. Tap the left or right arrows on either side of the current month to move to the previous month or following month, respectively. You can also swipe to the left and right in the calendar to move to the following or previous month, respectively.

12. If you want to set the due date in a different year, tap the year. You can swipe up and down in the pop-up menu to view past and future years as well as the current year. When you find the year, tap it in the menu.

13. When you see the calendar for the month in which you want to set the due date, tap the due date in the calendar. The date is highlighted with a green circle.

14. Tap Done.

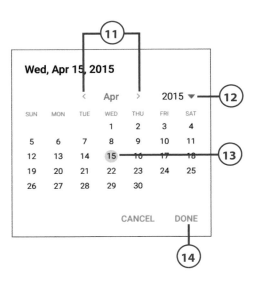

15. Tap My Task to open the Task window and determine where you want to store the task. By default you store tasks on your Galaxy S6, but you can store tasks in another account such as your Samsung account.

16. Tap Reminder to open the Reminder window and set a reminder type. You can set a reminder on the due date or set a customized reminder, which is on a date of your choosing.

17. Tap Notes to type a description for the task.

18. Tap Priority and then tap High in the Priority tile that appears. In the menu, you can change the priority level to High, Medium, or Low. The default priority is High.

19. Tap Save to complete the task and save it to your calendar.

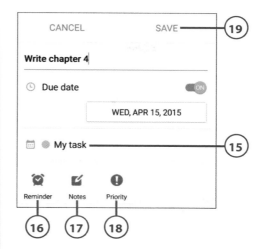

View the Task List and Remove Tasks

After you save the task, the task appears on the date within the calendar. Tasks are categorized by due date, and the task list is sorted from newest to oldest; that is, tasks with the closest due date appear at the top of the list, and future tasks appear further down the list.

View the task details in the Tasks screen by tapping the task in the list. When you complete the task or you decide to remove it from the list, tap the check box to the left of the task name. After you tap the check box, tap the Delete All button below the Enter New Task field.

How Can I Keep the Task After I Tap the Check Box?

If you tapped the check box next to a task and decide that you don't want to delete it, just tap the check box again. The check mark in the check box and the Delete All button disappear.

View More Task Options

As with the Month and Agenda, Week, and Day views, you can access more options in the Tasks view so you can search for events and tasks, manage your calendars, and change settings. You can also delete one or more tasks from the list as well as share your tasks using a variety of methods.

1. Tap More in the menu bar.

2. Tap Edit to open the Edit screen and then select one or more tasks you want to delete. After you select one or more tasks, tap Delete in the menu bar that appears at the top of the Edit screen.

3. Tap Share to open the Select Tasks screen and select one, several, or all your tasks to share. You can share the task using your phone carrier's mail service (if any), Android Beam, Bluetooth, OneNote, the Google Drive online file storage service, the Email or Gmail apps, the Messages app, Samsung Quick Connect, or Wi-Fi.

4. Tap Search to open the Search screen and search for one or more events or tasks.

5. Tap Manage Calendars to open the Manage Calendars screen so you can add an account with a calendar to create a combined task view across all accounts. You can also hide tasks on your device or stored in other accounts such as your Samsung account.

6. Tap Settings to change app setting information including changing how you are notified of upcoming task due dates including what notification sound plays and/or if you want the Galaxy S6 to vibrate when there's a task coming due.

>>>Go Further
EDIT A TASK

When you edit a task by tapping Edit in the More menu, you're not editing the task at all—you're deleting it. When you want to edit the task, tap the task name within the Tasks screen. You can also edit a task from within the Month and Agenda, Week, or Day views by tapping the task name below the current date or the week you're viewing, depending on the calendar view.

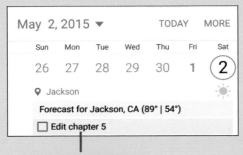

The task appears below the calendar week in Day view

Learn how to browse the
Web and view websites
using the built-in
Internet app

The Galaxy S6 comes with two built-in browsers: Google Chrome and Samsung's Internet app. In this chapter, you see how to browse the Web using the Samsung Internet app, which is designed specifically so you can get the most from the Web on your Galaxy S6. This chapter covers the following topics:

5

→ Browsing to a URL

→ Searching the Web

→ Viewing web pages

→ Bookmarking websites

→ Returning to previously visited websites

→ Deleting bookmarks

→ Filling in web forms

→ Copying text and images from web pages

Browsing the Web

The Galaxy S6 is a great tool for viewing web pages, whether you're at home or you're on the go. No matter which Galaxy S6 model you use, the screen is much larger than a mobile phone, so you can see more on the Galaxy S6 screen. Because you can touch the screen, you can interact with web content in ways that a computer typically cannot.

Browsing to a URL

It's likely that you already know how to browse to different web pages in your favorite web browser on your computer. The Internet app on the Galaxy S6 works much the same as the browser on your computer, but there are some differences.

1. On the Home screen, tap Internet.

2. Swipe down the screen to view the Address field.

3. Tap the Address field at the top of the screen. The keyboard opens at the bottom of the screen so you can type a Uniform Resource Locator (URL), which can be a website name or a specific page in a website.

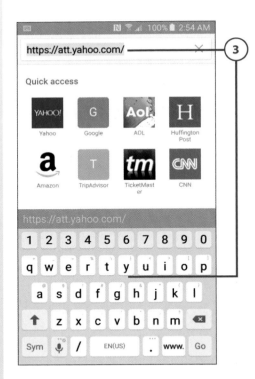

4. Start typing a URL, such as sam-sung.com or play.google.com. You can also tap an icon within the Quick Access site list that appears below the Address field.

5. Tap Go on the keyboard when you finish typing.

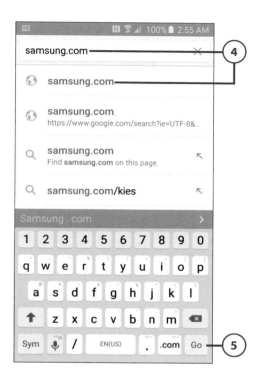

Tips for Typing a URL

The Internet app doesn't require you to type the "http://" or the "www." at the beginning of the URL. For example, if you type samsung.com or www.samsung.com, you still go to the Samsung Home web page. However, there might be some instances when you need to type in "http://" or even "https://" (for a secure web page) at the beginning of the URL. If you do, the Internet app lets you know so that you can type in the "http://" or "https://" in the Address field.

Searching the Web

The Internet app makes it easy for you to search the Web, so you don't need to know every URL of every web page out there (which is good considering there are literally billions of web pages). As you type, the Internet app suggests search terms you've used in the past as well as search terms you might be looking for.

1. On the Home screen, tap Internet.

2. Swipe down the screen to view the Address field.

3. Tap the Address field at the top of the screen. The keyboard opens at the bottom of the screen so you can type the URL. Start typing your search term. As you type, a list appears underneath the address bar with suggestions. You can stop typing at any time and scroll down the list to find your search term; tap the search term to select it and start the search.

4. If the list doesn't include what you're looking for, open the Google search page by tapping Go in the keyboard.

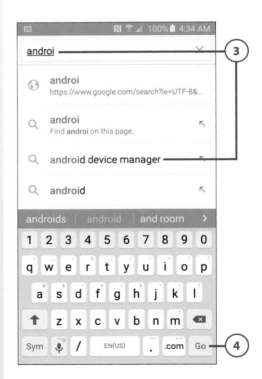

5. Tap any link on the Google search results page to go to that web page.

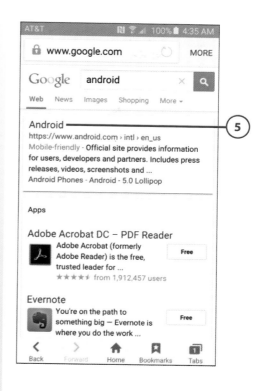

>>>Go Further
TIPS FOR SEARCHING THE WEB

You can search deeper within Google itself. For example, if you put a + in front of a search term, you're telling Google that you require the word in the search results. If you put quotes around a search term ("term"), you're telling Google that you want to search for results that contain that term. Scroll to the bottom of the search page and then tap Help to get more information about how you can get the most from your Google searches. You then see the Search Help screen where you can swipe up and down the screen to view help articles in a variety of topics.

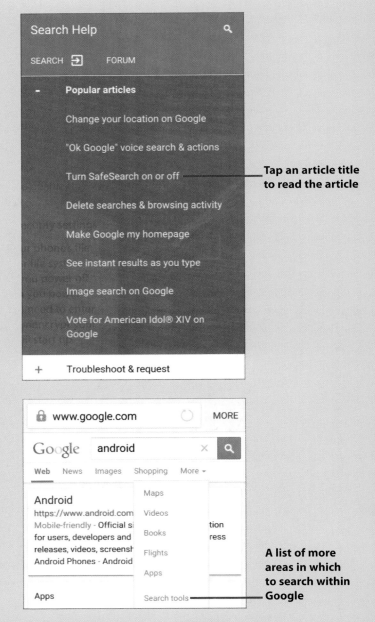

Tap an article title
to read the article

A list of more
areas in which
to search within
Google

If you look at the top of Google's search results page, you see links so you can search for more than text terms, including Images and Videos. If you click the More link, a pop-up list displays so you can search a variety of other areas within Google.

Viewing Web Pages

After you open a website, you can control what you view on the web page in several ways. These techniques enable you access the entire web page and navigate between web pages in the Internet app.

1. Navigate to a web page using one of the two methods described in the previous tasks in this chapter.

2. As you view a page, you can drag up and down the page with your finger. You can also flick with your finger to scroll quickly. After you flick, the screen scrolls, decelerates, and then comes to a stop.

Why Can't I Zoom In and Out on a Web Page?

Many websites have pages that are optimized for reading on a mobile device. What's more, many websites can automatically detect the device you're using to view the website and will load pages that are maximized for best use on your screen. When you're viewing a website page designed for a smartphone like the Galaxy S6, you can't zoom in and out on the page because the page is already sized to the dimensions of your screen.

3. Zoom in by pinching out on the screen. Zoom out by pinching in on the screen.

4. While you're zoomed in, you can touch and drag left and right to view different parts of the web page.

5. Move to another web page from a link in the current web page by tapping a link. Links are usually an underlined or colored piece of text, but they can also be pictures or images that look like buttons.

Hunting for Links

Unfortunately, it isn't always easy to figure out which parts of a web page are links and which ones aren't. Back in the early days of the Web, all links were blue and underlined. As web page elements have become more enhanced over time, it's now more common to find links in any color and any text style. What's more, graphics that are links aren't underlined, either.

On a computer's web browser it's easy to find out which element is a link when you move the mouse pointer over the link because the pointer changes shape. In Android, there is no cursor, so you can't find out if a web page element is a link unless you tap it and see what happens.

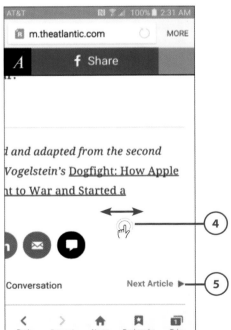

Working with Bookmarks

As you browse websites, you might want to save some of the websites in a list of your favorites so you can go back to them later. In browser parlance, this saving process is called "bookmarking." If you find there are websites that you don't visit anymore or that go to obsolete or missing web pages, you can delete a bookmark from the Bookmarks list or from the History list.

Create a Bookmark

1. Navigate to any page in the Internet app.

2. Swipe down the screen to view the Address bar at the top of the screen and the menu bar at the bottom of the screen.

3. Tap Bookmarks to open the Bookmarks screen.

4. Add a bookmark by tapping Add.

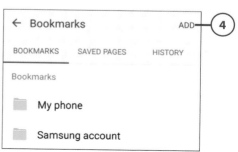

5. Edit the title of the bookmark. The official title of the web page is filled in and highlighted for you, but you can change the name by typing the new name using the keyboard. To change the folder in which the bookmark is stored, proceed with Step 6. Otherwise, skip to Step 11.

6. To change the folder in which the bookmark is stored, tap the folder name, which is My Phone in this example.

7. Create a new bookmarks folder by tapping Create.

8. Tap the Enter Folder Name field and then type the name of your new folder.

9. Tap Save.

10. Tap the name of the folder into which you want to place the bookmark.

11. Tap Save.

12. Tap the parent folder in the folder list.

13. Tap the new folder name in the folder list; the new bookmark appears within the folder on the screen.

14. Tap Bookmarks to return to the main Bookmarks folder.

Should I Edit a Bookmark Title?

Because the titles of web pages are usually long and descriptive, it's a good idea to shorten the title to something you can recognize easily in your bookmarks list. Every bookmark also includes a thumbnail picture of what the web page looks like so you can identify the bookmark more easily. If you would rather view bookmarks by title, tap and hold the bookmark title until a green check box with a white check mark appears to the left of the bookmark. Next, tap More at the right side of the menu bar and then tap Edit Bookmark in the menu.

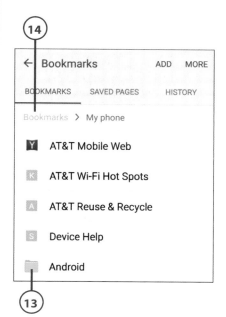

Delete a Bookmark from the Bookmarks List

1. Tap Bookmarks in the menu bar at the bottom of the Internet screen as described in the "Create a Bookmark" task. In the Bookmarks screen, tap the folder (and, if necessary, the subfolder) that contains the bookmark.

2. Tap and hold your finger on the bookmark you want to delete until a green check box with a white check mark appears to the left of the bookmark.

3. Delete the bookmark instantly by tapping Delete.

Sync Your Bookmarks

You can sync the bookmarks in your favorite web browser on your desktop or laptop computer with the Internet app so you have maximum control over your bookmarks. You can read more about syncing your Galaxy S6 in Chapter 11, "Sharing and Synchronizing Data."

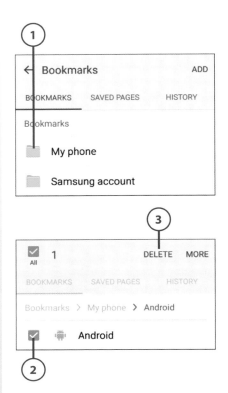

Delete a Bookmark from the History List

1. Tap the Bookmarks button in the menu bar at the bottom of the Internet screen.

2. In the Bookmarks screen, tap the History tab. This brings up a list of web pages you've viewed recently.

3. Tap and hold your finger on the website entry you want to delete until a green check box with a white check mark appears to the left of the bookmark.

4. Tap Delete.

5. The website no longer appears in the list of web pages.

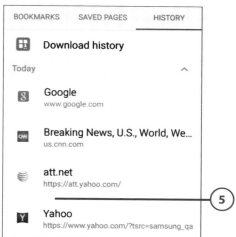

Returning to Previously Visited Pages

It's easy to return to the last page you visited in the Internet app—just press the Back button. As you keep pressing the Back button, you keep going back to pages you visited. In the History page, the Internet app also keeps a list of all web pages you've visited during your browsing session.

Browsing Forward

Like with any web browser, you can browse more recent pages you've viewed in your current browsing session by tapping the Forward button, which is the right-arrow button immediately to the right of the Back button.

1. Visit several web pages in the Internet app if you haven't done so already.

2. Swipe down the screen to view the Address bar at the top of the screen and the menu bar at the bottom of the screen.

3. Tap Bookmarks.

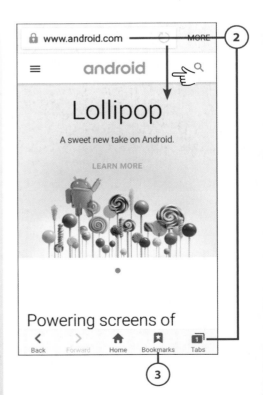

4. Tap the History tab in the Bookmarks screen.

5. The list of web pages you visited for the current date appears within the Today section.

Tips for Using History

If you want to hide the history for a specific day so you can see history for another day, tap the header for the specific day. For example, if you want to hide all the web pages for today, click the Today header above the first web page in the Today list. The Today header is still visible, but you won't see the web pages. You can view the web pages again by tapping the Today header.

You can also clear the entire history database by tapping More at the right side of the menu bar that appears at the top of the screen. In the menu, tap Clear History.

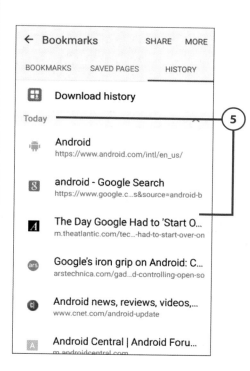

Filling in Web Forms

On many web pages, you are asked to fill in forms, such as for signing up for a company's email newsletter or to get more information about a product. Filling out web forms on your Galaxy S6 is similar to filling out forms on a computer's web browser, but there are differences.

1. Navigate to a page that you know contains a form. (The sample page is at http://code.google.com/p/android/issues/entry.)

2. Tap in a text box.

3. The keyboard appears at the bottom of the screen. Use the keyboard to type text into the box; the screen enlarges so you can see the text box more easily. Tap the Go button when you finish typing.

4. Select an item in a pull-down menu by tapping the box.

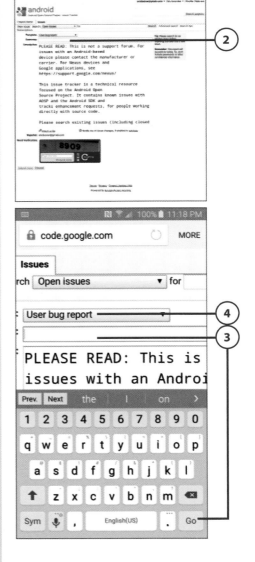

5. Tap an item in the menu to select it. If the menu list is long, touch and drag up and down to view more selections.

6. The menu closes and the selected item appears in the field.

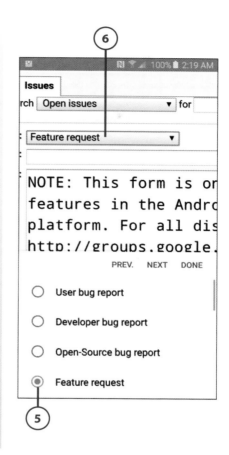

Special Menus

Some websites use special menus that are built from scratch. In these cases, the menu looks exactly like the one you get when you view the web page on a computer. If the web page is well constructed, it should work fine on the Galaxy S6. However, it might be a little more difficult to make a selection.

Copying Text and Images from Web Pages

The Internet app treats web pages like other documents. That is, you can copy text and images from a web page you view in a browser to another app.

Copy a Block of Text

You can select text from web pages to copy and paste into other documents such as email messages or your own text documents.

1. Navigate to a web page in the Internet app if you haven't done so already.

2. Hold down your finger on the first word in the block of text and then release your finger. The first word is highlighted in blue with "handles" at the beginning and end of the word.

3. Hold down your finger on the bottom handle (the one on the right side of the word) and drag over the text you want to copy. When you are finished, release your finger. The selected text is highlighted in blue.

4. In the pop-up menu that appears above the selected text, tap Copy. Android informs you that the text has been copied to the clipboard. You can now go to another application, such as Gmail (or an email form on another web page), and paste the text into a text area. For example, in Gmail you tap and hold on the cursor in the message for a second or two and then tap Paste in the pop-up menu that appears above the cursor.

Copy an Image

In addition to being able to copy and paste text from the Internet app, you can also copy images from a web page and save them to an email message or a photo collection.

1. Go to a web page that includes an image on the page.

2. Tap and hold your finger on that image for a couple of seconds and then release your finger. The image menu window appears on the screen.

3. Tap Save Image. This saves your image to the Galaxy S6 so you can view and use it in any app where you select images from your photo albums. Note that the menu options may differ depending on the image you select.

Why Do I See Save Instead of Save Image?

You see the Save Image option for an image after you select an image that has a web page link included. If there is no link included with an image, then you see a smaller image menu window with three options: Save, Copy, and View. Tap Save to save the image to your Galaxy S6.

HM1900 Bluetooth Headset, Dark Gray
BHM1900NDACSTA
★★★★★ (10) Write a review
PRICE: **$39.99**

ADD TO CART

LEARN MORE

http://www.samsung.com/us/
mobile/cell-phones...

Open

Open in new tab

Save link

Copy link

Save image

Copy image

View image

4. As the file downloads, the download icon appears in the Status bar.

5. Hold your finger on the Status bar and swipe down to open the Quick Settings and Notification Panel.

6. Scroll down the notification area if necessary and then tap the image filename to open the file in the Gallery or Photos app.

Personal and company email

Gmail and other personal email

Text messages

In this chapter, you discover your Galaxy S6's email applications for Gmail and other accounts, such as POP3, IMAP, and even Microsoft Exchange. In addition you discover how to use the Messages app for text messaging. Topics include the following:

→ Sending and receiving email
→ Working with attachments
→ Sending and receiving text messages
→ Sending and receiving multimedia messages

Email and Text Messages

Your Galaxy S6 has two email programs: the Gmail app, which works with Gmail, POP3, and IMAP email accounts, and the Email app that works with POP3, IMAP, and Microsoft Exchange (corporate email) accounts. In addition, you can use the Messages app to send and receive text messages

Gmail

When you first set up your Galaxy S6, you set up a Gmail account. The Gmail application enables you to have multiple Gmail accounts, which is useful if you have a business account and a personal account. If you don't want to add a second Gmail account, you can skip this section.

Add a Google Account

When you first set up your Galaxy S6, you added your first Google (Gmail) account, but you might have other Gmail accounts that you'd also like to access through your Galaxy S6. The following steps describe how to add a second account.

1. Pull down the Notification Panel and tap the Settings icon.

2. Tap Accounts under the Personal section.

3. Tap Add Account.

4. Tap Google.

5. Enter your existing Google account name. This is your Gmail address.

6. Tap Next.

What If I Don't Have a Second Google Account?

If you don't already have a second Google account but want to set one up, in Step 5, tap Create a New Account. Your Galaxy S6 walks you through the steps of creating a new Google account.

7. Enter your existing Google password.

8. Tap Next.

9. Tap Accept.

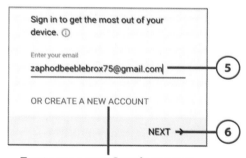

Tap to get a new Google account

10. Select Remind Me Later and tap Next to bypass setting up payment information for Google Wallet for this Google account. Right now you just want to set up the email account.

11. Select what components of your Google account you want to synchronize with your Galaxy S6.

12. Tap Next to finish the Google account setup.

Why Multiple Google Accounts?

You are probably wondering why you would want multiple Google accounts. Isn't one good enough? Actually, it is not that uncommon to have multiple Google accounts. It can be a way to compartmentalize your life between work and play. You might run a small business using one account, but email only friends with another. Your Galaxy S6 supports multiple accounts, but still enables you to interact with them in one place.

Add a POP3/IMAP Account

Unlike previous versions of the Gmail app, the latest version supports the non-Gmail account types of POP3 and IMAP. If you don't want to add a POP3 or IMAP account to the Gmail app, you can skip this section.

1. Pull down the Notification Panel and tap the Settings icon.

2. Tap Accounts under the Personal section.

3. Tap Add Account.

4. Tap Personal (IMAP) or Personal (POP3). This example uses an IMAP account type. However, the steps are the same for a POP3 account type.

5. Enter your IMAP account's email address.

6. Tap Next.

What Is Manual Setup?

If you are using an email service provider that is not well known, or you are using email from your personal domain, the Gmail app may not be able to automatically work out the server settings. In that situation you might want to tap Manual Setup, which enables you to enter all information manually.

7. Enter the password for the email account you are adding.

8. Tap Next.

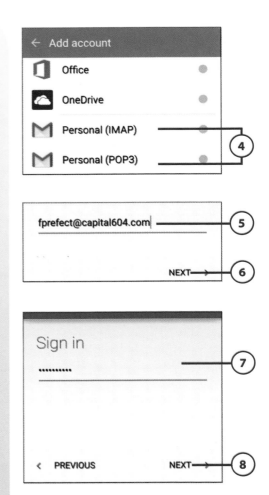

9. Verify the incoming server name and change if needed.

10. Verify the port number and change if needed.

11. Verify the security type and change if needed.

12. Tap Next.

13. Verify the outgoing server name and change if needed.

14. Verify the port number and change if needed.

15. Verify the security type and change if needed.

16. Check the box if your email provider requires that you use your username and password when sending email. This is almost always the case.

17. Tap Next.

Carried over from previous screens

Carried over from previous screens

18. Tap to choose how often the Gmail app automatically looks for and downloads new email in this account. You can also set it to Never, which means that email from this account is only downloaded when you open the Gmail app.

19. Check the box to be notified when new email arrives in this account.

20. Check the box if you want to synchronize mail from this account. Unchecking this box means that you don't want email to synchronize (not common).

21. Check the box if you want the Gmail app to automatically download email attachments when it detects that your Galaxy S6 is connected to a Wi-Fi network.

22. Tap Next.

23. Enter a friendly name for this account.

24. Enter the name you want to use when sending email from this account.

25. Tap Next to complete the setup of the email account.

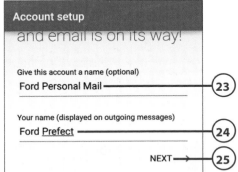

Be Secure If You Can

If your mail provider supports email security such as SSL or TLS, you should strongly consider using it. If you don't, emails you send and receive go over the Internet in plain readable text. Using SSL or TLS encrypts the emails as they travel across the Internet so that nobody can read them. Set this under the Advanced settings for the Incoming and Outgoing Servers.

Navigate the Gmail App

Let's take a quick look at the Gmail app and find out how to navigate the main screen.

1. Tap the Gmail icon to launch the app. Your initial view will be of the Inbox of your primary Google (Gmail) account, which is the account you used when setting up your Galaxy S6.

2. Tap to search the current folder for an email.

3. Tap to compose a new email.

4. Tap to see only new messages received from your social networking sites, such as Facebook and Google+. When you have tapped it once, the Social option disappears until new social media emails arrive.

5. Tap to see any new emails that are promotions for products. When you have tapped it once, the Promotions option disappears until more promotional emails arrive.

6. Tap to see any new updates. Updates include messages about updating an app but can also include update email relating to things you have purchased, bills you need to pay, and even updates to meeting invites. After you have tapped Updates once, this option disappears until there are more new updates.

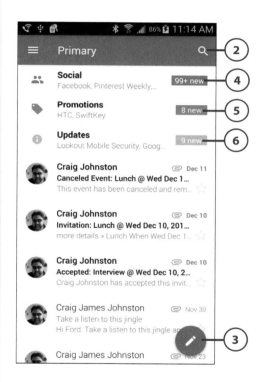

7. Swipe in from the left to reveal the menu.

8. Tap to switch between your email accounts, if you have more than one.

9. Tap to view Social, Promotions, and Updates. These are only visible when viewing Google (Gmail) accounts.

10. Tap to view messages in any forums you are participating in. This is only visible when viewing Google (Gmail) accounts.

11. Tap to switch between your different folders (or *labels*, as the Gmail app calls them).

12. Scroll down to see all of your labels.

13. Swipe the vertical action bar to the left to close the menu.

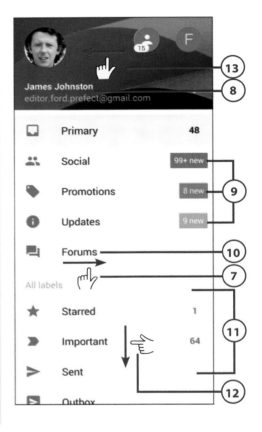

>>>Go Further

STARS AND LABELS

In the Gmail app, you use stars and labels to help organize your email. In most email clients you can create folders in your mailbox to help you organize your emails. For example, you might create a folder called "emails from the boss" and move any emails you receive from your boss to that folder. The Gmail app doesn't use the term *folders;* it uses the term *labels* instead. You can create labels in Gmail and choose an email to label. When you label the email, it is actually moved to a folder with that label. Any email that you mark with a star is actually just getting a label called "starred." However, when viewing your Gmail, you see the yellow star next to the email. People normally add a star to an email as a reminder of something important.

Compose an Email

1. Tap the compose icon.

2. Tap to change the email account from which the message is being sent (if you have multiple accounts).

3. Type names in the To field. If the name matches someone in your Contacts, a list of choices is displayed and you can tap a name to select it. If you only know the email address, type it here.

4. Tap to add Carbon Copy (CC) or Blind Carbon Copy (BCC) recipients.

5. Tap the paperclip icon to add one or more attachments or insert links to one or more Google Drive files.

6. Type a subject for your email.

7. Type the body of the email.

8. Tap to save the email as a draft or discard it.

9. Tap to send the email.

Add Attachments or Insert Drive Links

Before sending an email, you can add one or more attachments or insert links to files you have in your Google Drive account. The Gmail app can attach files that you've saved on your Galaxy S6 and in your Google Drive account. Here is how to add attachments and link Drive documents.

1. After filling in the fields as described in the "Compose an Email" task, tap the paperclip icon.

2. Tap either Attach File or Insert from Drive. This example uses the Attach File option.

3. Choose where you want to search for the file. This can include your recent downloads, your Google Drive account, the Downloads folder, or the Photos app.

4. Tap the file to attach it. In this example the attachment is a document in my Google Drive account.

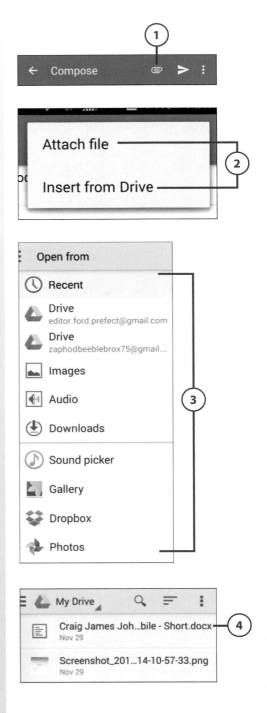

5. Tap Send.

What Is the Difference Between Attaching and Inserting?

When you choose to attach a file to an email, you can choose a file located on your Galaxy S6, in the Photos app, or in your Google Drive account. The file is then copied from that location and attached to the email. If you choose to insert a file from Google Drive, the file you choose is not actually copied out of Google Drive and attached to the email. Instead, a link to that file is placed in the body of the email. The link enables the recipients to tap the link and open the document right in your Google Drive account.

Links to Drive files

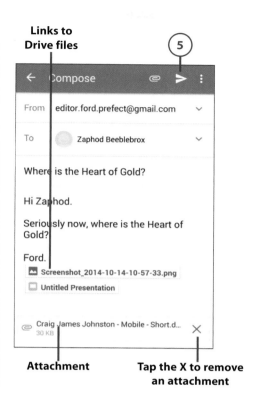

Attachment   **Tap the X to remove an attachment**

Read an Email

1. Tap an email to open it. Unread emails are in bold, and emails that you have already read are not bold.

Rich Text Formatting

A Rich Text Formatting (RTF) message is a message formatted with anything that is not plain text. RTF includes bulleted lists, different fonts, font colors, font sizes, and styles such as bold, italic, and underline. Although you cannot type an email on your Galaxy S6 with the standard keyboard using RTF, when you receive an RTF email, your Galaxy S6 preserves the formatting and displays it correctly.

2. Tap to mark the email as unread and return to the email list view.

3. Tap to reply to the sender of the email. This does not reply to anyone in the CC field.

4. Tap the Menu icon to reply to the sender of the email and any recipients in the To and CC fields (Reply All). You can also choose to forward the email or print it. See Steps 11 and 12 for an alternative method for replying to and forwarding messages.

5. Tap to expand the email header to see all recipients and all other email header information.

6. Tap to "star" the message, or move it to the "starred" label.

7. Tap the sender's contact picture to see more contact information about the person.

8. Tap to move the email to the Trash label.

9. Tap to move the email to a different label.

10. Scroll down to see the rest of the email and extra actions you can take.

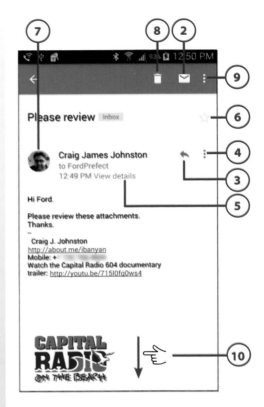

What Are Conversations?

Conversations are Gmail's version of email threads. When you look at the main view of the Gmail app, you are seeing a list of email conversations. The conversation might have only one email in it, but to Gmail that's a conversation. As you and others reply to that original email, Gmail groups those messages in a thread, or conversation.

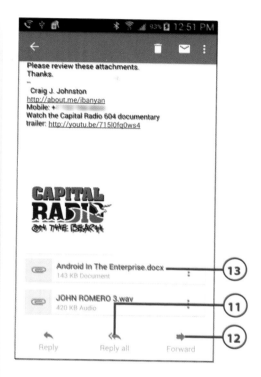

11. Tap to reply to the email and all recipients (Reply All).

12. Tap to forward the email.

13. Tap attachments to open them.

> >> *Go Further*

GMAILS HAVE EXTRA OPTIONS

If you are receiving email in your Gmail Inbox, you see a few extra options that are specific to Gmail. You can archive an email as well as send it to Trash. You can also mark an email as important, mute the email conversation, report an email as spam, and report an email as a phishing scam. When you mute a conversation, you will no longer see any emails in that conversation (or email thread). For more information on printing emails, and an explanation on what an important email is, see the Go Further sidebar and note later in the chapter.

Archive email

Tap for more options

>>>*Go Further*

HOW DO I PRINT EMAILS?

When you choose to print an email, the print dialog enables you to choose to print the email to a PDF, which turns the email into a Portable Document Format (PDF) file, or to print the email to any printers you have previously connected to Google Cloud Print using your desktop Chrome web browser. To learn more about how to connect your printers to your Google Cloud Print account, see the instructions at https://support.google.com/chrome/answer/1069693?hl=en.

What Is Important?

Gmail tries to automatically figure out which of the emails you receive are important. As it learns, it might sometimes be wrong. If an email is marked as important but it is not important, you can manually change the status to "not important." Important emails have a yellow arrow whereas emails that are not important have a clear arrow. All emails marked as "important" are also given the Priority Inbox label.

What Happens to Your Spam or Phishing Emails?

When you mark an email in Gmail as spam or as a phishing scam, two things happen. First, it gets a label called Spam. Second, a copy of that email is sent to Gmail's spam servers so that they are now aware of a possible new spam email that is circulating around the Internet. Based on what the servers see for all Gmail users, they block the emails that have been marked as spam and phishing emails from reaching other Gmail users. So the bottom line is that you should always mark spam emails because it helps all of us.

Customize Gmail App Settings

You can customize the way the Gmail app works, and you can also customize how each independent email account functions.

1. Swipe in from the left and tap the current email account to reveal its folders.

2. Tap Settings.

3. Tap General Settings.

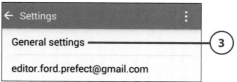

4. Tap to choose what must be shown when you choose to archive or delete a message in Gmail accounts. The choices are Archive and Delete.

5. Check the box to enable the ability to swipe an email left or right to archive it.

6. Check the box to enable showing the email sender's contact image in the conversation list.

7. Check the box to enable making Reply All the default reply action.

8. Tap to enable automatically shrinking the emails to fit on the screen.

9. Tap to choose what happens when you archive or delete a message. Your choices are to show newer messages, older messages, or the conversation list.

10. Choose which actions you want to show a confirmation screen for.

11. Tap to save your changes and return to the main Settings screen.

12. Tap one of your accounts to change settings specific to that account, and then follow the steps in the following sections.

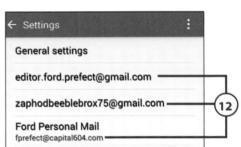

Additional Options in General Settings

While in the General Settings screen, if you tap the Menu icon, you can clear your email search history or your picture approvals. When you clear picture approvals, you are clearing your previous decisions on which emails you wanted to automatically load the images for.

Tap to clear email search history

Tap to clear the setting for automatic image downloads

What Is the Priority Inbox?

Google introduced the Priority Inbox as a way to automatically figure out which emails are important to you and place them in a folder called Priority Inbox. It does this by analyzing which emails you open and reply to. If it makes a mistake, you can mark a message as less important or more important. Over time, Google's handle on which emails are important to you gets more accurate. Because the Priority Inbox probably has the most-important emails, you might want to open it first and then go to the regular Inbox later to handle less-important emails. Read more about the Priority Inbox at http://mail.google.com/mail/help/priority-inbox.html.

Customize Google Account Settings

1. Tap to choose whether you want to see your Priority Inbox instead of your regular Inbox (Default Inbox) when opening the Gmail app.

2. Tap to choose what Inbox categories are shown. As shown earlier in the chapter, by default the Social and Promotions categories are displayed. You can also show Updates and Forums.

3. Tap to enable or disable notifications when new email arrives for this Gmail account.

4. Tap to select how to get notified when new email arrives for this account. You can choose a different notification for each label and also decide which labels in addition to the Primary label you will be notified for.

5. Tap to enter a signature to be included at the end of all emails composed using this account.

6. Tap to set your Vacation Responder. This is a message that is automatically sent to people when you are on vacation.

7. Scroll down for more settings.

Email Signature

An *email signature* is a bit of text that is automatically added to the bottom of any email you send from your Galaxy S6. It is added when you compose a new email, reply to an email, or forward an email. A typical use for a signature is to automatically add your name and some contact information at the end of your emails. Email signatures are sometimes referred to as *email footers*.

8. Tap to choose whether to synchronize Gmail to your Galaxy S6. Turning this off stops Gmail from arriving on your phone.

9. Tap to choose how many days' worth of email to synchronize to your phone.

10. Touch to manage labels. Labels are like folders. You can choose which labels synchronize to your Galaxy S6, how much email synchronizes, and what ringtone to play when new email arrives in that label.

11. Check the box to automatically download attachments to recently received emails while connected to a Wi-Fi network.

12. Tap to choose how images embedded in emails are handled. They can be automatically downloaded, or you can be prompted before they are downloaded for each email.

13. Tap to save your changes and return to the main Settings screen.

Customize POP/IMAP Account Settings

1. Tap to change the name of your account. This is the friendly name you may have typed when you originally set it up on your Galaxy S6.

2. Tap to change the full name you want people to see when you reply to emails using this account.

3. Tap to enter a signature to be included at the end of all emails composed using this account.

4. Tap to change the frequency with which your Galaxy S6 checks for new email for this account. You can set it to Never, which means that your Galaxy S6 only checks for email when you open the Gmail app, or you can set it to automatically check between every 15 minutes to every hour.

5. Check the box to automatically download attachments to recently received emails while connected to a Wi-Fi network.

6. Tap to enable or disable notifications when new email arrives for this email account.

7. Tap to select the ringtone to play when you are notified of new email for this account.

8. Scroll down for more settings.

9. Check the box if you also want to feel a vibration when new email arrives for this account.

10. Tap to change the incoming email server settings for this account.

11. Tap to change the outgoing email server settings for this account.

12. Tap to save your changes and return to the main Settings screen.

Email Application

The Email application supports all email accounts with the exception of Gmail. This includes any corporate email accounts that use Microsoft Exchange or corporate email systems, such as Lotus Domino/Notes, that have an ActiveSync gateway. In addition to corporate email accounts, the Email application also supports POP3 and IMAP accounts. POP3 and IMAP accounts are also supported by the Gmail app, so this is a duplication of functionality.

Add a Work Email Account

Your Galaxy S6 can synchronize your contacts from your work email account as long as your company uses Microsoft Exchange or an email gateway that supports Microsoft ActiveSync (such as Lotus Traveler for Lotus Domino/Notes email systems). It might be useful to be able to keep your work and personal contacts on one mobile device instead of carrying two phones around all day.

1. From the Home screen, pull down the Notification Panel and tap the Settings icon.

2. Tap Accounts under the Personal section.

3. Tap Add Account.

Error Adding Account? Guess the Server.

Your Galaxy S6 tries to work out some information about your company's ActiveSync setup. If it can't, you are prompted to enter the ActiveSync server name manually. If you don't know what it is, you can try guessing it. If, for example, your email address is dsimons@allhitradio.com, the ActiveSync server is most probably webmail.allhitradio.com or autodiscover.allhitradio.com. If options like these don't work, ask your email administrator.

4. Tap Microsoft Exchange ActiveSync.

5. Enter your full corporate email address.

6. Enter your corporate network password.

7. Tap Next.

8. Tap to agree that your mail administrator may impose security restrictions on your Galaxy S6 if you proceed.

Add POP3 or IMAP accounts in the Email app instead of the Gmail app

9. Tap to choose how many days' worth of email to synchronize to your Galaxy S6.

10. Tap to choose how often your corporate email is delivered to your Galaxy S6. Auto means that as it arrives in your Inbox at work, it is delivered to your phone. You can set it to Manual, which means that your work email is only delivered when you open the Email app on your phone. You can also set the delivery frequency from every 5 minutes to every hour.

11. Tap to choose how much of each email is retrieved. You can also set this to have no size limit so that the entire email is downloaded.

12. Tap to choose how many days in the past calendar items are synchronized to your Galaxy S6.

13. Scroll down to see more settings.

14. Tap to enable or disable being notified when new email arrives from your corporate Inbox.

15. Tap to enable or disable synchronizing your corporate contacts to your Galaxy S6.

16. Tap to enable or disable synchronizing your corporate calendar to your Galaxy S6.

17. Tap to enable or disable synchronizing your corporate tasks to your Galaxy S6.

18. Tap to enable or disable synchronizing SMS (text) messages you receive on your Galaxy S6 to your corporate Inbox.

19. Tap Next.

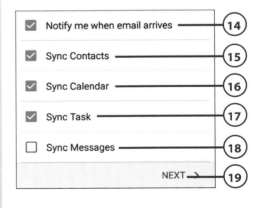

20. Tap Activate to allow your company's mail server to act as a device administrator for your Galaxy S6.

21. Enter a name for this email account. Use something meaningful that describes the purpose of the account, such as Work Email.

22. Tap Done to complete the setup.

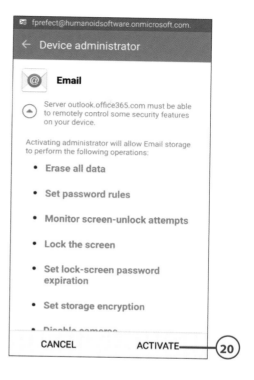

fprefect@humanoidsoftware.onmicrosoft.com

← Device administrator

@ **Email**

Server outlook.office365.com must be able to remotely control some security features on your device.

Activating administrator will allow Email storage to perform the following operations:

- **Erase all data**
- **Set password rules**
- **Monitor screen-unlock attempts**
- **Lock the screen**
- **Set lock-screen password expiration**
- **Set storage encryption**
- Disable cameras

CANCEL ACTIVATE — (20)

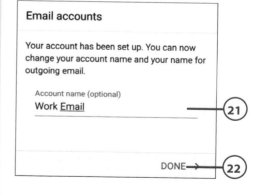

Email accounts

Your account has been set up. You can now change your account name and your name for outgoing email.

Account name (optional)
Work Email — (21)

DONE → (22)

>>>Go Further

CAN YOU TRULY KEEP WORK AND PRIVATE DATA SEPARATE?

More and more companies are adopting a Bring Your Own Device (BYOD) policy, which means that they expect you to use your personal phone to get access to company emails, contacts, calendar, and internal apps. As you have seen, your Galaxy S6 fully supports accessing your company's email system, but when you activate, you have to agree to allow your administrator control over your phone. This is not ideal because the administrator can see what apps you have installed, and he can send a self-destruct command to your Galaxy S6, which means you could lose all your private data and apps. *Dual persona* is fast becoming the way for you to truly keep your private data private and not allow your company to wipe your phone or see what you have installed. A few companies today provide this service, including Enterproid (the product is called Divide, www.divide.com/), Good Technology (the product is called Good, www1.good.com/), and Samsung (the system is called KNOX, https://www.samsungknox.com). The idea is that your Galaxy S6 has two personalities—a work persona and a private persona. All work data is kept in its own separate area on your phone, and administrators from your company have no control over the rest of your phone.

Add a New POP3 or IMAP Account

Remember that the Gmail app also supports POP3 and IMAP accounts, so you may not want to use the Email app for this type of account. It is up to you.

1. Pull down the Notification Panel and tap the Settings icon.

2. Tap Accounts under the Personal section.

3. Tap Add Account.

4. Tap Email.

Why Manual Setup?

Your Galaxy S6 tries to figure out the settings to set up your email account. This works most of the time when you are using common email providers such as Yahoo! and Hotmail. It also works with large ISPs such as Comcast, Road Runner, Optimum Online, and so on. It might not work for smaller ISPs, in smaller countries, or if you have created your own website and set up your own email. In these cases, you need to set up your email manually.

5. Enter your email address.

6. Enter your password.

7. Tap Next.

8. Tap POP3 or IMAP. IMAP has more intelligence to it, so select that option when possible.

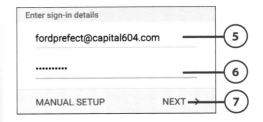

Where Can I Find This Information?

If you need to manually set up your email account, you must have a few pieces of information. Always check your ISP's (or email service provider's) website, and look for instructions on how to set up your email on a computer or smartphone. This is normally under the Support section of the website.

9. Ensure that the information on the incoming server screen is accurate.

10. Tap Next.

Username and Password

On the Incoming Server and Outgoing Server screens, your username and password should already be filled out because you typed them in earlier. If not, enter them.

11. Ensure that the information on the outgoing server screen is accurate.

12. Tap Next.

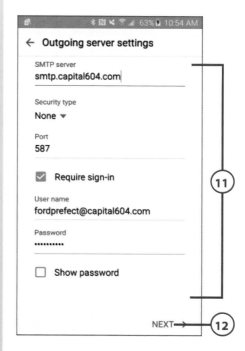

13. Tap to change how far back in the past email must synchronize.

14. Tap to change the frequency with which email from this account synchronizes to your Galaxy S6.

15. Tap to check the box if you want to be notified when new email arrives into this account.

16. Tap Next.

17. Enter a friendly name for this account, such as Home Email.

18. Enter your full name or the name you want to be displayed when people receive emails sent from this account.

19. Tap Done to save the settings for this account and return to the Add Accounts screen.

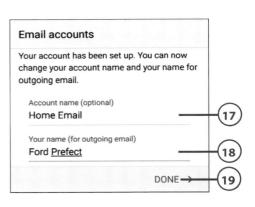

Be Secure If You Can

If your mail provider supports email security, such as Secure Sockets Layer (SSL) or Transport Layer Security (TLS), you should strongly consider using it. If you don't, emails you send and receive go over the Internet in plain readable text. Using SSL or TLS encrypts the emails as they travel across the Internet so nobody can read them. Set this under the Advanced settings for the incoming and outgoing servers.

Working with the Email App

Now that you have added two new accounts, you can start using the Email application. Everything you do in the Email application is the same for every email account. The Email app enables you to work with email accounts either separately or in a combined view.

Navigate the Email Application

Before you learn how to compose or read emails, you should become familiar with the Email application.

1. Tap to launch the Email app.

2. Tap to switch between email accounts or select Combined Inbox, which shows all emails from all accounts.

3. Tap the star to mark a personal account (POP3/IMAP) email as flagged.

4. Each color represents a specific email account.

5. Tap to compose a new email.

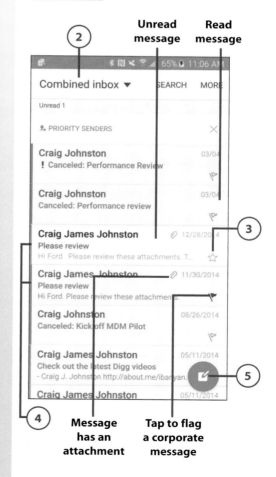

Unread message   **Read message**

Message has an attachment   **Tap to flag a corporate message**

Compose an Email

1. Tap to compose a new email.

2. Enter one or more recipients. As you type, your Galaxy S6 tries to guess who you want to address the message to. If you see the correct name, tap it to select it. This includes names stored on your Galaxy S6 and in your company's corporate address book.

3. Enter a subject.

4. Type the body of the email.

5. Tap to send the message.

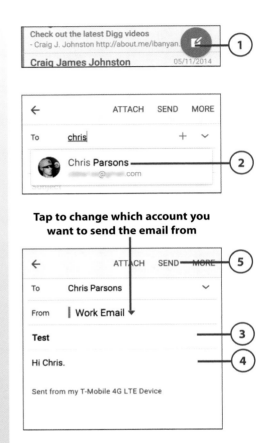

Tap to change which account you want to send the email from

Enable Rich Text

If you want to format your email using different fonts, bold, italic, and embedded images, you can tap More and then tap Turn On Rich Text. A bar with formatting options displays. Scroll left and right over the formatting bar to see all formatting options. To change the formatting of a specific word, touch and hold the word, drag the end markers to select more words if needed, and then change the formatting using the formatting bar.

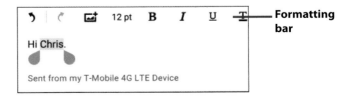

Formatting bar

Add Attachments to a Message

Before you send your message, you might want to add one or more attachments. You can attach any type of file, including pictures, video, audio, contacts, and location.

1. Tap Attach.

2. Choose the type of attachment. If you choose My Files, you can browse your Galaxy S6 and attach any file type, including documents, presentations, spreadsheets, and so on.

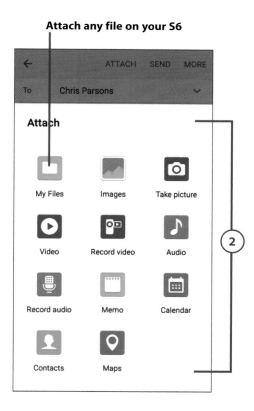

Attach any file on your S6

3. Tap the red minus symbol to the right of an attachment to remove it from the email.

4. Tap to send your email.

Other Options Before Sending

Before you send your email, you can change a few additional options. To see these additional options, tap More. Tap Priority to change the priority of the email to high, normal, or low. Tap Security Options to Encrypt the email, or digitally sign it. To encrypt or sign an email, you need certificates installed on your Galaxy S6. When you are sending an email using your company's Exchange email system, tap Permissions to set the permissions for what happens to the email after it has been sent, including preventing it from being forwarded or setting an expiration date on the email. The permissions options made available to you are set by your email administrator.

Read Email

Reading messages in the Email application is the same regardless of which account the email has come to.

1. Tap an email to open it.

2. Tap to reply to the sender of the email. This does not reply to anyone in the Cc field.

3. Tap to forward the email.

4. Tap to expand the email header to see all recipients and all other email header information.

5. Tap to mark the message as starred (personal email) or flagged (company email).

6. Tap to delete the message.

7. Tap to see the attachments on a separate screen.

8. Tap to preview the attachment. In this example it is an audio file.

9. Tap to save the attachment to your phone.

10. Tap to return to the email view.

Tap to use Reply All

Tap to see more options

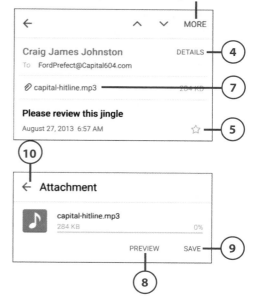

11. Tap More to see other options.

12. Tap to mark the message as unread.

13. Tap to move the message to a different folder.

14. Tap to save the email as a file on your phone (outside the Email app).

15. Tap to set yourself a reminder to respond to this email.

16. Tap to mark the message as spam or junk mail.

17. Tap to add the sender to the Priority Sender list. Email from people in the Priority Sender list is displayed in the Priority Sender view.

18. Tap to compose a new email.

19. Tap to print the email on a Samsung printer available on the Wi-Fi network, or save the email as a Portable Document Format (PDF) file.

Change Email App Settings

1. Tap More from the main Email screen.

2. Tap Settings.

General Settings

General settings are settings that take effect no matter what type of email account you are working with.

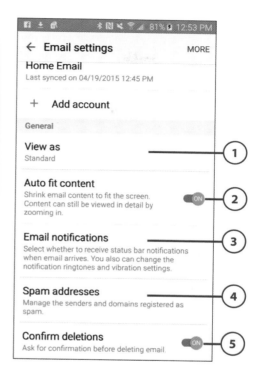

1. Tap to choose whether you want your email shown in the standard way, where each received email is on its own line, or in Conversation mode, where emails are grouped together based on the email subject line, to form an email conversation.

2. Tap to enable or disable auto-fit. When Auto Fit Content is enabled, your Galaxy S6 adjusts emails so they fit on the screen properly when you read them.

3. Tap to manage when you will receive notifications of new emails. You can choose to receive notifications when senders you have placed on the Priority Senders list send you email, and you can choose which email accounts to receive notifications from.

4. Tap to manage your spam address list. This includes manually adding email addresses and removing ones already on the spam list.

5. Tap to choose whether you want to see a confirmation screen when you delete emails.

What Is the Priority Sender List?

Emails received from people whom you have listed in the Priority Sender list are shown in the Priority Sender Inbox as well as in the regular Inbox. Opening the Priority Sender Inbox folder shows only emails from these people, which can be a way of filtering email so that you respond to the important people first and then switch to the regular Inbox and respond to everyone else.

Corporate Account Settings

You are able to change your email signature as well as control what components are synchronized and how often they are synchronized.

1. Tap your corporate email account.

2. Tap to choose whether you want this account to synchronize with your Galaxy S6.

3. Tap to change the friendly name for this account.

4. Tap to choose whether to always Bcc or Cc yourself on emails you send.

5. Tap to enable or disable using an email signature, add an email signature, or edit a signature.

6. Tap to enable or disable automatically loading embedded images in emails sent to you on this account.

7. Choose whether you want email attachments automatically downloaded when your Galaxy S6 is connected to a Wi-Fi network.

8. Scroll down for more settings.

Tap to choose which is the default account

Remove account

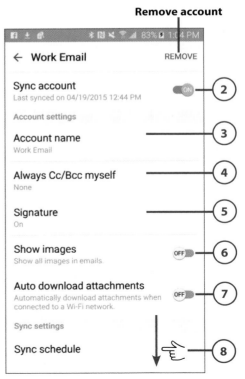

9. Tap to manage the synchronization settings for this account.
   This includes choosing different
   synchronization options
   depending on peak and off-peak
   times.

10. Tap to choose how far back in the
    past your email synchronizes.

11. Tap to choose how much of each
    email is retrieved.

12. Tap to choose how much of each
    email is retrieved when you are
    roaming outside your home
    cellular provider network.

13. Tap to set whether you are out of
    the office and your out-of-office
    message. This synchronizes to
    the out-of-office feature on your
    corporate mailbox so your out-of-
    office messages are sent by your
    mail server.

14. Tap to choose which folders
    (excluding Inbox and Outbox) you
    want to synchronize from your
    office email account and when
    they synchronize based on the
    peak and off-peak schedule.

15. Tap to choose how far back in the
    past your calendar synchronizes.

16. Tap to empty your Trash folder on
    the email server back in the office.

17. Scroll down for more settings.

Why Empty the Office Trash Folder?

Step 16 describes how you can choose to empty your Trash folder back in the office. This feature is useful because sometimes your email administrator sets a limit on the size of your mailbox, and when you reach that limit, you are unable to send emails. By emptying your Trash folder back at the office, you might be able to clear a little bit of space in your mailbox so you can send that important email.

How Are There Conflicts?

A conflict can occur if you or someone who has delegate access on your email account makes a change in your mailbox using a desktop email client such as Outlook (for example, your delegate moves an email to a folder) and you then make a change on your Galaxy S6 (say, you delete that same email). Now there is a conflict because an email has been both moved and deleted at the same time. If you set the server to have priority, then the conflict is resolved using your rule that the server wins. In this example, the email is not deleted but rather is moved to a folder.

18. Tap to change which device wins if there is a conflict between your phone and your email account back at the office.

19. Select what to synchronize between your Galaxy S6 and your office email account.

20. Tap to set advanced security options, including whether you want to encrypt your emails, sign emails with an electronic signature, and email certificates to use with S/MIME (if your company supports it).

21. Tap to change the Exchange mail server settings for this account. This includes your account username and password if these have changed.

22. Tap to return to the previous screen.

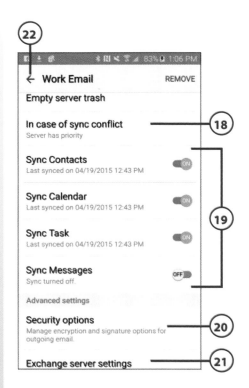

POP/IMAP Account Settings

1. Tap your POP3 or IMAP email account.

2. Tap to choose whether you want this email account to synchronize with your Galaxy S6.

3. Tap to change the friendly name for this account.

4. Tap to edit the name that is displayed when you send email to others.

5. Tap to choose whether to always Bcc or Cc yourself on emails you send.

6. Tap to enable or disable using an email signature, add an email signature, or edit a signature.

7. Tap to enable or disable automatically loading embedded images in emails sent to you on this account.

8. Tap to enable or disable automatically downloading email attachments when your Galaxy S6 is connected to Wi-Fi.

9. Scroll down for more settings.

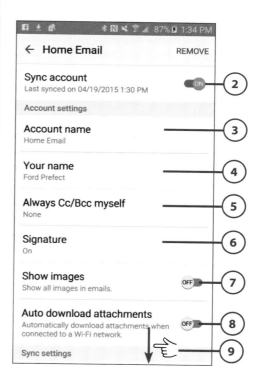

10. Tap to manage the synchronization settings for this account.
This includes choosing different
synchronization options depending on peak and off-peak times.

11. Tap to choose how far back in the
past your email synchronizes.

12. Tap to choose how much of each
email is retrieved.

13. Tap to choose how much of each
email is retrieved when you are
roaming outside your home
cellular provider network.

14. Tap to set advanced security
settings for this account,
including choosing to encrypt
emails, sign them with a
digital signature, and manage
encryption keys on your phone
for use with encrypting emails.

15. Tap to change the incoming
server settings for this account.

16. Tap to change the outgoing
server settings for this account.

17. Tap to return to the Settings main
screen.

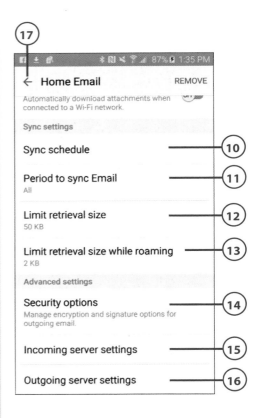

SMS and MMS

Short Message Service (SMS), also known as text messaging, has been
around for a long time. Multimedia Message Service (MMS) is a newer form
of text messaging that can contain pictures, audio, and video as well as text.
Your Galaxy S6 can send and receive both SMS and MMS messages.

Get to Know the Messages App

The Messages app is what you use to send and receive text messages. This app has all the features you need to compose, send, receive, and manage these messages.

1. Tap the Messages icon.

2. Tap to compose a new text message.

3. Tap the picture of someone who has sent you a message to show their contact card. You can then contact the person using email, phone, and other methods.

4. Tap a message thread to open it.

5. Tap More to see other options.

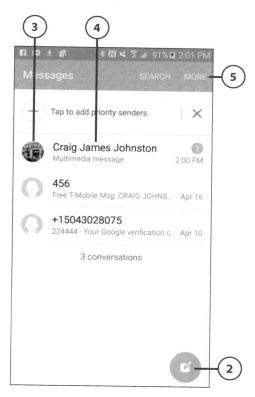

6. Tap to select one or more message threads and delete them or mark them as spam.

7. Tap to open the Locked Messages folder. Locked messages are messages that you have chosen to lock so they are not accidentally deleted. See the "How Do I Lock a Message?" margin note for more information.

8. Tap to select from a list of Quick Responses to send and manage the current Quick Responses. When you select a Quick Response, a new message opens with that Quick Response added to the text field.

9. Tap to choose to use your Galaxy S6's built-in font size, or select a smaller or larger size while you have the Messages app open.

10. Tap to open the Settings screen. See the next section for more on Settings.

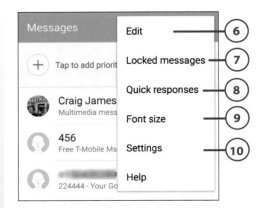

How Do I Lock a Message?

You might want to lock a message so that it does not get accidentally deleted when you delete the message thread. To lock a message, touch and hold on the message and choose Lock when the menu pops up. The lock symbol displays just below the locked message. To unlock the message, touch and hold on the message and choose Unlock.

>>>*Go Further*
SWIPE TO CALL

If you would like to call the sender of an SMS or MMS message, swipe the message from left to right to dial that person's number.

Swipe to call

Manage Settings for the Messages App

You use the settings of the Messages app to manage how the app handles your SMS and MMS messages.

1. Tap More on the main Messages screen.

2. Tap Settings.

3. Tap to manage how the Messages app looks. You can choose what kind of bubble style is used for text message display, and choose which background the app uses for messages.

4. Tap to manage the settings for detecting spam messages. Spam messages are unwanted commercial messages. You can also choose what mobile numbers and text phrases are treated as spam.

5. Tap to manage which emergency alerts you want to receive. These alerts are sent out by your government or law enforcement (for example, AMBER alerts).

6. Tap to see more settings.

7. Tap to control and manage text messages. This includes choosing to receive a delivery report for text messages you send, choosing the input mode (leaving it set to Automatic is recommended), and managing text messages that may still be on your old SIM card.

8. Tap to control how the Messages app handles multimedia messages. Settings include the ability to request delivery and read reports as well as to control whether to automatically retrieve multimedia messages while roaming outside your wireless carrier's home area.

9.   Tap to enable or disable receiving messages "pushed" from the server. Push messages arrive at your Galaxy S6 shortly after they arrive at the server, which is usually faster than waiting until the Galaxy S6 checks for messages. You can also choose how to handle remote requests to load services. Your choices are Always, Prompt, and Never.

10. Tap to enable or disable automatically deleting old text or multimedia messages when the limit you set is reached. When the limit is reached, messages within the thread or conversation are deleted using the FIFO method.

11. Tap to save your changes and return to the previous screen.

What Does the Manage SIM Card Messages Option Do?

Many old cell phones store text messages on the SIM card and not in the phone's memory. If you have just upgraded from an older phone, you might still have text messages on the SIM card that you would like to retrieve. If you choose the option to manage text messages on your SIM card, as mentioned in Step 7, you can then copy the messages to your Galaxy S6's memory and copy the senders to your contacts in the Contacts app.

Don't Auto-Retrieve MMS While Roaming

Disable the automatic retrieval of multimedia messages when you travel to other countries because automatically retrieving these messages when you're roaming can result in a big bill from your provider. International carriers love to charge large amounts of money for people traveling to their countries and using their networks. The only time it is a good idea to leave this enabled is if your carrier offers an international SMS or MMS bundle, where you pay a flat rate up front before leaving. When you have the auto-retrieve feature disabled, you see a Download button next to a multimedia message. You have to tap it to manually download the message.

What's the Difference Between a Delivery Report and a Read Report?

A delivery report indicates that the message has reached the destination device. A read report indicates that the message has been opened for viewing. There is still no guarantee that whoever opened the message has actually read it, let alone understood it.

Compose Messages

When you compose a new message, you do not need to make a conscious decision whether it is an SMS message or an MMS message. As soon as you add a subject line or attach a file to your message, your Galaxy S6 automatically treats the message as an MMS message.

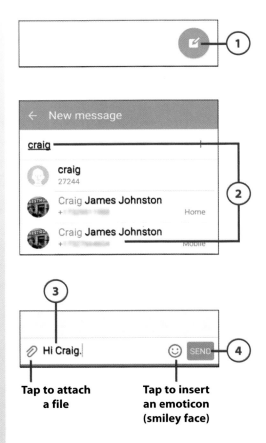

Tap to attach a file

Tap to insert an emoticon (smiley face)

1. Tap the pencil compose icon to compose a new message.

2. Start typing the recipient's name or phone number, or if the person is in your contacts, type the name. If a match is found, tap the mobile number.

3. Tap and start typing your message.

4. Tap to send your message.

It's Not All Good

Inserting Smiley Icons

By tapping the smiling face icon, you can insert emoticons (also known as smiley faces or emojis). Just be aware that the very first emoticon you insert into a new text message counts as 92 characters. Each additional emoticon counts only one character each. Each text message is limited to 160 characters, so after inserting your first emoticon, you'll only have 68 characters left.

Delay Sending the Message

You might decide that you want a text message to be sent automatically at a later time. To do this, before sending the message, tap More and choose Schedule Message. Choose the date and time you want your message to be sent and tap Done. Then tap the Send button, and your message will only send when you set it to.

>>>Go Further

MESSAGE LIMITS AND MESSAGES

Text messages can only be 160 characters long. To get around this limit, most modern phones simply break up text messages you type into 160-character chunks. Your Galaxy S6 displays a readout showing the number of characters remaining and the number of messages it will send: The readout starts at 160/1 when you begin a new message and runs down to 1/1; then it starts at 145/2 (fewer characters because there is some overhead in linking the messages). The phone receiving the message simply combines them into one message. This is important to know if your wireless plan has a text message limit. When you create one text message, your Galaxy S6 might actually break the message into two or more.

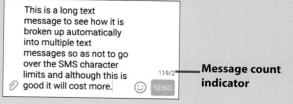

Message count indicator

Attach Files to Messages

If you want to send a picture, audio file, or video along with your text message, all you need to do is attach the file. Be aware that attaching a file turns your SMS text message into an MMS multimedia message and may be subject to additional charges.

1. Tap the paperclip icon to attach a file.

2. Choose a picture that you recently took on your Galaxy S6.

3. Choose other attachment types, including the option to take a picture or record a video and attach it directly.

4. Tap to send your MMS.

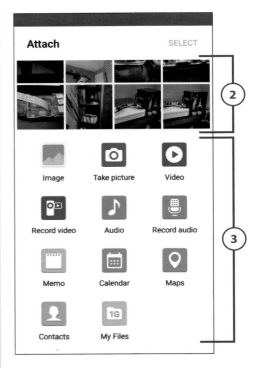

It's Not All Good

Is It Worth Attaching Files?

Attaching files to text messages is not as useful as you might desire. Most carriers limit the attachment size to around 300KB. This means that you can only really attach about 60 seconds of very low-quality video; pictures with low resolution, high compression, or both; and very short audio files. The Messaging app automatically compresses larger picture files to make them small enough to send, but you will often find that it simply refuses to send video files because they are too large. Choosing the option of capturing pictures, capturing video, or recording audio when you choose to attach is the only way you can guarantee that the files are small enough. This is because when you do this, the camera and audio recorder apps are set to a mode that makes them record low-quality audio and take low-quality pictures.

Receive Messages

When you receive a new SMS or MMS message, you can read it, view its attachments, and even save those attachments to your Galaxy S6.

1. When a new SMS or MMS message arrives, your Galaxy S6 plays a ringtone and displays a notification in the status bar.

2. Pull down the Notification Panel to see newly arrived messages.

3. Tap a message alert to display the message and reply to it.

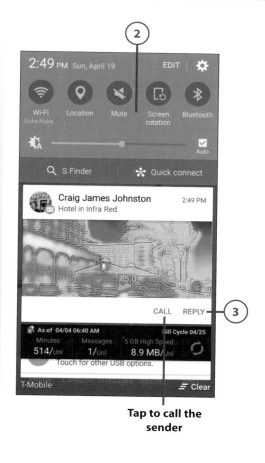

Tap to call the
sender

4. Tap an attachment to open it for viewing.

5. Touch and hold a message to display the Message Options dialog. Skip to Step 7 for more about the additional options.

6. Tap to write a reply to the message.

7. Tap to delete the message. This deletes just the message and not the entire thread.

8. Tap to copy the message text so you can paste it elsewhere.

9. Tap to forward the message and attachment to someone else.

10. Tap to share the message via social media or other methods.

11. Tap to lock the message against deletion if you later decide to delete the message thread.

12. Tap to save the attachment to your Galaxy S6.

13. Tap to view a slideshow of attached images.

14. Tap to view the message details, such as its size and the date and time it was sent.

Usable Content

If a text message contains links to websites, phone numbers, or email addresses, tapping those links makes the Galaxy S6 take the appropriate action. For example, when you tap a phone number, your Galaxy S6 calls the number; when you tap a web link, the Galaxy S6 opens the page in Chrome or your other default browser.

>>>*Go Further*

USING GOOGLE HANGOUTS FOR SMS AND MMS

You may decide that because you already use Google Hangouts to instant message your friends and family, as well as to video chat with them, it makes sense to set the Google Hangouts app to handle text messages (SMS) and multimedia messages (MMS) so that all communications with your friends and family are in one place. To set this, open the Google Hangouts app. Swipe in from the left of the screen and tap Settings. Tap SMS. Under General tap SMS Disabled and tap Yes when prompted. The way in which you interact with SMS and MMS while using the Hangouts app is very similar to the way it works in the Messages app, so the steps in this chapter should help you. Even the settings for handling SMS and MMS are similar. When one of your contacts has signed up for a Google account and has started using Google Hangouts, you can switch from sending and receiving SMS and MMS messages with them and start using Hangouts messages instead. Doing this saves you from costly SMS and MMS charges and just uses your data plan.

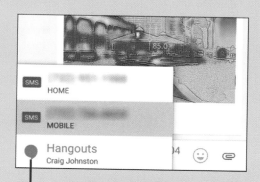

Switch to using Hangouts to save money

Search Google

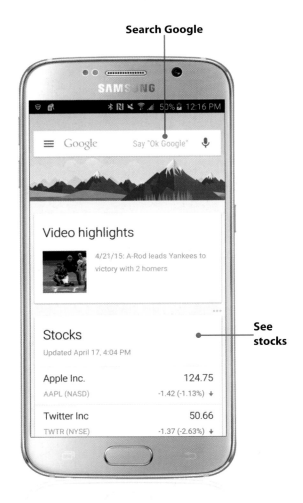

See stocks

In this chapter, you find out how to use Google Maps for step-by-step navigation and Google Now. Topics include the following:

→ Using Google Now
→ Using Google Maps for navigation
→ Taking map data offline

Google Now and Navigation Using Google Maps

You can use your Samsung Galaxy S6 as a GPS navigation device while you walk or drive around. Your phone also includes an app called Google Now that provides all the information you need when you need it.

Google Now

You can access Google Now from any screen (except the Lock screen), which enables you to search the Internet. Google Now provides you with information such as how long it takes to drive to work and the scores from your favorite teams.

Access Google Now

You can access Google Now from any app or the Home screen pane by pressing and holding the Home button.

Press and hold

1. Cards automatically appear based on your settings. Examples of these cards are scores for the sports teams you follow, upcoming meetings, weather in the location where you work, and traffic on the way to work.

2. Say "OK Google" to speak a search, or to command Google Now to do something. You can also type your search terms.

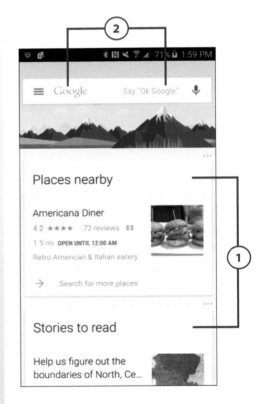

3. Information relevant to your
   search appears.

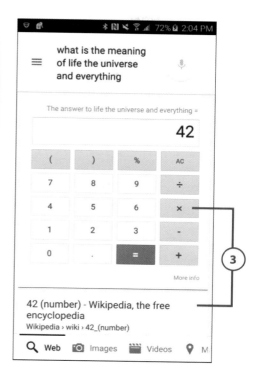

Commanding Google Now

In addition to searching the Internet using Google Now, you can command Google Now to do things for you. For example, you can tell Google Now to set an alarm for you, compose a text message, or even send an email. This is just a small list of the types of things you can have Google Now do for you. To see a comprehensive list of commands, visit http://trendblog.net/list-of-google-now-voice-commands-infographic/.

Setting an alarm

Set Up Google Now

For Google Now to work for you, you need to set it up correctly. This also means sharing your location information with Google.

1. Swipe in from the left of the screen to reveal the menu.

2. Tap to add and manage reminders.

3. Tap Customize to customize what kinds of Google Now cards are displayed. This includes choosing sports teams, stocks, places, and TV and video.

4. Tap Settings.

5. Tap to manage what Google Now can search for. This can include apps you have installed, bookmarks and web history in the Chrome web browser, your contacts, Google Play Books, Movies & TV, and Music.

6. Tap Voice to manage how and when Google Now responds to your voice.

7. Tap to choose the languages that Google Now responds to.

8. Tap to choose whether Google Now should be listening for you to say "OK Google."

9. Tap to choose whether Google Now works with a connected headset. You can choose to let Google Now use a paired Bluetooth device, or a headset connected by a cable, or both.

10. Tap to choose when Google Now speaks back to you. Your choices are On (which means Always), Off (which means never), or only when you are using a hands-free device (such as a Bluetooth headset or your car's built-in Bluetooth connection).

11. Tap to manage whether Google Now speech recognition can work even when there is no Internet connection. This is achieved by downloading one or more languages to your phone.

12. Tap to block offensive words being spoken when search results are returned by voice.

13. Tap to allow Google Now to record your voice using your Bluetooth headset or built-in car Bluetooth.

14. Tap to save your changes and return to the main Google Now settings screen.

15. Tap Accounts & Privacy.

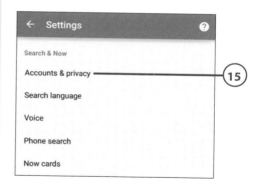

It's Not All Good

S Voice Replaced Google Now

On non-Samsung phones, Google's "OK Google" phrase detection can be set to work not only while Google Now is open, but from any screen, from any app, and even from the lock screen. On Samsung phones, like your Galaxy S6, Samsung's S Voice overrides Google's "OK Google" phrase detection with the S Voice "Hi Galaxy" phrase detection. Many Android phone users prefer Google's Google Now compared to Samsung's S Voice, however there is no easy way to use Google's "OK Google" instead of S Voice's "Hi Galaxy."

16. Tap to choose which of your Google accounts (if you have more than one) you want to use for Google Now.

17. Tap to manage whether apps can share your data with Google and clear any data that apps on your phone have shared with Google.

18. Tap to enable or disable the SafeSearch Filter that blocks offensive content.

19. Tap to choose whether you want to share your commute status, such as when you leave for home or leave for work. People need to be in your Google+ Circles to receive your Commute updates.

20. Tap to enable or disable high-contrast text if you have a vision disability.

21. Tap to enable or disable Google Now's ability to send Google information on how you use Google Now.

22. Tap to save your changes and return to the main Google Now settings screen.

23. Tap to manage how Google Now alerts you when new cards are ready, and choose the ringtone that plays when they are ready to view.

24. Tap to save your changes and return to Google Now.

Tell Google Maps Where You Live and Work

Google Now can be even more effective if you configure your work and home addresses in Google Maps. Google Now uses that information to tell you things such as how long your commute to work will be, whether there is heavy traffic on the route, and so on. See Step 3 in the "Configure Google Maps Settings" task later in this chapter for information about how to do that.

Google Maps

Google Maps enables you to see where you are on a map, find points of interest close to you, get driving or walking directions, and review extra layers of information, such as a satellite view.

1. Tap to launch Google Maps.

2. Tap to type a search term, the name of a business, or an address.

3. Tap to speak a search term, the name of a business, or an address.

4. Tap to get walking or driving directions from one location to another. You can also choose to use public transit or biking paths to get to your destination.

5. Tap to switch between the top-down view that always points North, and the 3D view that follows the direction your phone is pointing.

6. Tap to explore points of interest near your current location.

7. Swipe in from the left of the screen to reveal the menu.

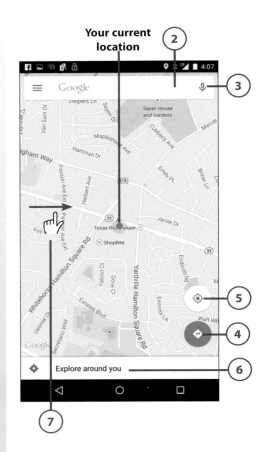

8. Tap to switch to a different Google account for use with Google Maps.

9. Tap to see your work and home address, plus addresses you have recently searched for.

10. Tap to toggle between the map view and the satellite.

11. Tap to show the current traffic conditions on the map or satellite view.

12. Tap to show all public transport locations on the map view or satellite view.

13. Tap to show all bicycling routes on the map view or satellite view.

14. Tap to see the terrain view.

15. Tap to launch the Google Earth app.

16. Touch to change the settings for Google Maps.

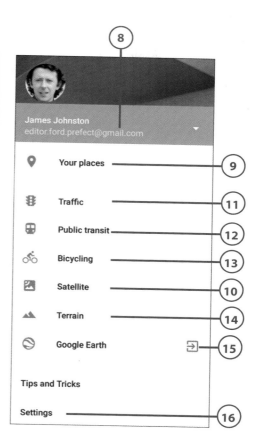

Changing Google Maps Settings

See the "Configure Google Maps Settings" task later in this chapter for more information about customizing Google Maps.

Get Directions

You can use Google Maps to get directions to where you want to go.

1. Tap the Directions icon.

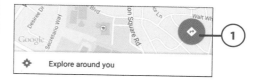

2. Tap to set the starting point or leave it as Your Location (which is your current location).

3. Tap to flip the start and end points.

4. Tap to use driving directions.

5. Tap to use public transportation.

Public Transportation

If you choose to use public transportation to get to your destination, you have two extra options to use. You can choose the type of public transportation to use, including bus, subway, train, or tram/light rail. You can also choose the best route (fewer transfers and less walking).

Scroll to see more previous destinations

6. Tap to walk to your destination.

7. Tap to use bike paths (if available).

8. Tap to choose a previous destination. If you need to type the address of your destination, go to Step 9, if not skip to Step 10.

9. Tap the Choose Destination field and then type or speak the destination address.

10. Tap to make changes to your route, including choosing alternative routes to travel, and modify options like avoiding toll roads. If you are happy with the route as-is, skip to Step 14.

11. Tap to decide whether you want to avoid highways, tolls, or ferries.

12. Tap to choose an alternative route. If you choose an alternative route, the screen automatically returns to the map view.

13. Tap to return to the map view.

14. Tap to start the navigation.

15. Tap to see and select alternative routes as they appear on the map.

16. Tap the Menu icon to mute the voice guidance, show traffic conditions, choose the satellite view, and show alternatives for the entire route.

17. Tap to speak commands such as "Show alternative route," "How's traffic ahead?" or "What time will I get there?"

18. Tap to cancel the route.

Configure Google Maps Settings

1. Swipe in from the left side of the screen.

2. Tap Settings.

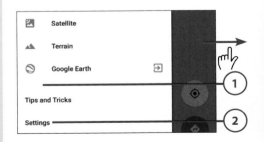

3. Tap to edit your work and home addresses. Telling Maps your home and work addresses is important for Google Now to work more efficiently, but it also helps you quickly plan new routes to work and home.

4. Tap to enable or disable the capability for your phone to report its location. You can also choose the accuracy of your location by changing the mode.

5. Tap to improve your location accuracy if you think that your phone is not reporting it correctly.

6. Tap to see addresses you have looked up and received directions to. You can also delete items in this list.

7. Tap to set the distance unit of measure. You can either set it to automatic so that Google Maps adjusts it based on where you are on the planet, or you can manually set it.

8. Tap to change the volume level for the voice that speaks the turn-by-turn directions, and choose whether you want to always start navigation using the Tilt Map. The Tilt Map is a view as if looking ahead from behind the navigation arrow.

9. Tap to save your changes and return to the main Google Maps screen.

Use Offline Google Maps

Google Maps enables you to download small parts of the global map to your phone. This is useful if you are traveling and need an electronic map but cannot connect to a network to download it in real time.

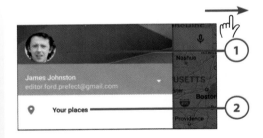

1. Swipe in from the left of the screen.

2. Tap Your Places.

3. Scroll down to the bottom of the Your Places screen, and tap View All and Manage. If you have never saved an offline map, move on to Step 4. If you're using a previously saved map, tap it to begin using it.

4. Tap Save a New Offline Map.

Tap to view previous saved maps

5. Pan around to find the area of the map you want to save offline.

6. Pinch to zoom out or unpinch to zoom in to the area of the map you want to save offline.

7. Tap Save when the area of the map fills the screen.

8. Type a name for the offline map and tap Save.

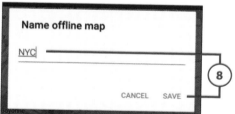

How Much Map Can I Take Offline?

When selecting the area of the map to take offline, you are limited to approximately 100Mb of map data. You don't need to worry about the size of the data because if you have selected an area that is too large, Google Maps gives you a warning.

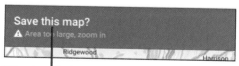

Warning that your selection area is too large

It's Not All Good

Offline Maps Have Limited Use

If you download some map data to your phone, you can use it to zoom in and out of the area you downloaded and also see where you are on the map in real time even though you have no network coverage. You cannot, however, get directions within the downloaded map area or use the Navigation app to get turn-by-turn directions. You also cannot search for things in the downloaded map area or see points of interest.

So how useful is having map data already downloaded to your phone? Because offline maps are already downloaded, they help when you have a network connection and are getting driving directions because Google Maps does not need to download the map data in real time, which could save you a lot of money in data roaming charges.

Play and manage music
from the Google Play Store

Download
and manage
podcasts

Purchase and
download
music to your
Galaxy S6

In this chapter, you find out how to get the most out of the audio and music playing capabilities of the Galaxy S6. Topics in this chapter include the following:

→ Purchasing music
→ Playing songs
→ Creating your own playlists
→ Adding a podcast app

Playing and Managing Music

Your Galaxy S6 is a digital media player packed with entertainment possibilities. You can play music using a variety of preinstalled apps for purchasing and downloading music: Music, Google Play Music, and Milk. You can also download apps from the Google Play Store to listen to podcasts and audiobooks.

Purchasing Music in Google Play Music

The Galaxy S6 includes the preinstalled Google Play Music app for finding, previewing, purchasing, downloading, and playing music. This app isn't the only one you can use, however—there are plenty of other music apps available for download in the Google Play Store.

1. Tap the Apps icon on the Home screen.

2. Tap Google.

3. Tap Play Music.

4. Tap Get Started to play any song in the Google Play Music catalog free for 30 days. After the 30-day trial period, you can choose to purchase a membership for $9.99 per month. After you open the Play Music app for the first time, you don't see the introductory screen and you can skip ahead to Step 8.

5. For now, tap Use Standard to continue.

6. Tap Learn More to discover more about adding songs and copying music to your phone.

7. Tap Shop if you want to shop for tracks.

8. For now, tap Done.

9. From the Listen Now screen, tap the Menu icon in the menu bar.

How Do I Know If a Song Has Explicit Lyrics?

If you don't want to listen to songs with explicit lyrics (and/or don't want your kids to listen to them), you can easily see which songs and albums have explicit lyrics by looking for the Parental Advisory warning within the song or album tile.

10. Tap Shop in the list.

11. The Music screen shows the latest free music and exclusive videos. Swipe up and down the screen to view more featured songs and albums in a variety of categories.

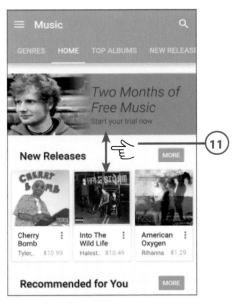

12. Tap More to view more songs and albums in the category.

13. Within the menu at the top of the page, swipe from right to left to view more options.

14. Tap Top Albums to view the best-selling albums in the Google Play Store.

15. Tap New Releases to view the newest albums in the Google Play Store.

16. Tap Top Songs to view the best-selling songs in the Google Play Store.

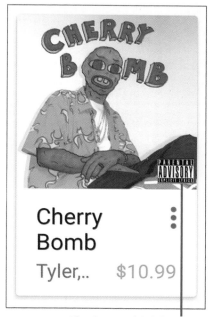

The Parental Advisory warning label in the album tile

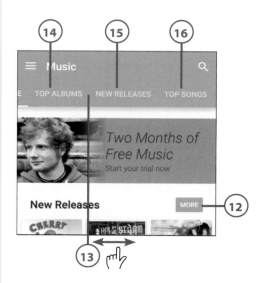

17. Swipe from left to right to view more menu options.

18. Tap Genres to view categories of music you can choose from.

19. View all the genres by swiping up and down in the list. When you find a genre you want, tap the genre name in the list.

20. Swipe up and down the screen to view different sections of the genre page.

21. Tap a category to view new releases and recommendations in the genre.

22. Tap Genres to view a list of sub-genres within the main genre.

23. Tap a subgenre in the list.

24. Top-selling albums in that sub-genre appear on the screen. Scroll up and down the screen to view all the top albums.

25. Tap New Releases to view newly released songs and albums within that subgenre.

26. Tap Top Songs to view the best-selling songs in the subgenre.

27. Tap the Back touch button to return to the genre page.

28. Tap the album or song tile on the screen to view more information.

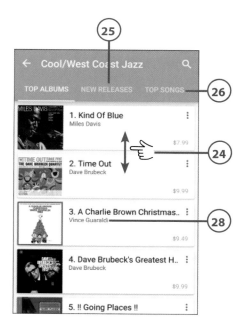

29. The title and album cover appear at the top of the screen. You can purchase the entire album by tapping the orange purchase button that contains the album price.

30. Swipe from bottom to top on the page to view a description of the album and artist, view songs in the album, read reviews from other Google Play users who downloaded the songs or album, see more albums by the artist, and also view similar artists.

31. Swipe from top to bottom of the screen if necessary until you see the Songs section, and then tap a song name to play a 90-second snippet of that song.

32. Tap Play All to play all the snippets in the album.

33. Purchase a song on the album by tapping the purchase button that contains the price of that specific song.

A Song Says It's "Album Only." What Does That Mean?

You may not be able to purchase one or more individual songs within the album. Instead, you need to purchase the entire album to hear the song(s). When you see a song in the list that says "Album Only" it means you can't purchase that individual song to download and listen to on your Galaxy S6.

34. Swipe from top to bottom of the screen until you see the album cover and then tap the orange price button.

35. The Google Play window appears with the price of the album and the credit card that the Google Play Store will use to process the transaction.

36. Tap Buy to purchase the album.

37. After you purchase the album, a Shopping bag with a check mark tells you that you successfully downloaded the album to your Galaxy S6.

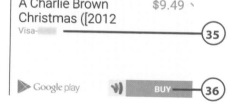

Playing Songs

The Music app on your Galaxy S6 was designed to make it easy for you to browse and play your music collection downloaded onto your Galaxy S6. A great set of headphones can enhance the enjoyment of your favorite music. The ability to browse your music library and understanding your playback options are big steps toward getting the most out of your many entertainment possibilities on the Galaxy S6.

Play Music in the Music App

In the Music app, you can play songs you added to your play queue within the app. You can also listen to music you downloaded from the Google Play Store within the Music app.

1. Tap the Apps icon on the Home screen.

2. Tap Music.

3. Tap Recently Added in the list.

4. The most recent song you added to the Galaxy S6 appears at the top of the Recently Added list. Swipe up and down in the screen to see other songs in the list.

Play a Song Even When the Music App Is Closed

After you start playing a song in the Music app, you see the play icon in the Status bar at the top of the screen. Pause the song by opening the Quick Settings and Notification Panel and then tapping the Pause button. When you close the Quick Settings and Notification Panel, you see the pause icon in the Status bar. You can read more about opening the Quick Settings and Notification Panel in the Prologue.

5. Tap a song in the list to listen to that song in the Music app.

6. The song plays automatically and the playback controls appear in a window at the bottom of the screen.

7. Tap the Pause button to pause playback.

8. Tap the Rewind icon to begin playing at the beginning of the song.

9. Tap the Fast Forward icon to move to the end of the song.

10. Tap Shuffle to have the Music app play songs in your Play Queue at random.

11. Tap the Back icon to go back to the Music screen.

12. Tap Playlists.

The Play icon in the Status bar

13. Tap Tracks in the menu to view all the tracks you can play in the Music app.

14. Tap and hold your finger on the selected track in the list. After a second or two, a green check box with a white check mark appears to the left of the track name.

15. Tap Delete to delete the song from the Music app.

16. Tap More.

17. Tap Add to Playlist to add the song to a playlist.

18. Tap Add to Favorites to add the song to your Favorites list.

19. Tap the Back touch button to close the menu.

20. Return to the list of tracks in the Tracks screen by tapping the Back touch button.

Play Music in the Google Play Music App

The Play Music app makes it easy for you to listen to music within the Google Play Store directly within the app.

1. Tap Google on the Home screen.

2. Tap Play Music.

3. From the Listen Now screen, tap the Menu icon at the left side of the menu bar, as discussed earlier in this chapter.

4. Tap My Library.

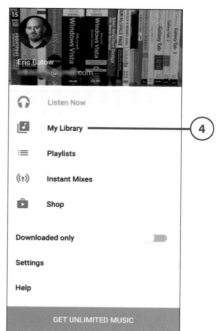

5. Tap Songs.

6. Swipe up and down the list of songs (if necessary) and then tap the song title in the list.

7. Tap the Pause button while you're playing the song to pause playback.

8. Tap the Play button to resume playing the song (not shown).

9. Tap the Play bar at the bottom of the screen to view more options.

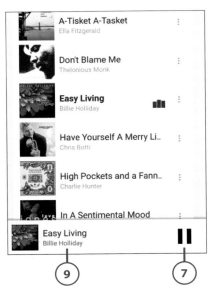

10. By default, the Repeat icon is active so the song will repeat when it finishes playing. Tap the icon to turn off the repeat feature; when the current song finishes playing, Google Music Player begins to play the next song in your queue.

11. Tap the Rewind icon to begin playing at the beginning of the song.

12. Tap the Pause button while you're playing the song to pause playback.

13. Tap the Fast Forward icon to move to the end of the song.

14. Tap the Shuffle icon to play a random song in your library after the current song ends.

15. Rate the song so other Google Play users can see your rating by tapping the thumbs up (good) or thumbs down (bad) icon.

16. Tap the Library icon to view all songs in your library; you can listen to another song in your library by tapping the song in the list.

17. Return to the My Library screen by tapping the Back touch button.

18. Have the Play Music app play all songs in the list randomly by tapping Start Instant Mix.

19. Play the next song in the list by tapping Play Next.

20. Download the song to your Galaxy S6 by tapping Add to Queue.

21. Add the song to a new playlist by tapping Add to Playlist.

22. Within the Add to Playlist window, tap a playlist to add the song to a playlist.

23. Tap New Playlist to add the song to a new playlist in the New Playlist window.

24. Type the playlist name in the Name field.

25. Type a description of your playlist in the Description field.

26. Share your playlist with all other Google Play Music users who view your profile by sliding the Public slider button from left (off) to right (on). Otherwise, only you are able to hear music in the playlist.

27. Tap Create Playlist. A pop-up box appears at the bottom of the screen that informs you that Play Music added the song to your playlist. Open the song options menu again by tapping the Menu icon to the right of the song title.

28. View all the artist's albums that you've added to your library by tapping Go to Artist.

29. View the album you've added to your library by tapping Go to Album.

30. Tap Delete to delete the song from your Galaxy S6 and from your playlist within the Play Music app.

31. Tap Shop This Artist to shop for more music from the artist in the Google Play Store.

32. Tap the Back touch button to return to the main Play Music screen.

Creating Your Own Playlists

Playlists are a great way to create a compilation of your favorite songs for playback in the Music app. Use playlists as an opportunity to organize the best songs from your favorite artists, acoustic selections, party music, classic rock, orchestral masterpieces, relaxation tracks, and more.

1. Tap the Apps icon on the Home screen.

2. Tap Music.

3. Tap Create Playlist.

4. Type the name for your new playlist.

5. Tap Create.

6. Tap the songs you want to appear in the playlist. After you tap a song, a green check mark appears in the check box to the left of the song name. Tap the song title again to clear the check box and remove the song from the playlist.

7. Tap Done when you've finished creating the playlist.

>>>Go Further
REMOVING AND ADDING SONGS IN A PLAYLIST

You can remove songs from a playlist by selecting the playlist and then tapping and holding on the song you want to remove. After a second or two, a green check box with a white check mark appears to the left of the song title. Remove the song by tapping Remove in the menu bar at the top of the screen. You can add a song to a playlist by opening the playlist to which you want to add the song and then tapping Add in the menu bar at the top of the screen. You can then select one or more songs in the Tracks screen. When you're finished, tap Done in the upper-right corner of the screen.

Adding a Podcast App

One popular podcast manager is BeyondPod, and the lite version of it is free. The lite version has all the features of the Pro version except that scheduling of updates is disabled, you can update only one feed at a time, and you can download only one podcast at a time.

During the first seven days after installation you can use the full version of BeyondPod at no charge. If you decide you want all the bells and whistles BeyondPod has to offer, you can purchase an unlock key for $6.99. If not, you can continue to use the free lite version indefinitely.

1. Find the BeyondPod app in the Google Play Store and install it. (Read Chapter 12, "Working with Android Applications," for more information on getting apps from the Google Play Store.) After you have installed the app, tap Open to launch the app.

2. Tap Let's Start in the Welcome screen.

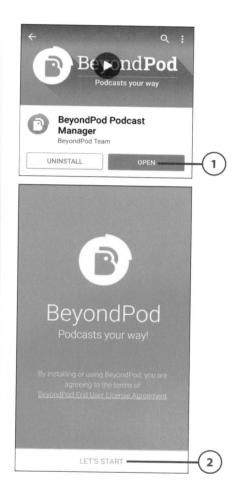

3. Swipe up and down in the window and tap one or more podcast categories. After you tap a category, a check mark appears in the upper-right corner of the category tile. When you're finished, tap Continue.

4. Keep the default settings and tap Finish.

5. Scroll up and down the feeds list in the What to Play window within the My Feeds screen. Tap the down arrow to the right of a feed category name to view podcasts within that category.

6. Tap a podcast to view the episodes.

7. Tap No, Thanks to close the Quick Tour box at the top of the screen.

8. In the My Episodes screen, each recent episode appears as a tile on the screen. Swipe up and down the screen if necessary to view all recent episodes. If you don't see the episode you want, tap See All Published Episodes at the bottom of the list.

9. Add an episode to your episode list by tapping the Menu icon within the episode tile and then tapping Add to My Episodes in the menu.

10. Return to the list of your episodes by tapping the podcast name in the menu bar.

11. Tap Download to download the episode to your Galaxy S6.

12. Tap Add to Playlist to add the episode to your playlist.

13. Tap the Menu icon to view a menu with more options.

14. Tap Delete Episode to delete the episode tile from the My Episodes screen.

15. Tap Set as Favorite to mark the episode as a favorite. After you add the episode as a favorite, the favorite icon (a red heart) appears to the left of the podcast publication date at the top of the tile.

16. Tap Mark Played to mark the episode as one you've already listened to. After you mark the episode as played, the episode tile is gray so you can't play the episode.

17. Tap Share Episode to share the episode using the Memo app, OneNote, Android Beam, your phone carrier's mail app, Facebook, Facebook Messenger, Facebook Pages Manager, Google+, Google Drive, Google Hangouts, the Messages app, Bluetooth, Wi-Fi Direct, Gmail or Email, or Samsung Quick Connect, or to copy the episode to the clipboard.

18. Tap Play to play the episode.

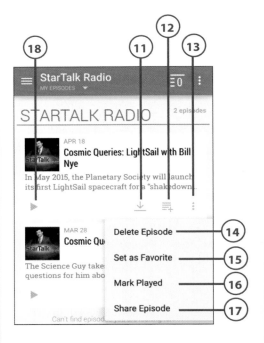

19. The number of episodes in your playlist appears in the upper-right corner of the podcast tile in the feeds list. View all episodes in your playlist for that feed by tapping the playlist number.

20. Tap the Car icon to view a large control area at the bottom half of the screen. This large control area includes a large Play button as well as buttons to rewind, fast forward, go to the beginning of the podcast, or skip to the end of the podcast.

21. Turn on sleep mode to pause the playback automatically after a certain period of time by tapping Sleep and then tapping the amount of time you want to play the podcast before it stops playing.

22. Change the playback speed by tapping 1x. Note that you can't change the speed of streamed podcasts, which are podcasts that play while the podcast app receives the rest of the podcast.

23. Use the slider to shuttle through the podcast. When the podcast ends, BeyondPod begins to play the next episode in the playlist, if any.

24. Use the playback controls to pause, play, or jump forward or backward in the podcast.

25. View a menu with more options by tapping the Menu icon.

26. Tap Share Episode to share the episode using the Memo app, OneNote, Android Beam, your phone carrier's mail app, Facebook, Facebook Messenger, Facebook Pages Manager, Google+, Google Drive, Google Hangouts, the Messages app, Bluetooth, Wi-Fi Direct, Gmail or Email, or Samsung Quick Connect, or to copy the episode to the clipboard.

27. Tap Play Videos as Audio to play the episode in audio mode only.

28. Return to the My Episodes screen by tapping the down arrow icon.

29. The podcast information appears in the playback box at the bottom of the screen so you can play the episode by tapping the Play icon.

30. View the options menu for the My Episodes screen by tapping the Menu icon.

31. Tap Update Feed to refresh the current feed on the page.

32. Tap Sort to sort episodes in the My Episodes list by a variety of criteria, such as listing the episodes alphabetically by name.

33. Tap Filter to filter episodes in the My Episodes list by a variety of criteria, such as viewing only those episodes you downloaded to your Galaxy S6.

34. Tap Share Feed to share the feed using the Memo app, OneNote, Android Beam, your phone carrier's mail app, Facebook, Facebook Messenger, Facebook Pages Manager, Google+, Google Drive, Google Hangouts, the Messages app, Bluetooth, Wi-Fi Direct, Gmail or Email, or Samsung Quick Connect, or to copy the episode to the clipboard.

35. Tap Edit Feed to edit feed settings such as changing the feed category.

36. Tap Search to search for a feed in the BeyondPod database.

37. Tap Compact Cards to hide the brief description of the episode in each episode tile.

38. Tap Play Videos as Audio to play all episodes within the feed in audio mode only.

39. Close the menu by tapping the Back touch button.

Automatically Updating Feeds

By default, feeds are set to automatically update on a configurable interval. You can change the interval by tapping and holding on the left edge of the screen and then swiping right. Within the menu, tap Settings. In the BeyondPod Settings screen, tap Feed Update Settings to change the interval.

Deleting Feeds

If you want to delete a feed, tap and hold your finger on the left side of the screen and then swipe right. Within the menu, tap and hold on the feed name for a couple of seconds. A pop-up menu displays that includes a Delete Feed option.

Edit and
share
photos

Capture
photos

Browse, manage, and share photos

In this chapter, you find out how to capture photos and screenshots, share photos via email and slideshows, and view and manage photos with Gallery:

→ Using the camera
→ Tips for capturing photos
→ Navigating Image Viewer
→ Working with Gallery
→ Editing and sharing images
→ Performing screen captures

Taking and Sharing Photos

Along with transferring images from other sources, such as your computer, to your Galaxy S6, you can also take high-quality photos with your Galaxy S6, which can house thousands of photos organized in categories. You also have the capability to take screenshots of the Galaxy S6 interface.

The high-resolution screen on your Galaxy S6 offers a great way to showcase photos to friends and family, but you don't have to stop there. You can also share pictures via Bluetooth, email, Facebook, Instagram, and more.

Using the Camera

Both the Galaxy S6 and S6 edge use a 16.0-megapixel rear-facing camera located on the back of the device to take photos, along with a 5.0-megapixel front-facing camera that you can use for self-portraits.

Taking a photo can be as simple as choosing a subject, composing your shot, and pressing a button. The Galaxy S6 is also equipped with some helpful features commonly found on dedicated photo cameras, including shooting modes, scene modes, manual exposure, white balance, flash, manual exposure, and ISO settings.

Why Does the Camera App Stop Running on Its Own?

If you don't use the Camera app for two minutes, then the app automatically minimizes and you return to the Home page. This approach helps conserve battery life as the app is resource intensive. You can return to the Camera app by tapping the Recent touch button and then tapping the Camera tile in the Recent Apps screen.

Change Quick Settings

1. On the Home screen, tap Camera.

2. The Quick Settings icons appear at the left side of the Viewer screen. Hide the Quick Settings icons by tapping the up arrow.

Vertical or Horizontal View?

You can take pictures in the view that's most comfortable for you: vertical or horizontal. The examples in this section starting with Step 2 are in horizontal view, so when you use the Camera app, keep in mind that the location of features on the screen in vertical view will be different from what is described here. For example, in vertical view the Settings icon is in the upper-left corner of the screen, but in horizontal view the icon is in the lower-left or upper-right corner of the screen depending on how you hold the Galaxy S6.

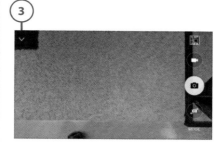

3. View the Quick Settings icons again by tapping the down arrow.

4. Select an effect to apply to your photo after you take the photo by tapping Effect.

5. Tap the Effect tile in the list; the selected effect appears with a check mark in the center of the tile. Tap Download to shop for and download another effect in the Galaxy Apps store.

6. An image that is too light or too dark degrades the appearance of your photos. The Galaxy S6 contains the HDR (High Dynamic Range) setting so the device automatically adjusts the brightness level for various bright or dark lighting conditions. Tap HDR Off to turn on HDR automatic mode, which means the Camera app checks the lighting conditions and applies the HDR feature if needed.

7. Tap HDR Auto to turn the HDR feature on for every photo you take.

8. Tap HDR On to turn the HDR feature off.

9. Tap the Timer icon to designate how long the Galaxy S6 should wait before the camera takes a photo. This is great when you want to set up the shot and then place yourself in the frame.

10. Select the timer option in the Timer window. The default option is Off, but you can select from 2 seconds, 5 seconds, or 10 seconds.

11. The camera flash is off by default. Tap the Flash icon to turn on automatic flash mode, which means the Camera app checks the lighting conditions and applies the flash if lighting is too dim.

12. Tap Flash Auto to turn the flash on for every photo you take.

13. Tap Flash On to turn the flash off.

View and Change Pro Settings

By default, the Camera app takes photos in Auto mode so you can take photos and know that they'll look great. If you need more control over how your photos look, you can access Pro settings and make manual changes to the color effect, focus mode, white balance, ISO value, and exposure value.

1. Tap Mode in the lower-right corner of the screen.

2. Tap Pro in the menu screen.

3. The Pro settings appear on the right side of the screen.

4. Tap Standard to apply a color effect after you take the photo.

5. Swipe up and down the color effect list to view the effects. The default effect is Standard, which contains the default color settings. The selected effect has a white check mark in the middle of the color effect tile.

6. Each tile shows you how the photo looks in comparison to the Standard effect.

7. Create a new custom effect by swiping down the list and then tapping Preset 1 or Preset 2. You can add up to two custom effects.

8. Change the effect by moving one or more of the six setting sliders up and down. You can change the color temperature, tint, contrast, saturation, highlight, and shadow levels. As you move each slider, the Viewer changes to show how your color effects will appear in a photo.

9. Reset effect settings to their default levels by tapping Reset.

10. Save your changes by tapping Save.

11. Return to the Viewer without making changes by tapping the Back icon.

12. Tap the Focus Mode icon to manually change the focus. The default is Auto, but you can slide the button on the slider bar up and down. You can swipe between close focus, which is signified by the flower icon, and broader focus, which is signified by the mountain icon.

13. The focus setting name below the Focus Mode icon (Auto in this example) changes to Manual after you have manually set the focus.

14. Tap the WB icon (WB stands for white balance) to adjust the white balance for the camera. The white balance features help accurately reproduce colors when you are shooting in various lighting situations so that neutral colors, such as white and gray, are truly neutral and all colors are rendered without undesired color casts, or tints of colors that affect the entire photo evenly.

15. Move the slider button up and down between Daylight, Cloudy, Incandescent, and Fluorescent white balances.

16. The white balance appears below the WB icon after you have selected a white balance mode.

Can I Select a Focus Between Auto and Close?

You can't select a focus on the slider bar between Auto and Close Focus. If you try, then after you release your finger from the slider button, the Camera app determines the setting to which the slider button is closest and then automatically moves to either the Close Focus or Auto setting in the slider bar.

17. Tap the ISO icon to adjust the brightness level in your photo. The default level in the slider bar is Auto.

18. Slide the button in the slider bar up to achieve a proper bright-ness level in a low-light shooting environment, or slide the button down for a bright shooting envi-ronment. You can select from one of five levels: Auto, 100, 200, 400, and 800. If you release your finger from the button between one of the levels, the button moves to the level closest to the button.

19. The level number appears below the ISO icon after you have selected the ISO level. (It's Auto in this example.) The Viewer also changes the light level so you can see whether the selected ISO level is appropriate for your environment.

20. Change the exposure value by tapping the Exposure icon. The exposure value determines how much light the camera's sensor receives.

21. Slide the button in the slider bar up if you're in a low-light environment or slide the button down for a bright shooting environment. You can slide to any level between +2 and −2. 0 is the default setting.

22. The value appears below the Exposure icon after you have selected the exposure value. The Viewer also changes the light level so you can see whether the selected exposure value is appropriate for your environment.

23. Tap Metering to set how the camera measures or meters the light source. This setting determines how the camera factors light in a scene to achieve the proper exposure.

24. Change the metering mode in the Metering Modes window.

>>>Go Further

LOOKING AT METERING MODES

The default Metering setting is Center-Weighted. Your other choices are Matrix, which measures light intensity in several points to achieve the best exposure, and Spot, where only a small area in the scene is measured. Matrix metering is usually considered the most accurate form of metering because it measures the entire scene and then sets the exposure according to an average. Spot metering is generally used to capture very-high-contrast scenes, such as when a subject's back is to the sun.

25. Save all your Pro settings so you don't have to set them each time you use the camera by tapping Custom.

26. Tap Save Current Settings in the Custom Settings window.

27. Tap one of the three custom setting names into which you can save your settings.

28. Tap Save.

29. The custom setting icon appears in the Viewer so you can tap the icon to change to your preferred camera settings automatically.

Set Camera Modes

You can apply special effects to your photos by selecting from one of three camera modes. If you don't see the camera mode you want, you can download other modes from Samsung's Galaxy Apps store.

1. Tap Mode in the lower-right corner of the Viewer.

2. If you want to have one or more specific objects in your photo stand out, tap Selective Focus. After you take the photo, you can specify which object(s) have sharper focus and which objects do not.

3. Tap Panorama to take a picture and then use the onscreen guide to move the viewfinder and take seven more shots. Then you can stitch each individual shot together to capture a wide vista, such as landscapes and cityscapes.

4. Tap Virtual Shot to take a series of photos around an object by moving the Galaxy S6 around the object. When the Camera app finishes taking the photos, the app stitches those photos together and creates a brief video that shows a 270-degree view of the object.

5. If you don't see a camera mode that meets your needs, tap Download to shop for other camera modes in the Galaxy Apps store.

6. Return to the Viewer by tapping the Back touch button.

Change Camera Settings

The Camera app contains a variety of settings you can view and/or change. Some of the settings allow you to change the video camera, but this section discusses camera settings only. Refer to Chapter 10, "Watching and Creating Videos," for more information about video settings within the Camera app.

1. In the Viewer, tap the Settings icon to customize camera quick settings.

2. The Camera Settings screen appears with five setting options in the list.

3. Tap Picture Size (Rear) to change the rear camera size and resolution for your photos. The default is 16.0 megapixels with 5312 × 2988 pixel resolution. Note that if you switch to the front-facing camera (as explained later in this chapter), this option is Picture Size (Front) so you can change the front camera size and resolution.

4. Slide the Tracking AF slider button from left (Off) to right (On) to focus on and track an object. If the object of your photo moves between the time the camera achieves focus and the time the photo is captured, the object will be blurred. With the Tracking AF feature on, the camera follows the moving object and keeps it in focus so your photo isn't blurry.

5. Slide the Grid Lines slider from left (Off) to right (On) to enable an onscreen grid that can help you with composition.

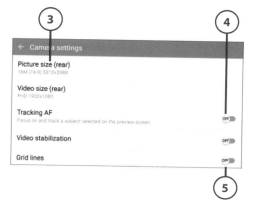

6. Swipe to view the next five setting options.

7. Slide the Location Tags slider to the left (Off) or right (On) to disable or enable, respectively, GPS tagging of the photos you capture. Embedded GPS information can come in handy if you use a photo-editing and -managing application such as Photoshop, which enables you to use the location information to manage and showcase photos.

8. Slide the Review Pictures slider to the right (On) or left (Off) to turn the review screen on or off, respectively. If Review is turned on, you see a preview of the photo you just shot in the Review screen.

9. By default, you can open the Camera app by quickly pressing the Home key two times. You can turn this feature off by sliding the Quick Launch slider button from right (On) to left (Off).

10. If you want to use your voice to take photos on the Galaxy S6, slide the Voice Control slider button from left (Off) to right (On). You can use one of four different voice commands to capture a photo: Smile, Cheese, Capture, or Shoot.

11. Tap Volume Keys Function to determine if the volume key acts as the zoom key, the video recording key, or the camera key. The default is the camera key, shown as "Take pictures" underneath the Volume Keys Function setting name.

12. Swipe to view the last three setting options.

13. By default, the Camera app makes a noise similar to an old camera shutter when you tap the Camera button. If you don't want to hear this sound, slide the Shutter Sound slider from right (On) to left (Off).

14. Tap Reset Settings to reset the Camera settings to their defaults.

15. Tap Help to get some quick onscreen help for the Camera app.

16. Return to the Viewer by tapping the Back icon.

Take a Photo

After you view and/or change Camera app settings, it's easy for you to take a photo with your Galaxy S6.

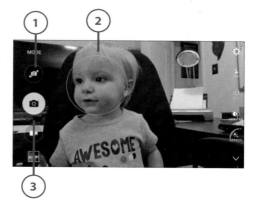

1. In the Viewer, tap to switch between the rear-facing and front-facing cameras. Tap again to return to the previous camera view.

2. Compose the subject in the Viewer. By default, Camera automatically focuses on what is in the center of the Viewer or on the face in your shot, as shown by the yellow circle around the face in this example.

3. Hold your finger on the Camera button, level the shot, and then remove your finger from the button to capture the image. A thumbnail of the image appears in the Image Viewer.

Why Are the Viewer Icons on Opposite Sides of the Screen?

There are two ways to hold your Galaxy S6 in horizontal view: with the Home button to your left or to your right of the screen. Most of the examples in this chapter show the icons when the screen is held in horizontal view with the Home button to the right. When you rotate the screen 180 degrees so the Home button is on your left, the icons switch sides on the screen so the Camera button and Image Viewer are on the left side of the screen, as you see in this example.

4. Tap the Image Viewer to review the image you just captured. You can also access your photos by tapping the Gallery icon under Applications from any Home screen.

Navigating Image Viewer

Image Viewer provides a quick-and-easy way to review the photos you have just taken. It also enables you to quickly share your pictures as soon as you capture them or set them as wallpaper. You can also edit and delete unwanted photos in Image Viewer.

As soon as you take a picture, a thumbnail of that photo appears next to the Camera button. You can tap that thumbnail to review the picture you have taken and browse other photos.

1. Tap the Image Viewer to review the image.

2. The image opens full screen, the controls appear, and then they fade away. Tap the middle of the screen to access the controls again.

3. Tap to add the photo as a favorite that you can view in the Gallery app, which is covered later in this chapter in the "Working with Gallery" section.

4. Tap to access many options for sharing your photos through services and apps including Google Drive, OneNote, the Memo app, Samsung Quick Connect, Wi-Fi Direct, Bluetooth, Google+, Flipboard, Hangouts, Instagram, Gmail, and Email. You can also view the photo on a connected device and print the photo, such as to a Bluetooth printer.

5. Tap to automatically adjust the photo for best viewing, rotate the photo, and crop the photo. You can also edit the photo in the Photo Editor app or create a collage of photos in the Collage app.

6. Tap to delete the currently displayed photo.

7. Swipe the image from left to right to navigate through all the photos you have captured.

8. Tap Album to view the album of all the photos you captured.

9. Tap More to access other options.

10. Tap to view details about the photo, including the time it was taken, the date it was captured, and the location where you took the photo.

11. Tap to begin a slideshow of your photos. After the slideshow begins, you can tap anywhere onscreen to end the slideshow.

12. Tap to set the current picture as a contact photo.

13. Tap to set the current picture as wallpaper on your Home screen, Lock screen, or the Home screen and Lock screens.

14. Close the menu by tapping the Back touch button.

15. With the menu closed, double-tap the image to zoom in. You can double-tap it again to zoom out and return the image to its normal size. You can also touch the screen with two fingers and then move them apart to zoom in on an image.

16. Tap the Back touch button to return to the Camera app and take more pictures.

>>>*Go Further*

TIPS FOR CAPTURING PHOTOS

Shutter lag is the amount of time that elapses between your press of the shutter release button and the moment the picture is captured. A longer shutter lag is common among most compact cameras and also the Galaxy S6. What this means for you is that you have to be particularly mindful of timing your shots when recording moving subjects. Shutter lag can cause you to miss out on a key action if you do not anticipate the shot.

One important thing to know about your Galaxy S6 is that the shutter does not fire as you place your finger down on the Camera button; the shutter fires when you lift your finger off the button. Use this knowledge to your advantage by pressing your finger on the shutter button and holding while you frame the shot and focus on an object about the same distance as where the subject will pass, to anticipate the shot, and then lift your finger. This means you need to hold your Galaxy S6 completely still for a little bit longer. Anticipating moving subjects to capture dynamic, moving shots can take some practice.

The slow shutter on the Galaxy S6 makes it prone to producing blurry photos if you do not remain perfectly still during capture. Even the smallest movement can have an adverse effect on your photographs; this is especially true in low-light situations. A photo might appear to be fine when you review it on the Galaxy S6 display, but when you download it and view it on a larger display, you can see the problem.

Working with Gallery

Gallery offers a more robust photo and video management system than Image Viewer, but it has similar options for viewing, sharing, and editing photos.

Manage Photos with Gallery

By default, you can access the Gallery icon by flicking the main Home screen from left to right, or you can access it from the Apps menu.

1. Tap the Apps icon on the Home screen.

2. Tap Gallery in the Apps screen.

3. Content is arranged in categories/albums. If you have downloaded photos with your Galaxy S6 and transferred images from your computer, they are in here, too.

4. Tap Albums to group your photos and videos in other ways. The name of this particular menu changes depending on which grouping method you have selected.

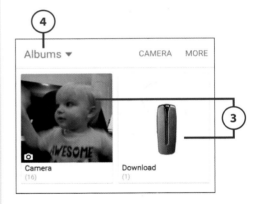

5. Tap Time to arrange photos based on the time they were captured. The most recent photos appear in the row at the top of the screen.

6. Tap Events to arrange photos by event, such as a birthday party. You can create events within the Events screen by tapping More in the menu bar, tapping Create Event, and then selecting the photos to add to your event.

7. Tap Categories to arrange photos based on various categories, such as People to show photos of people.

8. Tap Favorites to view photos you identified as a favorite within the Camera app Image Viewer as described in the "Navigating Image Viewer" section.

9. Tap the Albums option to arrange photos based on the folder in which they are stored. This example shows photos in albums.

10. Tap Camera in the menu bar to access the Camera feature from Gallery and take more photos.

11. Tap More.

12. Tap Edit to select one or more complete albums to delete.

13. Tap Search to search for a photo by typing search term(s) in the Search box, or you can search in different categories such as events and location where the photo was taken.

14. Tap Create Album to create a new album.

15. Tap Help to get quick help for the Gallery app.

16. Close the menu by tapping the Back touch button.

17. Tap an album to view all photos in it.

18. If you have more photos in the album than can fit on the screen, swipe up and down on the screen to view all thumbnail-sized photos in the album.

19. Tap and hold your finger on a photo for a couple of seconds to select it. The selected photo has a green check box with a white check mark in the upper-left corner of the photo.

20. Tap Share to view options for sharing the selected image(s) in an email or Gmail message, on Google Drive, to OneNote or a memo, to another device using Samsung Quick Connect or a Wi-Fi Direct or Bluetooth connection, on Hangouts or Skype, Google+ or Facebook, or within the Instagram and Photos apps. You can also use your phone carrier's messaging, mail, and/or file storage services if applicable. And you can print the photo, such as to a Bluetooth printer.

21. Tap Delete to delete the photo from the album and the Galaxy S6 altogether.

22. Tap More to either copy or move the photo to another album.

23. Select all photos in the album by tapping the All check box.

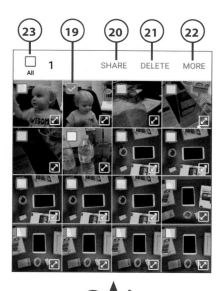

24. Turn off the image selection feature by tapping the Back touch button, and then tap a photo in the album to open it full screen.

25. Touch the middle of the screen to reveal the controls if necessary and then tap the left arrow icon in the menu bar to return to the previous screen.

>>>Go Further
MORE PHOTO-EDITING OPTIONS

The preinstalled Photo Editor and Collage apps offer many more options for enhancing your photographs. You can send your photos from the Gallery app to Photo Editor by opening a photo full screen, tapping the center of the screen, tapping the Edit icon at the bottom of the screen, and then tapping Photo Editor in the menu. Send photos from the Gallery app to the Collage app by tapping the Edit icon and then selecting Collage. In Photo Editor you find options to rotate, resize, crop, color, and add effects. Spot healing is also an option that enables you to retouch blemishes in your photographs. Collage enables you to create a collage of two or more photos that you can show to others on your Galaxy S6.

Email Photos from Gallery

Emailing your photos to friends and family can be accomplished in just a few taps on your Galaxy S6. The following instructions presume you have set up an email account. If you haven't, bookmark this page and read Chapter 6, "Email and Text Messages," before you email your photos in the Gallery app.

1. Open the album that has the photo you want to email, and then touch and hold your finger on that photo to access more Gallery options.

2. Touch more photos that you want to share. A green check mark appears within the check box that appears in the upper-left corner of each photo, letting you know that it is selected. Email providers have varying file size limitations, so make sure you are aware of your provider's limitations before emailing photographs.

3. Tap Share to access the options in the Share Via window that appears in the bottom half of the screen. You can access these same Share options even if you are viewing a single photo in full screen mode.

Additional Sharing Options

Keep in mind that as you add an email account or Facebook account on your Galaxy S6, those options also display in the Share Via window.

4. Swipe to the appropriate page with the Email app icon.

5. Tap Email.

6. The Email app opens and displays the Resize Images window so you can resize all the selected images when you include them in the email message. Tap the size you want. The resize options are Original, Large (70 percent of the original size), Medium (30 percent), and Small (10 percent).

7. A list of the photo files you've attached appears below the Subject field and includes a small thumbnail image of each photo as well as the filename.

8. Remove the attachment from the message by tapping the red minus icon located to the right of the photo name.

9. Type the recipient's email address into the To field. If you see the name of the recipient in the drop-down list as you type, tap the name of the recipient. After you add a recipient to the list, you can add another one by typing the recipient name; you don't need any separator characters, such as a semicolon.

10. Tap in the Subject field and then type a subject for the email.

11. Tap in the Compose Email field to compose a message.

12. Tap Send to send the message.

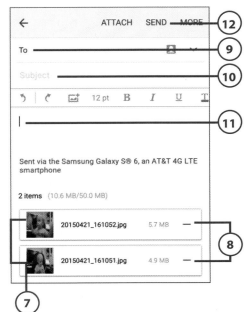

>>>Go Further
EMAILING FROM CAMERA

You can also email a photo from Camera within Image Viewer. After you tap the Camera button to capture the image, a thumbnail of the image appears in the Image Viewer. Tap the Image Viewer to review the image, and then tap the Share icon to access your email. Email providers have varying file size limitations, so make sure you are aware of your provider's limitations before emailing photographs.

Creating Screen Captures

Your Galaxy S6 has a very helpful feature that enables you to take screen captures of its interface. The ability to take screenshots can come in handy for educational purposes, especially if you want to post a few Galaxy S6 tips online.

1. Open the screen that you want to take the screenshot of and position the Galaxy S6 into the orientation in which you want to grab the screen capture: vertical or horizontal.

2. Press and hold the Power button and Home button at the same time, or use your hand to swipe across the screen. Refer to the Prologue to learn how to set up the Palm Swipe to Capture feature.

3. You hear the shutter sound effect as it takes the screen capture. The screenshot is saved to the Screenshots folder in the Gallery app, and the image is also saved to the clipboard.

4. Swipe down in the Status bar to open the Quick Settings and Notification Panel.

5. In the Screenshot Captured tile, tap Edit to edit the screenshot in the Gallery app.

6. Tap Delete to delete the screenshot. In the Delete window that appears, finish the deletion process by tapping Delete.

7. Tap Share to share the selected image(s) in an email or Gmail message, on Google Drive, to OneNote, to another device using Samsung Quick Connect or a Wi-Fi Direct or Bluetooth connection, on Hangouts or Skype, Google+ or Facebook, or within the Instagram and Photos apps. You can also use your phone carrier's messaging, mail, and/or file storage services if applicable.

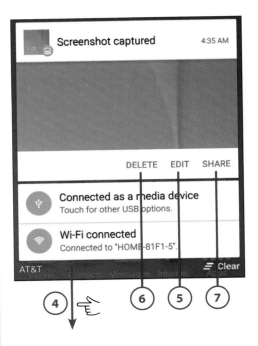

It's Not All Good

Difficulties Taking Screen Captures

It might not be possible to capture some of the Galaxy S6 menus using the Screen Capture function. For example, if you're playing a video, and then press and hold the Power button and Home button at the same time, the app you're using to view the video (such as YouTube) is minimized and the screen-shot is not captured. You can resume playing the video by tapping the Recent touch button and then tapping the video app tile in the Recent Apps screen.

Record video

Download and watch
movies and TV shows

Play and manage videos

In this chapter, you find out how to get the most out of the video recording and playback capabilities of the Galaxy S6. Topics in this chapter include the following:

→ Purchasing movies and TV shows
→ Playing videos
→ Viewing YouTube videos
→ Recording video

Watching and Creating Videos

Your Galaxy S6 allows you to play movies, TV shows, and videos on its high-resolution screen using several preinstalled apps. What's more, the Galaxy S6 is camcorder capable, which you can use to record 1080p HD video.

Downloading Movies and TV Shows

The Google Play Store makes it easy for you to browse, purchase, and download the latest music, movies, and popular TV shows to your Galaxy S6. If you want to find movies and television shows within the Google Play Store more quickly than shopping in the Play Store itself, try using the preinstalled Play Movies & TV app.

The Play Movies & TV app enables you to shop for movies and television shows, pay for a movie or show if necessary, download the movie or show, and then watch the movie or show within the app.

Download a TV Show

In this example, you find out how to download a free television featurette.

1. Tap Google on the Home screen.

2. Tap Play Movies & TV.

3. Tap Next in the bottom-right corner of the first introductory screen. If you've opened the Play Movies & TV app before, you won't see this introductory screen and you can skip ahead to Step 6.

4. Tap Next in the bottom-right corner of the second introductory screen.

5. Tap Done.

6. Tap the Menu icon in the menu bar.

7. Tap Shop.

8. Tap TV to view TV shows. This example walks through downloading a free TV show featurette.

9. Swipe up in the TV page until you see the Free Featurettes section. Tap More.

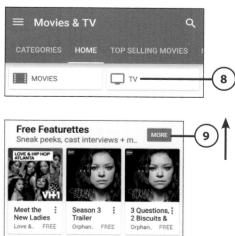

10. Swipe up in the Featurettes page until you see the tile that contains the featurette you want to download and then tap the tile.

11. In the middle of the page, information about the selected featurette appears below the title, including an image, summary, and reviews from other Google Play Store users who have watched the video. Swipe up in the page to read more reviews and view a list of episodes and featurettes.

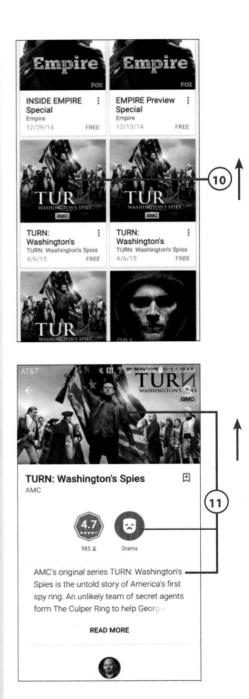

12. Tap Free to the right of the featurette title.

13. The video begins to play in horizontal screen orientation.

14. When you finish viewing the featurette, tap the Back touch button. View the featurette again by tapping the tile.

15. Return to the My Library screen by tapping the Back icon in the menu bar. You'll learn more about the My Library screen in the next section.

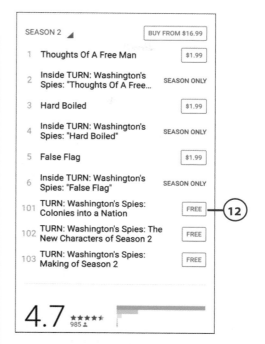

SEASON 2 ◢		BUY FROM $16.99
1	Thoughts Of A Free Man	$1.99
2	Inside TURN: Washington's Spies: "Thoughts Of A Free...	SEASON ONLY
3	Hard Boiled	$1.99
4	Inside TURN: Washington's Spies: "Hard Boiled"	SEASON ONLY
5	False Flag	$1.99
6	Inside TURN: Washington's Spies: "False Flag"	SEASON ONLY
101	TURN: Washington's Spies: Colonies into a Nation	FREE ── 12
102	TURN: Washington's Spies: The New Characters of Season 2	FREE
103	TURN: Washington's Spies: Making of Season 2	FREE

4.7 ★★★★✭
985 ±

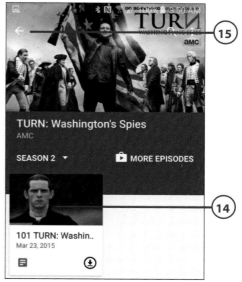

TURN: Washington's Spies
AMC

SEASON 2 ▼   ▶ MORE EPISODES

101 TURN: Washin..
Mar 23, 2015

Play the TV Show

The TV show you downloaded appears within the My Library section so you can play it whenever you want.

1. On the Movies & TV app home screen, open the menu by tapping the Menu icon at the left side of the menu bar.

2. Tap My Library.

3. Tap My TV Shows. The shows you have downloaded appear in each section; the most recent videos you downloaded appear at the top of the screen.

4. Tap a tile to view more information about each video within the section.

5. Tap a tile to begin playing the video in horizontal screen orientation.

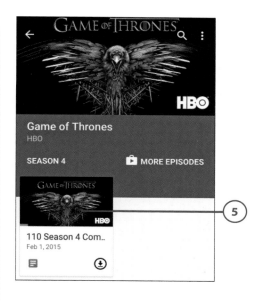

Shop for a Movie

It's easy to shop for movies that you can buy and keep on your Galaxy S6 so you can watch them any time you want.

1. From the Play Movies & TV app's home screen, open the menu by tapping the Menu icon at the left side of the menu bar.

2. Tap Shop.

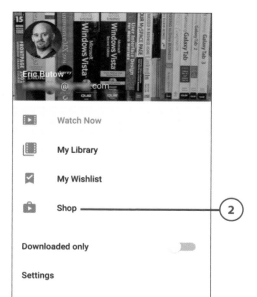

3. Tap Movies.

4. Tap Categories.

5. Tap the category you're interested in.

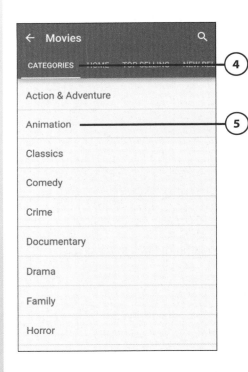

6. Swipe up and down in the page to view all the Top Selling movies in the category you selected. You can view new releases in the category by tapping New Releases.

7. Tap the tile with the movie you want more information about.

8. The name of the movie, the release year and movie rating, the movie run time, and buttons to either rent or buy the movie at the stated price appear on the screen.

9. Swipe up and down the information area to view the video trailer; rate and review the movie; view user reviews; read the synopsis, cast, and credits; and get rental period information if any.

10. Tap one of the Buy options.

11. The Buy window shows you the credit card that you have saved, which you need in order to buy a movie or TV show (even free ones) from the Google Play Store. If you don't have a card on file, the app takes you through the steps to register your credit card.

12. Buy the movie by tapping Buy. Google Play charges the card you have on file and downloads the movie to your Galaxy S6 so you can view it.

Playing Videos

There are two ways to view movies, TV shows, and other videos on your Galaxy S6. One is to watch in the Play Movies & TV app. The other is to use the Video app, which makes it easy for you to browse and play your downloaded and recorded videos.

Play Movies and TV Shows in the Play Movies & TV App

The Play Movies & TV app makes it easy for you to watch movies and TV shows from the Google Play Store directly within the app.

1. Tap Google on the Home screen.

2. Tap Play Movies & TV.

3. Swipe up and down in the Watch Now screen to view movies and TV shows you downloaded as well as get recommendations for movies and TV shows from Google Play.

4. Open and watch the video by tapping the movie or TV episode tile.

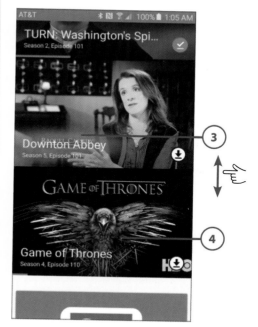

Play Videos in the Milk Video App

Samsung preinstalled its Milk Video app so you can watch videos on different "channels." These channels are websites that offer videos in a variety of categories, such as television entertainment shows, news sources, and technology websites. Milk Video makes it easier to find video content online without having to search for it in your web browser app.

After you select a channel, you can browse videos and select a video to watch.

1. Tap the Apps icon on the Home screen.

2. Tap Milk Video.

3. Tap Start in the Welcome screen.

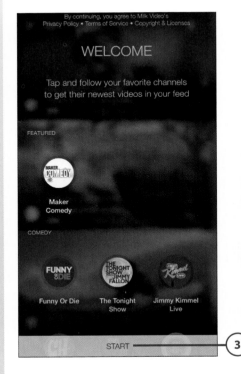

4. Tap the Menu icon in the upper-left corner of the screen.

5. Swipe up and down in the Channels screen until you find a channel you want.

6. Tap the channel name to view videos within the channel.

7. Swipe up and down in the channel page to view a list of available videos.

8. Tap the video tile to view the video on the screen.

9. Tap within the video tile to pause the video, and resume playing the video by tapping within the video tile again.

10. Swipe up and down within the videos list to view more videos you can play.

11. Tap a video tile if you want to view that video at the top of the screen.

12. Close the video by tapping the Back touch button.

13. Return to the main channel page by tapping the Back icon in the upper-left corner of the screen.

14. If you don't find a channel you want within the category and there are more channels available in the category, tap More to view more channels.

15. Tap Follow to follow the channel.

16. When you are following a channel, the Follow button is replaced by the Following button. You can unfollow a channel by tapping the Following button.

17. Follow more channels by tapping Follow to the right of the channel name.

18. When you're finished following channels, tap the Close icon.

19. Swipe up and down the Following page to see videos you can view in your favorite channel(s). Tap a video in the list to play it on the channel screen.

Play Videos in the Video App

If you've downloaded movies to your Galaxy S6 or if you've recorded videos using the device's video camera, you can play videos even without access to the Internet within the Video app.

1. Tap the Apps icon on the Home screen.

2. Tap Video.

3. By default, the Video Player screen displays videos in Thumbnails view. That is, a thumbnail-sized image from the video appears in the list so you can get an idea of what's in the video. You can play the video by tapping the thumbnail image.

4. Change the screen view by tapping Videos.

5. View your video files and the folder that contains those files by tapping Folders.

6. Tap a folder tile in the left pane, and then tap a video thumbnail image in the list to begin playing it.

7. After the video has started, tap in the middle of the screen to bring up the playback controls.

8. Tap the Pop-Up icon to view the video in a small video player window that you can move around on the screen. Though the video player window appears on the Camera screen, you can access any other screen (such as the Home screen) and the video player window still appears.

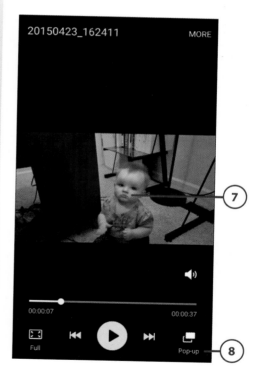

9. Tap the window to access the playback controls so you can pause playback or resume playing the video, rewind to the beginning of the video, and fast forward to the end of the video.

10. Close the window by tapping the Close icon.

11. View the video again by tapping the video tile in the Camera screen.

Return to Viewing the Video from Another Screen

If you open a screen other than the Camera screen and then close the video, you can view the video again by tapping the Recent Apps touch button and then tapping Video. The Camera screen appears again so you can tap the tile with the video you want to view.

12. Adjust the volume of the video by tapping your finger on the Volume icon and then sliding your finger on the Volume slider.

13. Tap the Viewfinder icon to change the size of the video between normal and full screen views.

14. Drag your finger across the Movie Timeline to advance through the video or jump to a new location. You can also tap the timeline in a new location to jump to that location.

15. The Play button, located in the Playback controls, turns into a Pause button as the video plays. Tap the Pause button to pause the video.

16. Tap the Rewind or Fast Forward button to move to the beginning or end of the video, respectively.

17. Tap More.

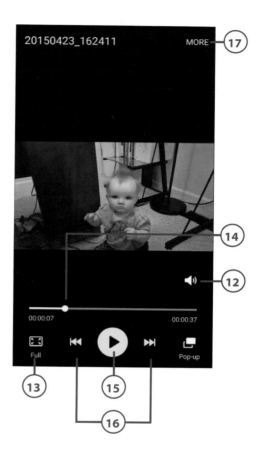

18. Tap Editor to edit the beginning and end of a video by performing a trim, adding an effect, and/or editing the audio. You can also download the Video Editor app from the Samsung Galaxy Apps store so you can edit the video with more powerful tools.

19. Tap Delete to delete the video from the playlist.

20. Tap Share to share the video using Samsung Quick Connect, OneNote, Google+, Google Drive, Bluetooth, Wi-Fi Direct, YouTube, Instagram, Photos, Facebook, Facebook Pages Manager, Facebook Messenger, Skype, Gmail, or Email. You can also share your video using your phone carrier's built-in messaging, mail, or storage apps. What's more, you can view content on another device.

21. Tap Listen via Bluetooth to share the video with other devices via Bluetooth.

22. Tap Turn On Play Audio Only to hide the video on the screen and play only the audio that was recorded with the video.

23. Tap Play Speed to change the play speed of the video so it plays faster or slower than the speed at which you recorded the video.

24. Tap Subtitles (CC) to set the app to view closed-captioned subtitles on the screen as you view the video.

25. Tap Details to view details of the video such as File Name, Resolution, Size, and Last Modified.

26. Close the menu by tapping the Back touch button.

Viewing YouTube Videos

The high-resolution screen of the Galaxy S6, along with its portability and built-in video camera, makes it great for viewing and sharing videos online. The preinstalled YouTube widget gives you the capability to browse and view videos posted by users from around the world. You can also upload videos as soon as you shoot them with your Galaxy S6.

1. Tap the Apps icon on the Home screen.

2. Tap YouTube.

3. Skip the introduction by tapping Skip. Note that the introduction screen only appears the first time you start YouTube. If you don't see this screen, skip to Step 5.

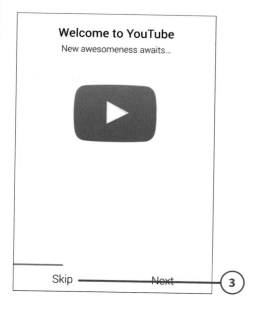

4. Tap OK.

5. Tap the Menu icon at the left side of the menu bar.

6. A list of your channels appears on the left side of the screen that overlaps a list of videos on the screen. In this example, the list of videos is within the selected What to Watch channel.

7. Swipe up in the list and then tap Browse Channels to view channels YouTube recommends for you.

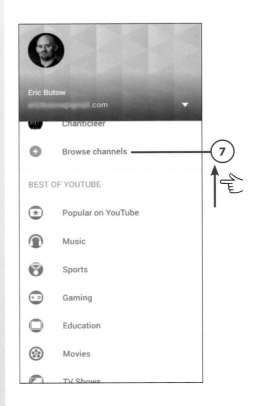

8. View channels by swiping up and down the screen. You can see videos and more information about the artist channel by tapping the channel tile.

9. Tap the Menu icon in the menu bar.

10. Return to the YouTube home screen by swiping down in the list and then tapping What to Watch.

11. Tap the Search icon to search for a YouTube video.

12. Type the search terms in the Search YouTube field. As you type, a list of potential matches appears under the field.

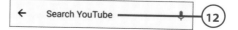

13. When you're finished typing, tap the Search button in the keyboard.

14. Swipe up and down the list of results in the Search page.

15. Tap the thumbnail image of the video or the video name to view the video on the screen.

16. Return to the What to Watch screen by tapping the Back icon.

17. Tap the Menu icon in the menu bar as described in Step 9.

18. Swipe up in the menu until you see the Subscriptions section; view videos within a subscription channel by tapping the channel name in the Subscriptions list.

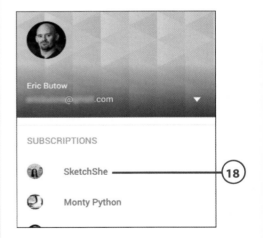

19. Tap a video tile to play the video on the screen. If you viewed the video previously, the Watched box appears in the upper-left corner of the tile.

20. Tap the Add icon to add the video to an existing playlist or create a new playlist.

21. Tap the Share icon to share a link to the current video using Samsung Quick Connect, OneNote, Google+, Google Drive, Bluetooth, Wi-Fi Direct, YouTube, Instagram, Photos, Facebook, Facebook Pages Manager, Facebook Messenger, Skype, Gmail, or Email. You can also share your video using your phone carrier's built-in messaging, mail, or storage apps. What's more, you can save the link to a memo or copy the link to the clipboard.

22. Tap the Info icon to see the group of videos to which the video belongs.

23. Tap the Menu icon so you can turn closed captioning on and off, change the video quality, and flag the video for inappropriate content so Google can review it.

24. Tap the Full Screen icon to view the video on the entire screen. If you view the full screen video in vertical screen orientation, you'll see black areas above and below the screen.

25. Tap to pause and play the current video.

26. Drag the button in the timeline slider to move through the current video.

Other Sharing Options

Other sharing options might appear in this list if you have downloaded apps that allow for additional sharing features, such as BeyondPod.

27. The video description appears below the video.

28. Tap to visit the channel of the user who posted this video.

29. Swipe up and down in the page to read more about the artists, view similar videos and artists, read comments about this video from other users, and create a response of your own.

30. Return to the channel screen by tapping the Back touch button.

31. The video continues to play in the window in the lower-right corner of the screen. View the video screen by tapping and holding in the window and then flicking upward. Close the video screen by tapping and holding in the window and then flicking to the right.

32. Return to the main YouTube screen by tapping the Menu icon in the menu bar and then tapping What to Watch as you learned about in Steps 9 and 10.

Recording Video

Your Galaxy S6 is capable of recording 1080p HD video with its main 16-megapixel camera, located on the rear of the device. The Galaxy S6 is also equipped with some very helpful features commonly found on dedicated camcorders, including white balance, a video light, manual exposure, and effects.

1. Tap Camera on the Home screen.

2. Switch to video mode by tapping the video button. The Camera app starts recording automatically.

3. The timer appears at the bottom of the screen so you can see how long you've been recording your video.

4. Pause recording by tapping the Pause button. After you tap the Pause button, the button changes to a Record button (with a red circle in the center). Resume recording by tapping the Record button.

5. Stop recording by tapping the Stop button.

6. The video you just recorded appears in the Image Viewer in the lower-left corner of the window. Tap the Image Viewer to review the recorded video in the Gallery app.

Change Camera App Settings

It's easy to change your app and camera settings so you can have the app work the way you expect each time you use it.

1. Tap the Settings icon.

2. In the Settings screen, tap Video Size (Rear) to set a size for the images you record. Note that if you switch to the front-facing camera as described later in this chapter, this option is Video Size (Front) so you can change the front camera size and resolution.

3. Slide the Video Stabilization slider button from left (Off) to right (On) to reduce or remove any blurriness that occurs in your video from the shaking of your hand and/or arm as you hold the Galaxy S6 to record your video.

4. Slide the Grid Lines slider from left (Off) to right (On) to enable an onscreen grid that can help you with the composition of the video.

5. Swipe upward to view the next five settings.

6. If you want to use your voice to take videos on the Galaxy S6, slide the Voice Control slider button from left (Off) to right (On). Say "record video" to begin recording the video.

7. Tap Volume Keys Function to determine whether the volume key acts as the zoom key, the video recording key, or the camera key. In the menu that appears, tap Record Video to tell the Galaxy S6 the volume key is the video recording key.

8. Swipe upward to view the last three settings options.

9. Tap Reset Settings to reset the Camera settings to their defaults.

10. Tap Help to get some quick onscreen help for the Camera app.

11. Return to the Viewer by tapping the Back icon.

View and Change Basic Settings

Several setting icons appear on one side of the Viewer depending on how you hold your phone. These icons allow you to add effects, change light settings, and set a time before the camera starts to record your video.

1. Tap to add camera effects to your videos as you capture them.

2. Apply an effect by tapping the effect tile. Your choices include Grayscale, Vignette, and Vintage. If you don't see an effect, you can shop for one in the Galaxy Apps app by tapping the Download tile.

3. Tap anywhere else on the screen to close the Effects area.

4. An image that is too light or too dark degrades the appearance of your videos. The Galaxy S6 contains the HDR (High Dynamic Range) setting so the device auto-matically adjusts the brightness level for various bright or dark lighting conditions. Tap HDR Off to turn on HDR automatic mode, which means the Camera app checks the lighting conditions and applies the HDR feature if needed.

5. Tap Timer to designate how long the Galaxy S6 should wait before the camera starts to record. This is great for allowing time for you to set up the shot and then place yourself in the frame.

Adding Video Effects

Keep in mind that when you use
any of the video effects, such as
Grayscale, Vignette, or Sepia, they
become a permanent part of your
videos. To give yourself more
choices in the future as to how
you use your images, consider
purchasing a video-editing app
that enables you to perform such
effects but still maintain your
original video.

View and Change Pro Settings

By default, the Camera app takes
photos in Auto mode so you can
record videos and know that they'll
look great. If you need more control
over how your videos look, you can
access Pro settings and make manual
changes to the color effect, focus
mode, white balance, ISO value, and
exposure value.

1. Access Pro settings to get more
   control over how your videos look
   by tapping Mode in the lower-
   right corner of the screen.

2. Tap Pro in the menu screen.

3. The Pro settings appear on one
   side of the screen depending on
   how you hold your Galaxy S6. In
   this example, the phone is being
   held with the Home button to the
   right of the screen so the Pro settings appear on the right side of
   the screen.

4. Tap Standard to apply a color effect before you take the video.

5. Swipe up and down the color effect list to view the effects. The default effect is Standard, which contains the default color settings. The selected effect has a white check mark in the middle of the color effect tile.

6. Each tile shows you how the video will look in comparison to the Standard effect.

7. Create a new custom effect by swiping down the list and then tapping Preset 1 or Preset 2. You can add up to two custom effects.

8. Change the effect by moving one or more of the six setting sliders up and down. You can change the color temperature, tint, contrast, saturation, highlight, and shadow levels. As you move each slider, the Viewer changes to show how your color effects will appear in your video.

9. Reset effect settings to their default levels by tapping Reset.

10. Save your changes by tapping Save.

11. Return to the Viewer without making changes by tapping the Back icon.

12. Tap the Focus Mode icon to manually change the focus. The default is Auto, but you can slide the button on the slider bar up and down. You can swipe between close focus, which is signified by the flower icon, and broader focus, which is signified by the mountain icon.

13. After you manually set the focus, the focus setting name below the Focus Mode icon (Auto in this example) changes to Manual.

14. Tap the WB icon (WB stands for white balance) to adjust the white balance for the camera. The white balance features help accurately reproduce colors when you are shooting in various lighting situations so that neutral colors, such as white and gray, are truly neutral and all colors are rendered without undesired color casts.

15. Move the slider button up and down between Daylight, Cloudy, Incandescent, and Fluorescent white balances.

16. After you select a white balance mode, the white balance appears below the WB icon.

Can I Select a Focus Between Auto and Close?

You can't select a focus on the slider bar between Auto and Close Focus. If you try, then after you release your finger from the slider button, the Camera app determines the setting to which the slider button is closest and then automatically moves to either the Close Focus or Auto setting in the slider bar.

17. Tap the ISO icon to adjust the brightness level in your photo. The default level in the slider bar is Auto.

18. Slide the button in the slider bar up to achieve a proper brightness level in a low-light shooting environment, or slide the button down for a bright shooting environment. You can select from one of five levels: Auto, 100, 200, 400, and 800. If you release your finger from the button between one of the levels, the button moves to the level closest to the button.

19. After you select the ISO level (Auto in this example) the level number appears below the ISO icon. The Viewer also changes the light level so you can see whether the selected ISO level is appropriate for your environment.

20. Change the exposure value by tapping the Exposure icon. The exposure value determines how much light the camera's sensor receives.

21. Slide the button in the slider bar up if you're in a low-light environment or slide the button down for a bright shooting environment. You can slide to any level between +2 and −2. 0 is the default setting.

22. After you select the exposure value, the value appears below the Exposure icon. The Viewer also changes the light level so you can see if the selected exposure value is appropriate for your environment.

23. Tap in the center of the screen to close the Exposure Value slider bar.

24. Save all your Pro settings so you don't have to set them each time you use the camera by tapping Custom.

25. Tap Save Current Settings.

26. Tap one of the three custom setting names into which you can save your settings.

27. Tap Save.

28. The custom setting icon appears in the Viewer so you can tap the icon to change to your preferred camera settings automatically.

Connect to other devices
using Wi-Fi Direct

Connect to the
cloud with the
Google Drive app

The Galaxy S6 is a great tool for sharing with other devices directly using Wi-Fi Direct and also for sharing files and media in the cloud. This chapter covers the following:

→ Connecting using Wi-Fi Direct
→ Printing wirelessly
→ Using the Google Drive app
→ Finding other cloud services
→ Sharing music and video

Sharing and Synchronizing Data

The Galaxy S6 enables you to synchronize data with other devices directly by using Wi-Fi Direct so you don't need to buy a cable or even a wireless router to connect your Galaxy S6 to another device. You can store and share data with online services on the cloud, which is file storage available on the Internet. What's more, you can share music and video between your Galaxy S6 and your computer using a USB cable and the Samsung Smart Switch app.

Connecting Using Wi-Fi Direct

If you need to wirelessly transfer data to or connect with another device such as your tablet, you can use the Galaxy S6 Wi-Fi Direct feature to connect to another device that also has Wi-Fi Direct enabled.

Set Up Wi-Fi Direct

Before you can transfer data between devices, you have to set up Wi-Fi Direct on the Galaxy S6 to connect with the other device.

1. On the Home screen, tap Apps.

2. Tap Settings.

3. Tap Connections in the menu bar.

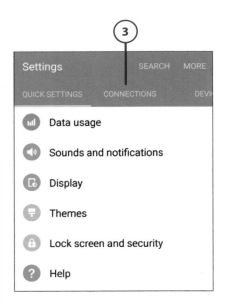

4. Tap Wi-Fi in the settings list.

5. Tap Wi-Fi Direct in the menu bar.

6. The name of your Galaxy S6 appears at the bottom of the list of connections and tells you the device is currently visible to other devices.

7. Tap the device name to which you want to connect.

8. The name of the other device turns blue, which signifies that you're connected to the other device via Wi-Fi Connect.

9. Disconnect from the device by tapping the device name.

10. Return to the Wi-Fi settings screen by tapping the Back icon.

How Do I Know I'm Connected to a Device Through Wi-Fi Direct?

If you're not sure you're connected to another device through Wi-Fi Direct, look in the Status bar at the top of the screen. The Wi-Fi Direct icon appears to the left of the Wi-Fi icon at the right side of the bar.

The Wi-Fi Direct icon

>>>Go Further
TROUBLESHOOTING CONNECTION ISSUES

If the Galaxy S6 can't find your Wi-Fi Direct device, check the other device's Wi-Fi connection and ensure the other device offers Wi-Fi Direct. You should also check the Wi-Fi Alliance website to learn whether your device is Wi-Fi Direct enabled. The Wi-Fi Alliance is a nonprofit group founded in 1999 that was formed to grow Wi-Fi acceptance in the marketplace, support industry standards, and provide a forum so Wi-Fi companies can collaborate and improve Wi-Fi technologies. You can begin searching for products that include Wi-Fi Direct functionality by opening the Internet app and then accessing the Certified Products page at http://www.wi-fi.org/product-finder.

Printing Wirelessly

It's easy to print a file such as a word processing document or spreadsheet from your Galaxy S6. You don't need any cables, and you don't need to transfer your files to another computer, either. There are some limitations to the printing functionality built in to the Galaxy S6, but you can download apps and use web-based services to get around those limits.

Connect a Wi-Fi Printer

Your Galaxy S6 automatically scans for wireless printers that are available through a Wi-Fi connection. Note that you might have to enable a Wi-Fi connection on the printer as well. For this example, I use my Hewlett-Packard (HP) Officejet Pro X576dw printer. This Officejet Pro requires the user to enable HP Wireless Direct functionality on the printer before any device can see it.

1. On the Home screen, tap Apps.

2. Tap Settings.

3. Tap Connections in the menu bar.

4. Tap Wi-Fi in the settings list.

5. Connect to the printer by tapping the printer name in the Wi-Fi Networks list.

6. If you need to enter a password, the password window appears so you can type the password in the Password field window.

7. Tap Connect.

8. The Galaxy S6 might take a few seconds to find the printer's IP address; after it does, the printer appears at the top of the Wi-Fi Networks list and displays the Connected status.

What If the Galaxy S6 Can't Find My Wireless Printer?

If the Galaxy S6 doesn't recognize your wireless printer, you might need to bring your Galaxy S6 closer to it. You can scan for the printer again by tapping Scan in the Settings menu bar that appears at the top of the screen. When the wireless printer appears in the Wi-Fi list, connect to the printer by tapping the printer name.

Connect a Bluetooth Printer

If you have a Bluetooth printer, you can also connect that printer to your Galaxy S6 so you can print wirelessly. The printer in this example is different from the HP Officejet Pro used in the previous section.

1. On the Home screen, tap Apps.

2. Tap Settings.

3. Tap Connections in the menu bar.

4. Tap Bluetooth in the settings list.

5. After the Galaxy S6 finds your Bluetooth printer, tap the printer name.

6. Type the printer's PIN in the Bluetooth Pairing Request window using the keypad at the bottom of the screen. If you aren't sure what the PIN is, try 0000 or 1234. If those PINs don't work, you need to consult your printer documentation and/or the printer manufacturer's website to find the PIN. When you're finished, tap Done.

7. Tap OK.

8. The paired Bluetooth printer appears in the Paired Devices section.

9. Tap the Settings icon to the right of the printer name to change the printer name and unpair, or disconnect, the printer from the Galaxy S6.

>>>Go Further

DOWNLOAD A PRINT APP

Samsung boasts that you can print directly from within an app on your Galaxy S6 to any compatible printer without having to connect to a Wi-Fi or Bluetooth printer. Unfortunately, what Samsung doesn't tell you is that you can only print to Samsung's printers. You find this out when you try to print from an app for the first time and see the message "You can only print to a Samsung printer." Fortunately, apps are available from the Google Play Store that enable you to print to other printers.

For example, if you have a Hewlett-Packard printer, as I'm using in this example, you can download the HP ePrint app. You can also search for your printer manufacturer in the Google Play Store to see if a printing app is available. There are also apps available from the Google Play Store for printing to a variety of devices. One such app is PrinterShare Mobile Print, which is free.

If you find a printing app in the Google Play Store that doesn't work for you (or doesn't work at all), another option is to use Google's Cloud Print service. This service connects your printers to the Web so any web-enabled device, including the Galaxy S6, can access a printer connected to Cloud Print. As of this writing, Google Cloud Print is still in beta test status, so be aware that the service's performance might not match your expectations.

You can access the Google Cloud Print website in the Internet app at www.google.com/cloudprint/learn. After you open the site, you're invited to log in using your Gmail account. After you log in, you can add a printer that's connected to a laptop or PC, or you can add a Cloud Ready printer, which is a printer that connects directly to the Web.

The Google Cloud Print website

Sharing Files

A "cloud storage" service enables you to upload files onto its server computers. Cloud storage services make it easy for you to share large files with others, especially because the maximum file attachment sizes in email messages can vary depending on the email service you use, and downloading email messages with large file attachments can take a long time.

Use the Google Drive App

The Google Drive app came installed on your Galaxy S6, and you might have set up your Google Drive account when you set up your Galaxy S6. You can give another Google Drive user access to one or more folders in your account so that other users can upload files to and download files from that folder.

What Do I Need to Use the Google Drive App?

These instructions presume that you already have a Google account and you logged into your Google account when you set up your Galaxy S6 or within the Settings screen, and that you already have a Google Drive account. If you don't have a Google Drive account, bookmark this page and set up the account at http://drive.google.com.

Add Galaxy S6 Photos to Google Drive and Create a Folder

When you first start Google Drive, the app takes you step by step through setting up your Galaxy S6 to work with Google Drive. Then you can start adding files.

You may want to start by adding photos on your Galaxy S6 to your Google Drive account so you don't lose them in case something happens to your device. Complete the following steps after you upload one or more photos to your Google Drive account.

1. On the Home screen, tap Google.

2. Swipe upward in the Google window and then tap Drive.

3. Swipe from right to left to view introductory information about Google Drive. Note that if you've already used Google Drive on your Galaxy S6, you can skip ahead to Step 5.

4. Tap Done in the last introductory screen.

5. Tap Got It to close the informational tile about organizing your files using drag and drop.

6. Tap the Add icon in the bottom-right corner of the screen.

7. Tap Upload in the New window that appears at the bottom of the screen.

8. Tap Images in the Open From list.

9. Tap the folder tile that contains the photos you want to upload to Google Drive.

10. Tap and hold on the first file you want to upload; this example uses photos. The selected photo contains a circle with a white check mark in the center of the photo.

11. Swipe up and down in the list and tap each photo tile you want to add.

12. Tap Open.

13. The photo(s) you added appear at the top of the Files section as a tile. Select the photo by tapping and holding your finger on the photo for a second.

14. The selected photo has a blue circle with a white check mark in the center of the photo.

15. Select another photo by tapping the photo tile.

16. Tap the Menu icon in the pop-up window at the bottom of the screen.

17. Tap Move To.

18. Tap the New Folder icon in the Select Destination Folder window.

19. Type the name of your album in the New Folder field.

20. Tap OK.

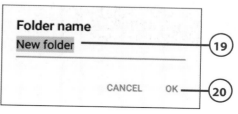

21. Your new folder appears in the window and shows you there are no items in the folder.

22. Tap Move.

23. The new folder appears in the Folders section. Tap the folder to open files within the folder.

View and Share Files in Google Drive

The Google Drive home screen contains all files and subfolders within the Google Drive folder.

1. View files within a folder by tapping the folder name within the Folders section.

2. Swipe up and down in the screen if necessary to view all the files within the folder. When you find a file that you want to view, tap the tile to view it. If the file is a photo or image file, as in this example, then the file opens within the built-in Google Drive image viewer.

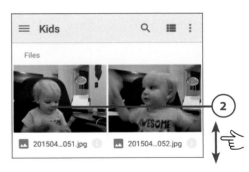

3. After a couple of seconds, the menu bar at the top of the image disappears so you can view the image in its entirety. Open the menu again by tapping the image.

4. Tap the Share icon to open the sharing menu.

5. Tap Share Link to share or copy a link to the file. You can share using Samsung Quick Connect, Bluetooth, Wi-Fi Direct, Email or Gmail, Google Hangouts, Google+, Facebook, Facebook Messenger, Facebook Pages Manager, OneNote, Skype, or your phone carrier's preinstalled messaging or mail apps. You can also share with another Google Drive account. What's more, you can copy the link to a memo to access in the Memo app or copy the link to the clipboard.

6. Tap Add People to give permission to another Google Drive user to access the file so they can either view, comment on, or edit the file.

7. Tap Send File to send the file using an app or service. You can send the file to a Gmail or Email message, a memo you can access with the Memo app, Google Photos, Instagram, Google Hangouts, Google+, Facebook, Facebook Messenger, Facebook Pages Manager, OneNote, Skype, or your phone carrier's preinstalled messaging or mail apps. You can send the file to another device using the Samsung Quick Connect, Bluetooth, or Wi-Fi Direct services. You can also send the file to another Google Drive account.

8. Tap the Info icon to view details about the file and perform more tasks.

9. Tap Add People to give permission to another Google Drive user to access the file so they can either view, comment on, or edit the file.

10. Tap Share Link to share or copy a link to the file as described in Step 5.

11. Tap the Star icon to add the file as a favorite to your Starred list. Read the "Access Menu Options" section later in this chapter for more information about the Starred list.

12. Tap Move to move the file to a different folder. You can also create a new folder as described earlier in this chapter and then move the file into the new folder.

13. Tap Send File to send the file using an app or service as described in Step 7.

14. Tap Download to download the file to your Galaxy S6.

15. Tap Rename to rename the file in the Rename File window.

16. Tap the Menu icon to view more options.

17. Tap Remove to remove the file from Google Drive. If you downloaded the file to your Galaxy S6 or the file is already on the device, then those files remain on your Galaxy S6.

18. Print the file, such as to a connected Bluetooth printer.

19. Close the menu pop-up window by tapping the Menu icon.

20. You can automatically copy the file to your Galaxy S6 by swiping the Keep on Device slider from left (Off) to right (On).

21. Swipe up and down to view information about the file, who has access to the file, and any activity related to the file.

22. Return to the image screen by tapping the Back icon.

23. Return to the folder screen by tapping the Back icon.

24. In the folder screen, return to the main Google Drive folder by tapping the Back icon.

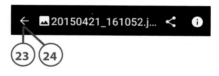

Access Menu Options

You can access a variety of tools and settings for the Google Drive app from within the menu bar at the top of the My Drive screen.

1. Tap the Menu icon at the left side of the menu bar.

2. Tap Shared with Me to view files and folders within other Google Drive users' accounts that those users are sharing with you.

3. Tap Google Photos to view, add, and delete photos and albums in your Google Photos account.

4. Tap the Starred icon to view all the files you marked as Starred as you learned about earlier in this chapter.

5. Tap Recent to order all files in your Google Drive account by the time it was last viewed. The most recently viewed files appear at the top of the list and the oldest files appear at the bottom of the list.

6. Tap On Device to view all files in your Google Drive account that are also stored on your Galaxy S6.

7. Tap Uploads to view all files uploaded from your Galaxy S6 to your Google Drive account.

8. Tap Settings to get information about your account, change your account settings, and learn more about Google Drive.

9. Tap Help & Feedback to get answers to your most common questions about Google Drive.

10. Close the menu by tapping My Drive.

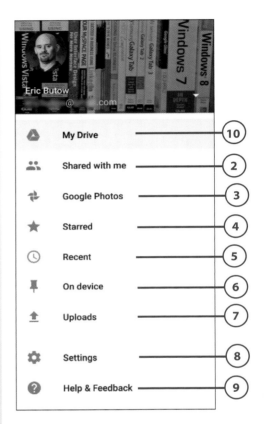

11. Tap the Search icon to search for files in Google Drive.

12. Type your search term(s) in the Search field.

13. As you type, files matching the description appear as tiles underneath the Search field.

14. If you don't see the search results you want, or there are more tiles than can fit on the screen, tap the Search button in the keyboard.

15. Swipe up and down the screen to view all the files in the list. Tap on a tile to view the contents of the file on the screen.

16. Return to the search results screen by tapping the Back icon.

17. Tap the List View icon to view all the files in a list. After you tap the icon, the icon changes to the Tile View icon; return to the tile view by tapping the Tile View icon.

18. View more options by tapping the Menu icon.

19. Tap Filter By to filter the files list by seven different criteria: Folders, Presentations, Spreadsheets, Text Documents, Images, Videos, and PDF files. After you select a filter, you see only those files that meet your filter criteria in the Filter screen. Return to the My Drive screen by tapping the Back touch button.

20. Tap Sort By to change the sort order. The default is by title, but you can also sort by the files' last modified date, when you last opened the file, when you last edited the file, or how much of your file storage quota was used.

21. Tap Select to select one or more files and/or folders in the My Drive screen. If you want to deselect all the files you selected, tap the Menu icon and then tap Clear Selection.

22. Tap Select All to select all files and folders in the My Drive screen. You can deselect all the files and folders by tapping the Menu icon and then tapping Clear Selection.

23. Tap Details to get information about your activities on My Drive. Activities are sorted from the most recent activity at the top of the Details list to the oldest activity at the bottom.

>>>*Go Further*

GET MORE GOOGLE DRIVE SPACE

Google gives you 15GB of space on its servers for storing photos on Google+ photos, storing your email messages on Google Mail, and storing files in Google Drive. If you find you need more storage, you can choose from five different monthly plans that give you from 100GB ($1.99 per month) to 30TB ($299.99 per month) of total storage. Google doesn't offer annual storage plans as of this writing.

When you visit the Google Drive Storage website (https://www.google.com/settings/storage), you'll see how much total space you have and how much of that total space is in use. You also see different ways to add more space to your account. After you choose your monthly plan, the Drive Storage website takes you through the checkout process.

Find Other Cloud Services

If you prefer to use a cloud storage app other than Google Drive, you can shop the Google Play Store for cloud storage apps that are optimized for the Android operating system.

1. Tap Play Store on the Home screen.

2. Tap Apps.

3. Tap the Search icon in the menu bar.

4. Type cloud storage in the Search Google Play field.

5. Tap the search button in the keyboard.

6. Swipe up and down within the list of apps in the search results screen. Tap a tile to view more information about the app. You learn more about shopping for apps in the Play Store in Chapter 12, "Working with Android Applications."

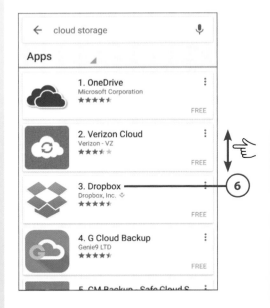

Sharing Music and Video

You have a number of ways to share your music and video between different devices or between your computer and your Galaxy S6. If you have a computer that runs Windows, you can connect the Galaxy S6 to your computer and copy files with Windows Media Player. You can also connect your Galaxy S6 to your Windows computer and tell Windows that your Galaxy S6 is a storage device. One other alternative is to connect your PC or Mac to your Galaxy S6 using Samsung's free Smart Switch application.

Copy Files with Windows Media Player

When you connect your Galaxy S6 to your PC with the data cable, you can choose how you want to connect and/or synchronize media files with your Galaxy S6. One option is to sync your PC and your Galaxy S6 with Windows Media Player. This example connects the Galaxy S6 to a PC running
Windows 8.1.

1. Connect the data cable from the Galaxy S6 to the USB port on your PC. If an AutoPlay window opens, click the window and then click Sync Digital Media Files to This Device: Windows Media Player in the list. If you don't see this window, open the Windows Media Player app on your PC.

2. Click the Sync tab within the Windows Media Player window.

3. Click and drag the music file(s) you want to copy to the Sync list.

4. The list of music files you select appears in the Sync list. You can deselect any files you do not want to copy by right-clicking the filename and then clicking Remove from List in the pop-up menu that appears.

5. Tap Start Sync to begin copying the files from your PC to your Galaxy S6.

6. After sync is complete, you can view the music files within the Music app on your Galaxy S6.

Connect as a Mass Storage Device

You can drag and drop files from a PC to your Galaxy S6 by connecting as a removable disk. Follow these steps to transfer music files from your PC to your Galaxy S6 using the Mass Storage USB mode.

1. Connect the data cable to the Galaxy S6 and the USB connector to the USB port on your computer. If an AutoPlay window opens, click the window and then click Open Device to View Files: File Explorer in the list. If you don't see this window, open the File Explorer app on your computer.

2. Your Galaxy S6 appears as a removable disk in the folder tree within the File Explorer window. Double-click the SAMSUNG-SM-G920A entry in the tree.

3. Open the list of folders on the Galaxy S6 by double-clicking the Phone folder in the tree.

4. Double-click the Music folder in the tree. The list of music files and subfolders appears in the file pane.

5. Locate the files you want to transfer from your computer and then drag them to the Music folder on your Galaxy S6. The files are copied to the device.

6. After you have finished copying files to your Galaxy S6 from your computer, remove the USB cable from the PC.

7. When you open the Music app on your Galaxy S6, the music you have transferred is available for playback.

>>>*Go Further*

CONNECTING TO A MAC

You need extra software to connect your Galaxy S6 to a Mac. Android File Transfer is an application for Macs running OS X 10.5 or later that enables you to view and transfer files between your Mac and Galaxy S6. This application works with Android devices running Android 3.0 or later. You can download Android File Transfer from www.android.com/filetransfer/.

Samsung Smart Switch for PCs and Macs

The Samsung Smart Switch application makes it easy for you to manage your music, movies, and photos between your computer and your Galaxy S6.

When you connect your Galaxy S6 to your PC or Mac, Samsung Smart Switch allows you to copy files from your computer and other devices (such as another smartphone) to your Galaxy S6. You can download Smart Switch for your PC or Mac on the Samsung website at www.samsung.com/us/support/smart-switch-support/.

After you transfer files to your Galaxy S6 with Smart Switch, you can download the Smart Switch app from the Google Play Store on your Galaxy S6 to view those transferred files.

Can I Use Samsung Kies?

Previous models of Samsung smartphones used the Kies app to synchronize data. With the introduction of the Galaxy S6 and Galaxy S6 edge, Samsung requires that you use Smart Switch. If you try using Kies on your computer with your Galaxy S6, a dialog box appears in Kies that informs you that you can only use Smart Switch with the device. After you close the window, Kies doesn't recognize the Galaxy S6 and asks you to connect a device. You need to close Kies before you can run Smart Switch.

1. After you have installed Samsung Smart Switch onto your computer, connect your Galaxy S6 to your PC or Mac.

2. Launch Samsung Smart Switch on your computer.

3. Tap the manufacturer button and then select from Apple, Blackberry, or Nokia in the list. This example uses Apple.

4. Select the backup file either on your existing iPhone or on your computer. If you don't see your backup file, click Locate Another Backup File button and then find the folder that contains the file within the Select Backup Data window.

5. Click Next.

6. By default, all data in the Personal Information, Multimedia, and the App List and Others categories is transferred. Deselect a data subcategory by clicking the associated check box to clear it.

7. As you add and/or remove a data subcategory at the right side of the slider bar, you can see a running total of the amount of data to be transferred (on the left) and the total amount of data (on the right).

8. Click the Music Playlist button to select the music playlist(s) you want to transfer to the Galaxy S6.

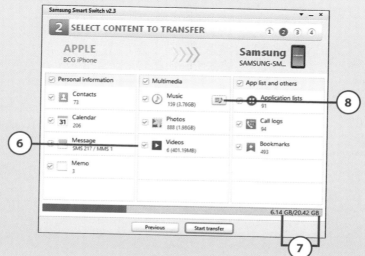

9. If you have one or more playlists on your iPhone, click the Selected Playlist button and then select one or more playlists in the list.

10. You can sync all playlists by keeping the All Synced Music button selected.

11. Click the Confirm button.

12. After you select the data categories and/or subcategories you want to sync, click the Start Transfer button.

13. During synchronization, you can cancel the process by clicking the Cancel Transfer button.

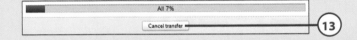

14. When the Smart Switch app finishes synchronizing your data, close the transfer information window by clicking the Close icon.

15. Close the Smart Switch program by clicking the Exit button.

16. On the Galaxy S6, open an app that contains one or more files you transferred. This example uses the Memo app. Tap the Apps icon on the Home screen.

17. Tap Samsung in the Apps screen.

18. Tap Memo in the Samsung window.

19. A list of your memos that you transferred from the other device appears on the All Memos screen. Tap the memo you want to read in the list.

Backing Up and Restoring Your Galaxy S6

Backing up the contents of your Galaxy S6 is a good practice for securing your important information and multimedia content. You can ensure that your contacts, photos, videos, and apps are copied to your PC or Mac in case something happens to your Galaxy S6.

Ensure Automatic Google Account Backup

Your Google account information—such as your Gmail inbox, Contacts list, and Calendar app appointments—automatically syncs with Google servers, so this information is already backed up for you. To ensure that your Google account information is being automatically backed up, follow these directions.

1. On the Home screen, tap Apps.

2. Tap Settings.

3. Swipe from right to left within the tabs section of the menu bar.

4. Tap Personal.

5. Tap Backup and Reset.

6. Make sure the slider buttons to Back Up My Data and Automatic Restore are in the On position. If they're not, slide the slider button from left (Off) to right (On). The information associated with your Google address is now automatically backed up.

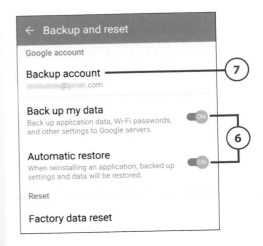

The Automatic Restore Option

Having the Automatic Restore option on ensures that any data or settings placed on third-party apps are restored when you restore those apps to your Galaxy S6.

7. If you want to change your backup account to a different Google account, tap Backup Account.

8. Tap Add Account in the Set Backup Account window. Then follow the steps to add another Google Account in the Add Your Account screen.

>>>Go Further

MANUALLY BACKING UP

When connected to your PC or Mac as a mass storage device, you can open File Explorer in Windows or Finder in Mac OS to view all of the data on your Galaxy S6's internal storage. The content is categorized into specific folders that you can copy from your card and internal storage such as DCIM, Download, Music, Pictures, Movies, Podcasts, and more. You can also copy all folders that have the names of apps installed on your Galaxy S6, such as Facebook, to your PC or Mac.

See the top free apps

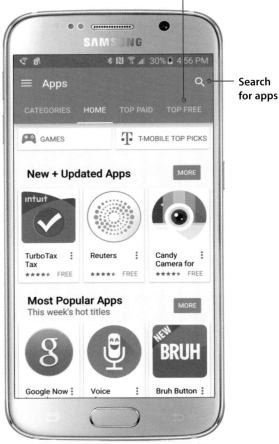

Search
for apps

In this chapter, you find out how to purchase and use Android applications on your Galaxy S6. Topics include the following:

→ Setting up Google Wallet
→ Finding applications with the Google Play Store
→ Working with the Galaxy Apps Store
→ Purchasing applications

Working with Android Applications

Your Galaxy S6 comes with enough applications to make it a worthy phone. However, wouldn't it be great to play games, update your Facebook and Twitter statuses, or even keep a grocery list? Well, you can use the Google Play Store to find these types of applications. Read on to discover how to find, purchase, and maintain applications.

Configuring Google Wallet

Before you start buying apps in the Google Play Store, you must first set up your Google Wallet account. If you plan to download only free applications, you do not need a Google Wallet account.

1. From a desktop computer or your Galaxy S6, open the web browser and go to http://wallet.google.com. Sign in using the same Google account you used to set up your phone.

2. Click or tap Payment Methods.

3. Click or tap Add a Payment Method, and select either Add a Credit or Debit Card or Link a Bank Account.

4. Enter the required information to add your payment method (not shown).

Navigating the Google Play Store

The Google Play Store is the place where you can search for and buy Android applications for your phone.

1. Tap the Play Store icon.

2. Swipe in from the left of the screen to see Google Play Store actions.

3. Tap to see any apps you have already purchased or downloaded.

4. Tap to select which Google account you want to use when you use the Google Play Store (if you have multiple Google accounts).

5. Tap to see your wishlist. This list shows all apps, music, books, and movies that you have placed on your wishlist.

6. Tap to see people you know on Google+ and see the apps they like.

7. Tap to redeem a Google Play gift card.

8. Tap to change the settings for Google Play. See the "Adjust Google Play Settings" section later in this chapter for more information.

9. Tap to manage payment methods and see your order history.

10. Tap anywhere outside the menu to return to the Google Play Store main screen.

11. Tap Apps to see only Android apps.

12. Swipe left and right to move between different top app lists, including Top Paid apps, Top Free apps, and Top New apps.

13. Tap to search the Google Play Store. This searches everything available in the store, including apps, music, movies, and books.

14. Tap Categories to see apps organized by Category.

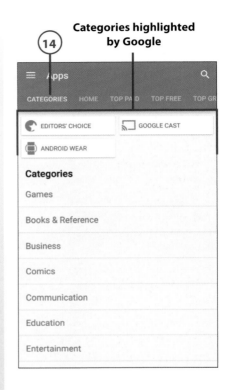

Categories highlighted by Google

Install Free Applications

You don't have to spend money to get quality applications. Some of the best applications are free.

1. Tap the free application you want to install.

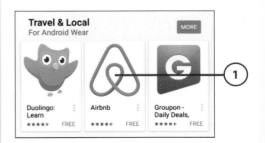

2. Scroll down to read about the app's features, reviews by other people who installed it, and information on the person or company who wrote it. Scrolling down also enables you to share a link to the app with friends.

3. Swipe left and right on the app screen shots to see all of them.

4. Tap Install to download and install the app.

5. Tap to accept the app permissions, and proceed with the installation.

Beware of Permissions

Each time you download a free app or purchase an app from the Google Play Store, you are prompted to accept the app permissions. App permissions are permissions the app wants to have to use features and functions on your Galaxy S6, such as access to the wireless network or access to your phone log. Pay close attention to the kinds of permissions each app is requesting, and make sure they are appropriate for the type of functionality that the app provides. For example, an app that tests network speed will likely ask for permission to access your wireless network, but if it also asks to access your list of contacts, it might mean that the app is malware and just wants to steal your contacts.

Tap to play a video about the app

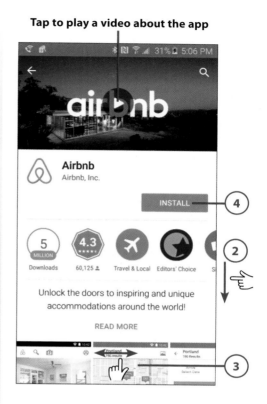

Permissions the app is requesting from your phone

Buy Applications

If an application is not free, the price displays next to the application icon. If you want to buy the application, remember that you need to have a Google Wallet account. See the "Configuring Google Wallet" section earlier in the chapter for more information.

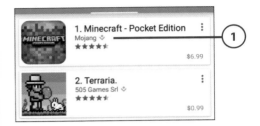

1. Tap the application you want to buy.

What if the Currency Is Different?

When you browse applications in the Google Play Store, you might see applications that have prices in foreign currencies, such as in Euros. When you purchase an application, the currency is simply converted into your local currency using the exchange rate at the time of purchase.

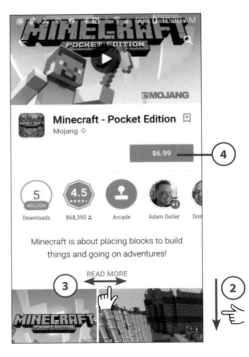

2. Scroll down to read the application features, reviews by other people who installed it, and information on the person or company who wrote the application. Scrolling down also enables you to share a link to the app with friends.

3. Swipe left and right on the app screen shots to see all of them.

4. Tap the price to purchase the app.

5. Tap to accept the app's requested permissions and proceed to the payment screen.

Permissions the app is requesting from your phone

What Are In-App Purchases?

An app you install that is either free or costs little may offer extra features that you need to pay for later if you want to take advantage of them. For example, an app might provide ways to edit photos and add effects to them, but some effects are not available until you pay extra for them. This is considered an in-app purchase.

6. Tap Buy to purchase the app. You receive an email from the Google Play Store after you purchase an app. The email serves as your invoice.

Tap to change the payment method

Checking App Permissions Anytime

To see what permissions you have granted to any app, swipe down from the top bezel, tap the Settings icon (the cog), tap Applications under the Device section, and tap Application Manager. Tap any app and scroll down to Permissions to see what permissions you previously granted for the app. Tap each permission to read a description of what it allows, and in some cases how it affects your device.

Manage Apps

Use the My Apps section of the Google Play Store to update apps, delete them, or install apps that you have previously purchased.

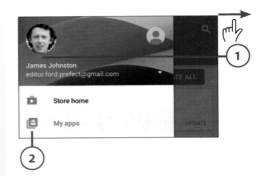

1. Swipe in from the left of the screen.

2. Tap My Apps.

3. Tap All to see all apps that are currently installed or previously were installed on all your Android devices.

4. The word Free indicates a free app that you previously installed but that is not installed on this phone. Tapping the app enables you to install it again for free.

5. The word Purchased indicates an app you previously purchased and installed but that is no longer installed on this phone. Tapping the app enables you to install it again for free.

Tap to see only apps you have installed on this device

Tap to update all apps

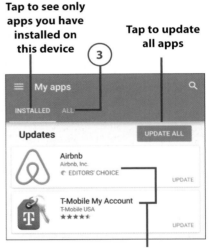

Tap each app to update it

Uninstalling an App

When you uninstall an app, you remove the app and its data from your Galaxy S6. Although the app no longer resides on your Galaxy S6, you can reinstall it as described in Steps 4 and 5 because the app remains tied to your Google account.

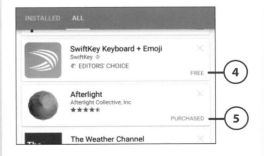

Allow an App to Be Automatically Updated

When the developer of an app you have installed updates it to fix bugs or add new functionality, you are normally notified of this in the System Tray so that you can manually update the app. Google Play enables you to choose to have the app automatically updated without your intervention. To do this, open the My Apps screen, and tap the app you want to update automatically. Tap the Menu icon and make sure that Auto-Update is checked. Automatic Updating is suspended if the developer of the app changes the permissions that the app requires to function. This enables you to review them and manually update the app.

Tap to allow automatic updating

Auto-update

Airbnb
Airbnb, Inc.

UNINSTALL   UPDATE

Tap to uninstall the app

Adjust Google Play Settings

1. Swipe in from the left of the screen.

2. Tap Settings.

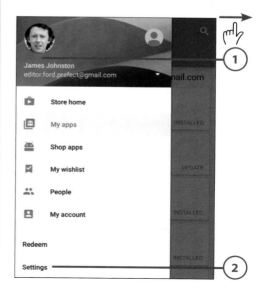

3. Tap to choose whether apps are updated automatically, and over what types of networks they are updated. For example you can set your apps to update automatically at any time, which means they will update over the cellular data network or Wi-Fi. Because cellular data charges apply, you may choose to have your apps only update over Wi-Fi.

4. Check the box to create an app shortcut icon to appear on your Home screen for each app that you install.

5. Tap to clear the Google Play Store Search History. This removes the log of searches you have made in the Google Play Store on this device only.

6. Check the box to enable notifications of app or game updates.

7. Check the box to enable notifications when app or game have automatically updated.

8. Scroll down for more settings.

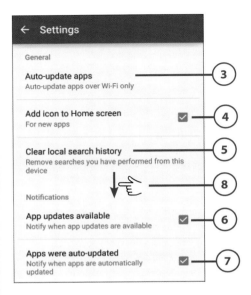

Accidentally Uninstall an Application?

What if you accidentally uninstall an application or you uninstalled an application in the past but now decide you'd like to use it again? To get the application back, go to the My Apps view in the Google Play Store. Scroll to that application and tap it. Tap Install to reinstall it.

9. Tap to adjust or set your content filtering level (for example, apps for everyone, or apps with medium maturity content, and so on). Use this to filter out apps, movies, music, or books that you deem to be inappropriate.

10. Tap to choose whether you want to enter your Google password for every Google Play Store purchase, or only every 30 minutes. If you choose 30 minutes, you can enter your password one time and then purchase content in the store for 30 minutes without retyping your password. After 30 minutes have elapsed, you are prompted to enter your password for your next purchase.

11. Tap the Back icon to return to the main screen.

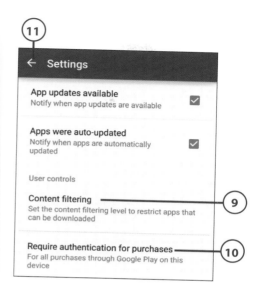

Install Apps Not from the Google Play Store

Although it is not recommended that you install Android apps not found in the Google Play Store, there is a way to do it. Open Settings, tap Lock Screen and Security, and tap the switch next to Unknown Sources. If you use your phone for work, your company's Mobile Device Management (MDM) system will likely require this setting to be enabled so that it can push down the MDM Agent app and enable you to install your company's internal apps. Outside the requirement to install non-Google Play Store apps for your company, it is dangerous to install non-approved apps. You open yourself up to apps that may contain malware, spyware, or viruses.

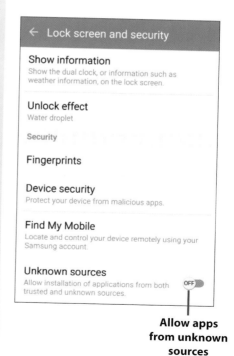

Allow apps from unknown sources

Galaxy Apps

Although you can find the majority of Android apps in the Google Play Store, Samsung has its own app store specially for the Galaxy phones. There are some apps that are exclusive to the Galaxy Apps Store; however most apps in the Galaxy Apps Store are also in the Google Play Store, with some possible price differences between the two stores for the same app.

1. Tap the Galaxy Apps icon.

2. Swipe left and right to see apps grouped by Staff Picks, Samsung Galaxy Exclusives, and Top apps.

3. Tap to search for an app.

4. Tap to see the Menu.

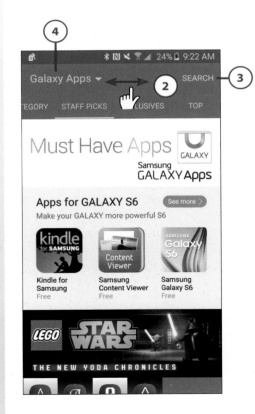

Adding a Payment Method for Galaxy Apps

Before you start buying apps in the Galaxy Apps Store, you must first set up a payment method. If you plan to download only free applications, you do not need to follow these steps.

1. Tap Galaxy Apps to see the menu.

2. Tap Payment Methods.

3. Tap Credit Card.

Tap to use coupons to buy apps

4. Tap Register Credit Card.

5. Enter the required information to add your credit card.

6. Tap Register.

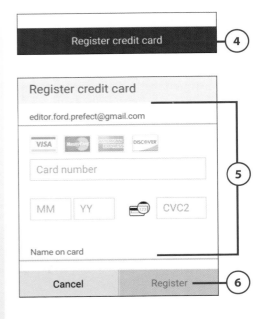

Install Free Applications

You don't have to spend money to get quality applications. Some of the best applications are free.

1. Tap the free app you want to install.

2. Scroll down to read about the app's features, reviews by other people who installed it, and information on the person or company who wrote it.

3. Tap to share a link to the app with friends.

4. Tap Install to download and install the app.

5. Tap to accept the app permissions and proceed with the installation.

Permissions the app is requesting from your phone

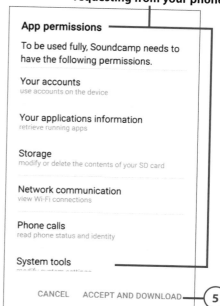

Buy Applications

If an application is not free, the price displays next to the application icon. If you want to buy the application, remember that you need to have set up a payment method, such as a credit card. See the "Adding a Payment Method for Galaxy Apps" section earlier in the chapter for more information.

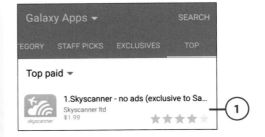

1. Tap the app you want to buy.

2. Scroll down to read the application features, reviews by other people who installed it, and information on the person or company who wrote the application. Scrolling down also enables you to share a link to the app with friends.

3. Tap to add the app to your Wish List.

4. Tap the price to purchase the app. If you have set up your fingerprint for purchase authentication, proceed to the next step. Otherwise, skip to Step 6.

5. Place one of your registered fingers over the Home button to authenticate that it is you who is making the app purchase.

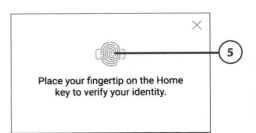

6. Tap to accept the app's requested permissions and proceed to the payment screen.

7. Tap to choose the credit card you added earlier.

8. Tap Buy to purchase the app.

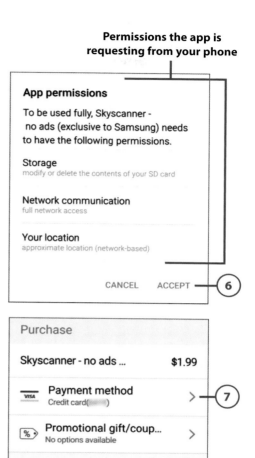

Permissions the app is requesting from your phone

App permissions

To be used fully, Skyscanner - no ads (exclusive to Samsung) needs to have the following permissions.

Storage
modify or delete the contents of your SD card

Network communication
full network access

Your location
approximate location (network-based)

CANCEL   ACCEPT — 6

Purchase

Skyscanner - no ads ... $1.99

VISA   Payment method   > — 7
         Credit card(   )

%>   Promotional gift/coup...   >
         No options available

Tax $0.13

Total $2.12

Cancel   Buy — 8

Install Apps Not from the Google Play Store

Your Galaxy S6 comes preinstalled with the Amazon.com app. With this app you can find and purchase items from Amazon.com, but it also allows you to purchase Android apps. Apps that appear in the Amazon.com app store are the same as apps that appear in the Google Play Store; however, they may be discounted or free. Before you start using the Amazon.com app, make sure that you have a payment method set up in your Amazon.com account. To do this, log in to your Amazon.com account, click Account, and click Add a Credit or Debit Card. When you open the Amazon.com app on your Galaxy S6, tap the Menu icon, and tap Apps & Games to see apps that Amazon.com is selling. Similar to buying apps from the Google Play Store or the Galaxy Apps Store, simply search for an app, and tap Buy to buy it.

Add a payment method

Tap to see apps and games

Tap to buy the app

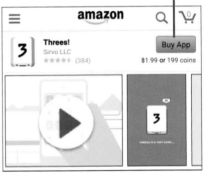

Tap a book to read it

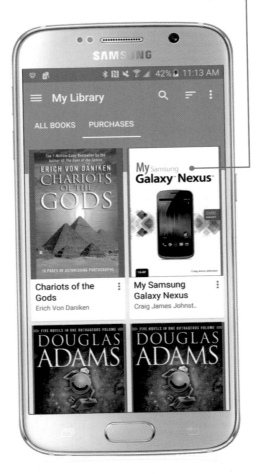

In this chapter, you find out how to buy books, read books, and subscribe to your favorite magazines. Topics include the following:

→ Buying and reading books
→ Buying and reading magazines

Books and Magazines

This chapter covers how you can use your Galaxy S6 for reading books and magazine subscriptions.

Books

The Google Play Store has a section that enables you to purchase (and, in some cases, get free) books in eBook form. After you have an eBook, you can read it at your leisure and even bookmark your favorite pages.

Navigate the Play Books App

The Play Books app enables you to read your books, bookmark pages, and find and purchase more books.

1. Tap the Google app folder on the Home screen.

2. Tap to launch Play Books. You see the Read Now screen that shows books you have recently opened and books that Google recommends you read.

3. Swipe in from the left of the screen.

4. Tap Shop to find and purchase more books.

5. Tap to see books already in your library.

6. Tap to change the Play Books app settings.

7. Tap to the switch to see only books that have been physically downloaded to your phone as opposed to all books you have purchased, some of which may still be stored in the Google cloud.

8. Tap to return to the Read Now screen.

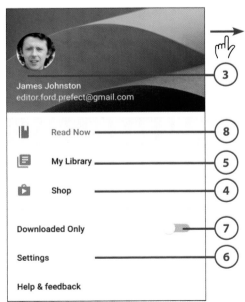

Buy Books

The procedure is the same for downloading a free book and buying a
book. The only difference is a free
book shows a price of zero.

1. Swipe in from the left of the
   screen.

2. Tap Shop to open the Google Play
   Store to the Books section. Bear
   in mind that at this point you are
   exiting the Google Books app and
   opening the Google Play Store.

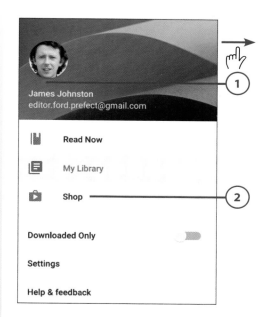

Searching for a Book

Finding books in the Google Play Store is easy. You can swipe left and right in
the blue area at the top of the screen to switch between different groupings of
books—for example, Top Selling books, New Releases in Fiction, Top Free books,
and so on. When you tap Categories, you see books listed by categories such
as Art & Entertainment, Education, Engineering, and so on. You can also use
the search icon to find books. When you choose to search, remember that you
can also speak your searches. One drawback of searching is that your search is
done across all stores, so you see related results for apps, movies, TV shows, and
books.

Search for books

3. Tap a book to open it.

4. Scroll down to read reviews on the book.

5. Tap to read a free sample of the book before you purchase it.

6. Tap to purchase the book.

7. Tap to change the method of payment if you need to.

8. Tap to buy the book. The book immediately starts downloading to your phone and appears in the Read Now screen.

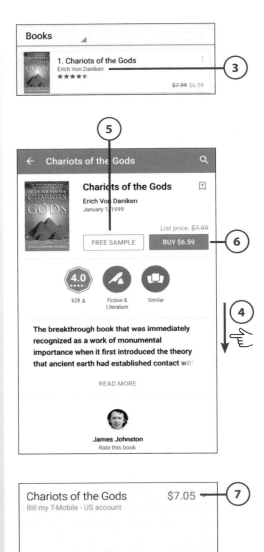

Read Books

As you read a book, you can book-mark certain pages, jump to different chapters, and even change the font size.

1. Tap a book to open it.

2. Swipe left and right across the screen to flip forward and backward through the book.

3. Tap near the middle of the screen to reveal the formatting controls and controls for quickly moving to specific pages.

4. Swipe down from the top or swipe up from the bottom to reveal the formatting and other controls.

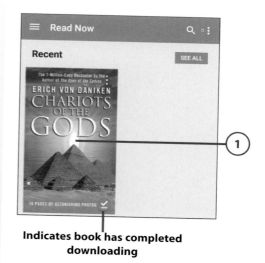

Indicates book has completed downloading

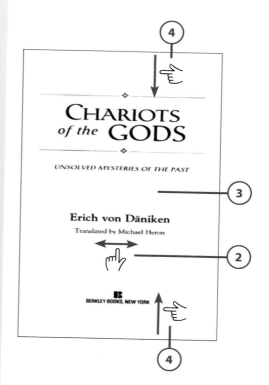

Jump to Pages Quickly

After you tap the middle of the screen you can quickly move to specific pages in the book.

1. Drag left and right to quickly jump to a specific page.

2. Swipe left and right to skim through the pages.

3. Tap a page to return to the reading view.

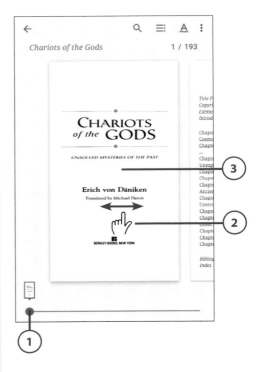

Formatting and Other Controls

After you tap the middle of the screen, swipe down from the top, or swipe up from the bottom, you can control the way the book is presented on the screen.

1. Tap to search the entire book for a word or phrase.

2. Tap to list all the chapters in the book and jump to them, see notes you may have taken, and bookmarks that you previously set.

3. Tap to change the way the book appears on your screen.

4. Tap to see more options.

Tap to go back to your library

Control the Visuals

Tap the Font icon to reveal ways to control how the book appears on your screen. You can choose black text on a white background (typically used during the day), white text on a black background (typically used at night), or a simulation of real book paper color. If you are viewing the book using the Flowing Text Mode, you can also change the typeface, text alignment, brightness, line height, and font size. Read more about what Flowing Text is in the "What Are Original Pages?" margin note later in this chapter.

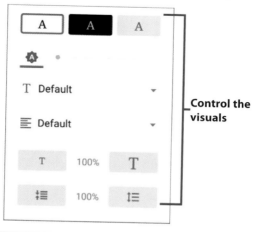

Control the visuals

5. Tap to switch between Original Pages and Flowing Text (if the book supports it).

6. Tap to share a link to the book you are reading via social media, email, and other methods.

7. Tap to add or remove a bookmark.

8. Tap to change the settings for the app.

What Are Original Pages?

When you read a book on your phone, the app defaults to showing the book using Flowing Text. This means that the text of the book is all there, but it's not structured in its original format per page. When viewing the book using Flowing Text you are able to change the font, font size, alignment, and so on. Some books allow you to switch to Original Pages, which makes it possible for you to page through the book as it was originally laid out, using the original typeface and alignment.

>>>Go Further
TRANSLATING TEXT AND TAKING NOTES

As you read through your book, you might need a translation of some foreign text, or you might want to highlight some text and make notes about it. To do either thing, touch and hold the text you want to translate or make a note on, and then drag the markers left and right until you have selected all the text you want. Tap the appropriate icon in the toolbar.

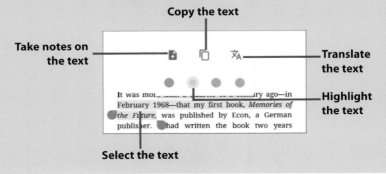

Copy the text

Take notes on the text

Translate the text

Highlight the text

Select the text

>>>Go Further
SAVE YOUR BOOK TO YOUR PHONE

When you buy and read a book, it is downloaded to your phone and stays there while you are reading it. If you know that you will be reading more than one book in an area with no Internet access (such as on a plane) you should first manually download any books you think you will be reading so that they are available. In the My Library screen, tap the Menu icon under the cover image of each book you want to download and then tap Download. A blue check mark indicates that the book has been downloaded.

Book already downloaded

Tap to download the book

Magazines and Newspapers

You can subscribe to magazines and newspapers on your phone and have them delivered in electronic form to read anytime. The Play Newsstand app enables you to subscribe to and read your magazines.

1. Tap the Google app folder on the Home screen.

2. Tap to launch the Play Newsstand app. The first screen you see is the Read Now screen. This screen shows stories from different publications that you can read without subscribing to those publications.

3. Tap a highlight to read it.

4. Scroll down to see more highlights.

5. Tap to search for magazines and newspapers to subscribe to.

6. Swipe left and right to scroll through the categories of stories. Highlights are a mixture of stories from all categories; other categories show only stories relevant to that category.

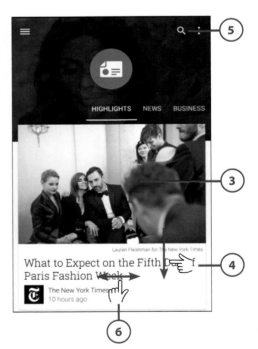

Purchase or Subscribe to Publications

You can subscribe to publications or just purchase a single edition.

1. Swipe in from the left of the screen.

2. Tap Explore.

3. Tap a category. This example uses the Automotive category.

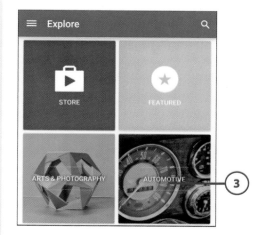

4. Tap a publication.

5. Tap Buy to buy only the latest edition of the magazine, or tap Subscribe to buy a subscription to the magazine.

6. Tap Subscribe to complete the transaction. If you chose to buy only the latest issue, the button is instead labeled Buy.

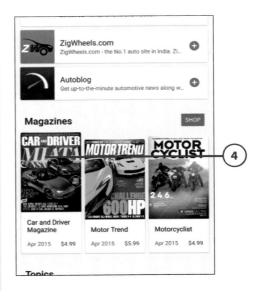

Add the magazine to your Wishlist

Read a Publication

1. Swipe in from the left of the screen.

2. Tap My Library.

Why Would I Download a Magazine?

When you open and read magazines, they are temporarily downloaded to your phone, but you are still required to be connected to the Internet before you read them. If you are going to be in an area with no Internet access (such as on a plane) and you want to read a magazine, while you are still connected to the Internet you need to manually download it. To do this, tap the menu icon under the magazine's cover and tap Download. A blue check mark indicates a downloaded magazine.

3. Tap the appropriate tab for the type of publication. This example uses a purchased magazine, which is on the Magazines tab.

4. Tap the publication to open it.

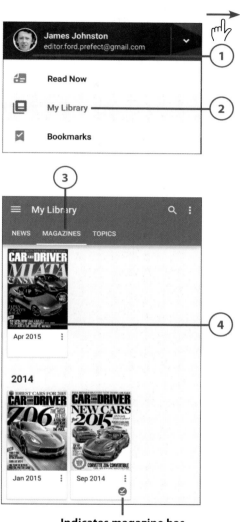

Indicates magazine has been downloaded

5. Scroll down to see all of the magazine's articles.

6. Tap the magazine cover to open the magazine at the cover, or tap one of the articles to open it.

Switch between page mode and article mode

6

5

Comparing Article Mode and Page Mode

If you tap the blue icon in the top-right of the screen, you can switch between viewing the magazine as it is laid out in the print version, page by page, or in article mode, which reformats the magazine so that you can move between the articles. When in page mode, if you tap on a page to jump to it, you can then continue to swipe left and right to page back and forth through the magazine. When in article mode, if you tap an article, you must scroll up and down to scroll through the article, and when you swipe left and right you can switch between articles.

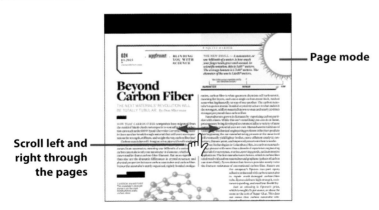

Page mode

Scroll left and right through the pages

Scroll left and right to switch articles

Scroll up and down through the article

Article mode

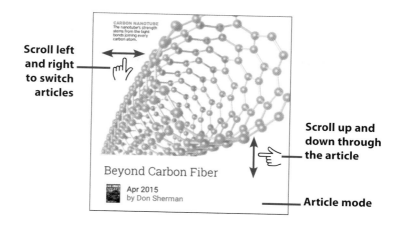

CARBON NANOTUBE
The nanotube's strength stems from the tight bonds joining every carbon atom.

Beyond Carbon Fiber

Apr 2015
by Don Sherman

Pair Bluetooth devices with
your Galaxy S6

Troubleshoot Galaxy S6
software, hardware,
and accessories

This chapter covers how to get the most from your Galaxy S6 using hardware accessories, plus ways that you can properly maintain your Galaxy S6 or S6 edge and troubleshoot basic software or hardware problems. Topics covered in this chapter include the following:

→ Finding Galaxy S6 and S6 edge accessories
→ Pairing Bluetooth devices
→ Maintaining your Galaxy S6
→ Updating the Galaxy S6 software
→ Backing up and restoring your Galaxy S6
→ Extending battery life
→ Solving Galaxy S6 issues
→ Troubleshooting connected devices
→ Getting help

14

Optimizing and Troubleshooting

Your Galaxy S6 is fully capable of providing an amazing multi-media experience right out of the box, but whether you are viewing movies, capturing photos and video, or composing a long email, you want your Galaxy S6 to be versatile. Accessories such as covers, Bluetooth headsets, battery packs, and wireless chargers can offer some much needed practical support for your Galaxy S6 use.

Although problems concerning the Galaxy S6 software, hardware, and accessories are rare, on occasion you might experience inci-dents where your Galaxy S6 or S6 edge does not perform properly. There are a few fixes you can try if you experience the occasional glitch that can occur with any hardware device.

Although your Galaxy S6 or S6 edge is a sophisticated piece of hardware, it is less complex than an actual computer, making any issue that might arise more manageable.

Finding Accessories

You can find accessories for the Galaxy S6 and S6 edge models in electronics stores such as Best Buy, or you can also shop your phone carrier's website, as they may offer accessories for the Galaxy S6 and S6 edge.

Online stores, such as Samsung.com and Amazon.com, are also great places to find hardware accessories for the Galaxy S6 and S6 edge. Visit the accessories page for the Samsung website at www.samsung.com/global/galaxy/galaxys6/accessories/.

The Samsung website Galaxy S6 and S6 edge Accessories page

Always make sure that you pick the right accessory for your Galaxy S6 model. As of this writing, none of the previous Galaxy S smartphone series accessories work with the Galaxy S6 or S6 edge.

It's Not All Good

Limited Accessories to Date

This section covers accessories that were available as the book was written. It's likely that shortly after this book finds its way onto shelves there will be new accessories for both Galaxy S6 models. For example, Samsung does not currently offer a multimedia desk dock for the Galaxy S6, but as of this writing desk docks from other companies are available for pre-order. We encourage you to keep up to date on what is available for your device by periodically checking the Samsung website, Amazon.com, and tech forums.

Pairing Bluetooth Devices

Along with the many other comfort features and conveniences found with the Galaxy S6, your Galaxy S6 gives you the capability to connect some external hardware devices wirelessly. The Galaxy S6 is equipped with Bluetooth 4.1 technology, enabling you to connect cable-free with Bluetooth-capable devices. By default, Bluetooth is enabled on your Galaxy S6. If you have already played with this setting, you can tell if Bluetooth is turned on by verifying that the Bluetooth symbol is visible in the status bar at the top of the screen.

Pair a Bluetooth Device

You can easily connect your Galaxy S6 to a Bluetooth device in two phases: discovering and pairing.

1. Turn on the wireless device that you want to pair with your Galaxy S6 and make it discoverable.

2. Tap the Apps icon on the Home screen.

3. Tap Settings.

Discoverability

Bluetooth devices broadcast their availability only after you instruct them to do so. If necessary, refer to your device's manual to learn how to make it discoverable.

4. Tap Connections in the menu bar.

5. Tap Bluetooth.

6. Tap your Bluetooth device in the list. (If you don't see your device, tap Scan in the menu bar above the list.) Your Galaxy S6 attempts to pair with the device.

Entering or Confirming Passcode May Be Required

You may need to enter a passcode for the Bluetooth device you're trying to pair with, such as a printer. For other Bluetooth devices, such as the Galaxy Tab S in this example, you may only need to tap OK in the Bluetooth Pairing Request window on both devices to confirm that each device has the same pairing passkey number.

7. The device appears under a newly created Paired Devices list.

8. If you need to refresh the list of devices, tap Refresh.

Paired Bluetooth Device Settings

After you have successfully paired your device to your Galaxy S6, a Settings icon appears next to the name of the Bluetooth device within the Paired Devices list. Tap that Settings icon to rename or unpair your device.

Maintaining Your Galaxy S6 and S6 Edge

Regular maintenance of your Galaxy S6 or S6 edge not only helps extend the life of your Galaxy S6, it also helps ensure peak performance. It's important that you make sure your Galaxy S6 software is up to date and that you understand basic troubleshooting concepts.

Properly cleaning and protecting the body of your Galaxy S6 or S6 edge can be equally important. The Galaxy S6 and S6 edge were designed to be sturdy, but, like any other electronic device, they can collect dust, and a simple drop on the sidewalk can prove disastrous. The first step in maintaining your Galaxy S6 or S6 edge is prevention. You can start by purchasing a protective case.

A sturdy case designed for the Galaxy S6 or S6 edge is important for the overall protection of your device. A number of companies have created a variety of cases for the Galaxy S6 and S6 edge, including Samsung. If you don't like Samsung's offerings, search the Internet or go to Amazon.com to see what's out there. The more padded the case, the better it can absorb a shock if you happen to drop your Galaxy S6.

A case can also help protect your Galaxy S6 or S6 edge from dust and keep it dry if you happen to get caught in the rain. Make sure you keep the inside of your case clean. Dust and sand can find its way into even the most well-constructed cases. Instead of using your sleeve to wipe off your Galaxy S6 display, invest in a microfiber cloth; you can find one in any office supply or computer store.

Your first instinct might be to wet a cloth to clean your Galaxy S6 touchscreen. Don't use liquids to clean the touchscreen, especially if they include alcohol or ammonia. These harsh chemicals can cause irreparable damage to the touchscreen, rendering it difficult to view content. Consider purchasing a screen protector at a local store or your favorite online retailer to keep the touchscreen dust and scratch free. Some screen protectors also come with a microfiber cleaning cloth.

Updating Galaxy S6 Software

Every so often, Google releases software updates for your Galaxy S6's Android operating system. To get the most from your Galaxy S6, it is good practice to update soon after an upgrade has been released. When an update is available, you receive a notification that indicates you can download a system upgrade. At that point, you have the option to initiate the software update. You can also check for system updates manually.

1. Tap the Apps icon on the Home screen.

2. Tap Settings.

3. Swipe from right to left within the tabs area in the menu bar.

4. Tap System.

5. Tap About Device.

6. Tap Software Update.

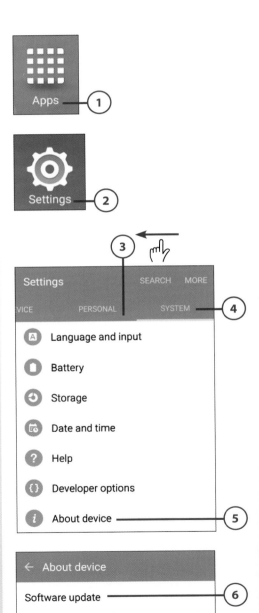

7. Tap Check for Updates.

8. The Software Update screen for your specific carrier appears, which is AT&T in this example. Tap OK.

Updating Firmware

The Android operating system is not the only software you need to update on your Galaxy S6. Your Galaxy S6 also uses software called *firmware* to run its internal functions. When an update is available, use your own discretion as to whether you want to update right away, just in case there are any issues with the update.

AT&T Software update

Check for updates ⎯⎯⎯⎯ ⑦

Continue update

AT&T Software update

Software update process will not delete any personal data on your phone.

Check the AT&T server for new software update?

CANCEL OK ⎯⎯ ⑧

9. If the software is up to date, tap OK to return to the About Device screen. If an update is available, follow the provided directions to upgrade your software.

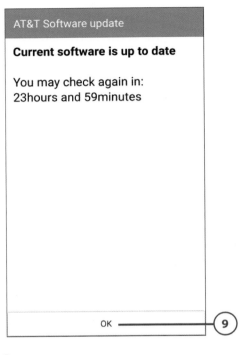

Extending Battery Life

Your Galaxy S6 is capable of up to at least nine hours of battery life, depending on the model you have. Battery life can also vary depending on how you use the Galaxy S6. Strenuous tasks, such as playing HD video, dramatically lower your battery life more than surfing the Web does.

You can monitor your battery power at the top of the screen in the Status area. The white battery status icon located on the right side of the Status bar lets you keep an eye on how much battery power you have left.

The battery status icon in the Status bar

When the battery gets low, a warning appears, informing you of the percentage of battery power you have left and instructing you to connect the charger. When the battery is too low, your Galaxy S6 automatically shuts down. There are a few things you can do to extend the life of your Galaxy S6 battery between charges.

Monitor Power Usage

On the Galaxy S6, you can use the Battery Usage screen to see which of the apps you use consumes the most power, and then you can reduce the use of those apps. Your battery power savings are small, but if you're running low on power with no way to recharge, every little bit counts. Follow these directions to access the Battery Usage screen.

1. Tap the Apps icon on the Home screen.

2. Tap Settings.

3. Swipe from right to left within the tabs area in the menu bar.

4. Tap System.

5. Tap Battery.

6. The screen shows you how many days you have left on your current battery charge and how long it's been since your battery was fully charged.

Adjust Screen Brightness

The high-quality touchscreen of the Galaxy S6 can consume plenty of battery power. The higher the brightness level set on your Galaxy S6, the more power the touchscreen uses. If you are viewing the screen in very bright conditions, you probably do not need a very high brightness setting. Consider dimming the screen to extend the battery life.

1. Tap the Apps icon on the Home screen.

2. Tap Settings.

3. Swipe from right to left within the tabs area in the menu bar.

4. Tap Device.

5. Tap Display.

6. Slide the slider button to the left to lower the brightness level or to the right to increase the brightness level.

7. Change the brightness level to the default level by tapping the Auto check box.

8. Return to the Device settings list by tapping the Back icon.

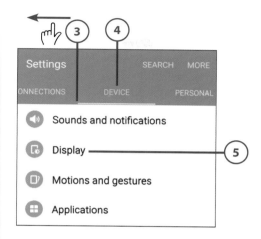

Quick Settings for Brightness

The Galaxy S6 offers a quicker way for you to access the brightness controls by changing the brightness level in the Quick Settings and Notification Panel. Open the Quick Settings and Notification Panel by swiping down from the top of the screen and then use the slider below the settings button row to adjust screen brightness.

Utilize Sleep Mode

Your Galaxy S6 goes to sleep after a specified period of inactivity, but you don't have to wait for it to fall asleep—you can put it to sleep manually. When your Galaxy S6 is awake, it is consuming battery power. Press and then immediately release the Power button on the side of your Galaxy S6 when you have finished using the device to conserve battery power.

Conserve Power by Turning Off Wi-Fi

When the Wi-Fi antenna is activated on your Galaxy S6, your device is incessantly looking for available Wi-Fi networks to join, which uses battery power. To see if Wi-Fi is turned on, check the right side of the status bar of your Galaxy S6 for the Wi-Fi symbol. If you do not need a Wi-Fi connection, turn it off to conserve battery power. If you are not wandering and are using Wi-Fi in a single location, look for a power outlet and plug in your Galaxy S6.

1. Tap Settings in the Apps screen.

2. Tap Connections in the menu bar.

3. Tap Wi-Fi.

4. Turn off Wi-Fi by sliding the Wi-Fi slider to the left.

5. The slider button displays the word Off with a gray background, and the screen asks you to turn on Wi-Fi to see available networks.

Quick Settings for Wi-Fi

The Galaxy S6 offers an even quicker way for you to access the Wi-Fi setting in the Quick Settings and Notification Panel. Simply swipe down from the top of the screen; within the Quick Settings and Notification Panel tap the Wi-Fi button with the green Wi-Fi icon to turn it off. When the icon turns gray, tap the Wi-Fi button to turn Wi-Fi on again.

Conserve Power by Turning Off Bluetooth

When Bluetooth is activated on your Galaxy S6, your device is constantly checking for other Bluetooth devices, which drains battery power. To see if Bluetooth is turned on, check the status bar in the top-left corner of your Galaxy S6 for the Bluetooth symbol. If you are not using a Bluetooth device, turn this function off. There are also security reasons why you should turn off Bluetooth when you are not using it, so get in the habit of turning Bluetooth off as soon as you finish using a wireless device with your Galaxy S6. You can easily deactivate Bluetooth in the Notification Panel.

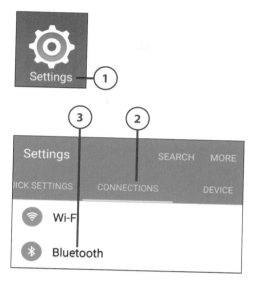

1. Tap Settings in the Apps screen.

2. Tap Connections in the menu bar.

3. Tap Bluetooth.

4. Turn off Bluetooth by sliding the Bluetooth slider to the left.

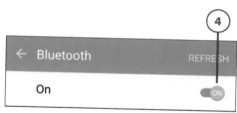

5. The slider button displays the word Off with a gray background, and the screen asks you to turn on Bluetooth to see paired and available devices.

Quick Settings for Bluetooth

The Galaxy S6 offers an even quicker way for you to access the Bluetooth setting in the Quick Settings and Notification Panel. Swipe down from the top of the screen to open the Quick Settings and Notification Panel. Then turn off Bluetooth by tapping the Bluetooth button with the green Bluetooth icon at the right side of the button bar. When the icon turns gray, tap the Bluetooth button to turn Bluetooth on again.

Conserve Even More Power Using Power Saving Modes

If you would rather not tweak individual settings to save battery life, the Galaxy S6 comes with two power saving modes: Power Saving Mode and Ultra Power Saving Mode. Each mode restricts the performance of the Galaxy S6 and requires a few setting changes on your part.

Set Up Power Saving Mode

By default, Power Saving Mode is turned off. When you turn on Power Saving Mode, the Galaxy S6 begins saving power immediately by limiting maximum CPU performance, reducing the screen brightness and frame rate, and turning off the touch key lights and vibration feedback. What's more, the device turns off the screen more quickly after you receive a notification.

You can change when Power Saving Mode goes into effect based on how much battery life you have left.

1. Tap Settings on the Apps screen.

2. Swipe from right to left within the tabs area in the menu bar.

3. Tap System.

4. Tap Battery.

5. Tap Power Saving Mode.

6. Slide the slider from left (Off) to right (On).

7. Tap Start Power Saving.

8. Tap the appropriate battery power level in the list to determine when you start power saving; the default level is Immediately. You can select between 5%, 15%, 20%, and 50% battery power. This example uses 50% power.

9. The Start Power Saving setting shows that the Galaxy S6 will go into Power Saving Mode when your battery life reaches 50%.

10. Turn off Power Saving Mode by sliding the slider button to the left.

11. Return to the Power Saving settings list by tapping the Back icon.

Set Up Ultra Power Saving Mode

Ultra Power Saving Mode automatically puts your display in grayscale mode and goes further by severely limiting the apps and services you can use on the Galaxy S6. These services include mobile data, Wi-Fi, and Bluetooth.

If you already have Power Saving Mode active, the Galaxy S6 closes Power Saving Mode so you can get the benefits of Ultra Power Saving Mode.

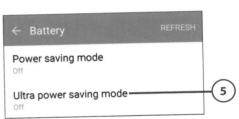

1. Tap Settings on the Apps screen.

2. Swipe from right to left within the tabs area in the menu bar.

3. Tap System.

4. Tap Battery.

5. Tap Ultra Power Saving Mode.

6. Swipe up in the screen to view more information about Ultra Power Saving Mode.

7. Slide the slider from left (Off) to right (On).

Save battery power by applying a simplified grayscale theme to your Home screen and limiting the number of usable apps.

More info
- Changing the color of the screen to grayscale

8. Tap the check box in the Terms and Conditions window. After you tap the check box, the box turns green and contains a white check mark. You only see this window the first time you start Ultra Power Saving Mode; if you don't see this window, proceed to Step 10.

9. Tap Agree.

10. The Galaxy S6 turns on Ultra Power Saving Mode by dimming the screen, placing the screen in grayscale mode, and turning off the screen after 15 seconds of no activity. The Ultra Power Saving Mode screen appears, and this screen opens every time you wake the Galaxy S6 from sleep mode.

11. The Ultra Power Saving Mode window tells you what your current battery percentage is and the maximum number of days your Galaxy S6 can stay in standby (another word for sleep) mode.

12. By default, you can use the Phone, Messages, and Internet apps. Run the app by tapping the app icon; when you finish using the app, tap the Back touch button.

13. Add an app to the list of apps you can run by tapping one of the Add (+) buttons. In the Add Application window that appears, tap Calculator, Clock, Facebook, Google+, Memo, or Voice Recorder. After you select the application, the app icon appears, replacing the Add icon.

Terms and conditions

The estimated usage time is calculated based on Samsung's research and test results using various network connections under default device settings.

The accuracy of this estimate may vary depending on your current network configuration, application usage, mode settings, signal strength, noise, features or tasks selected, actual usage patterns, operating temperature and other surrounding factors and conditions.

☑ I have read and agree to all the terms and conditions above.

DISAGREE   AGREE

Ultra power saving mode   MORE

Save power with a simple Home screen and access to a limited number of apps.

Phone   Messages

Internet   +

+   +

Battery percentage   Estimated usage time remaining

100%   4.9 Days

14. Tap More to open the menu so you can remove one or more apps from the list of apps you can run; change various settings including Wi-Fi, Bluetooth, Airplane Mode, Location, Sound, and Brightness; and turn off Ultra Power Saving Mode.

15. When you select to turn off Ultra Power Saving Mode, there's a delay of a few seconds and then the Home screen appears in full color. All apps and services return to normal operation.

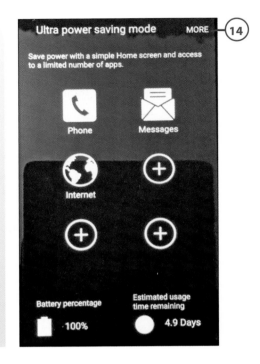

Solving Random Galaxy S6 Issues

The occasional hardware or software glitch happens to even the best of electronic devices. You might encounter an issue, although rare, where an app you are using freezes, a wireless device proves difficult to pair with your Galaxy S6, the touchscreen becomes unresponsive, or landscape orientation is not available at all times. Fortunately, it is not very difficult to troubleshoot some of these issues. If you should happen to come across a problem that you can't solve yourself, there are plenty of channels for you to find technical support.

Difficulty Turning Your Galaxy S6 On or Off

On rare occasions, you might find that your Galaxy S6 is stubborn when you try to turn it on or off. It might appear that the device has locked or become unresponsive. If this happens to you, hold the Power button for 8 seconds to see if it responds. If this does not work, you might need to let your Galaxy S6 sit for a few seconds before you again try holding the Power button for 8 seconds.

Touchscreen Becomes Unresponsive

This tip assumes that your Galaxy S6 and any app you are using is responsive, but the touchscreen is not responding to your touch. If you attempt to use your Galaxy S6 touchscreen while wearing conventional gloves, it does not work. This can prove inconvenient on a very cold day, so you might want to consider a capacitive stylus for your Galaxy S6.

Your Galaxy S6 uses a capacitive touchscreen that holds an electrical charge. When you touch the screen with your bare finger, capacitive stylus, or special static-carrying gloves, it changes the amount of charge at the specific point of contact. In a nutshell, this is how the touchscreen interprets your taps, drags, and pinches.

The touchscreen might also be unresponsive to your touch if you happen to have a thin coat of film on your fingertips. So no sticky fingers, please.

Force Stop an App

Sometimes an app might get an attitude and become unruly. For example, an app might provide a warning screen saying that it is currently busy and is unresponsive, or it might give some other issue warning to convey that a problem exists. If an app is giving you problems, you can manually stop the app.

1. Tap Settings on the Apps screen.
2. Swipe from right to left within the tabs area in the menu bar.
3. Tap Device.
4. Tap Applications.

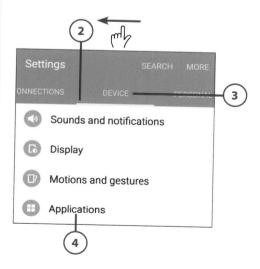

5. Tap Application Manager.

6. Tap the Running tab.

7. Swipe down the list of apps if necessary.

8. Tap the problem app in the list.

9. Tap Stop. The app stops running.

10. Tap Report to send a problem report to the app's developer.

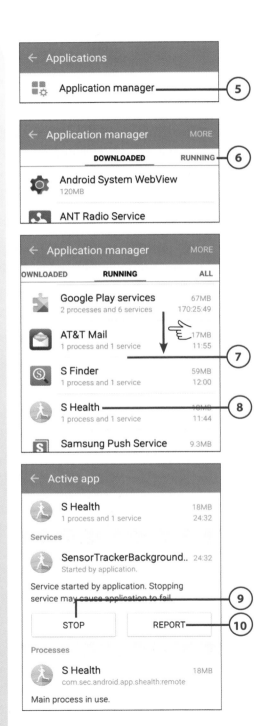

Battery Does Not Charge

If you find that your battery is not charging, first start with the power outlet. Is the outlet supplying power? Is the power strip turned on? Plug something else into the outlet to see if it works, or try another outlet.

Make sure that everything is connected properly. Is the adapter secure on both ends? If the outlet supplies power and the cables are connected properly, but the battery still does not charge, try another cable. If this does not solve the issue, your battery might be defective. Contact Samsung technical support. (See the "Getting Technical Help" section later in this chapter for more information about how to contact Samsung.) There is no way for you to remove the battery yourself.

Overheating

Overheating is rare, but if your Galaxy S6 becomes too hot and regularly turns itself off, you might need to replace the battery. You can tell if your Galaxy S6 is getting too hot by holding it in your hands. Use caution.

Landscape Orientation Does Not Work

The orientation setting on your Galaxy S6 could be set so that your Galaxy S6 stays in either portrait (vertical) or landscape (horizontal) mode, regardless of how you hold the device. If your Galaxy S6 no longer utilizes landscape orientation, first check the setting for screen orientation.

The Galaxy S6 has a Screen Rotation setting that must be selected for the screen to adjust from portrait to landscape mode, depending on how you hold the device. You can easily confirm that the Screen Rotation setting is selected from the Quick Settings and Notification Panel.

1. On the Home screen, open the Quick Settings and Notification Panel by tapping and holding on the top edge of the screen and then swiping downward.

2. Locate the Screen Rotation setting button and confirm that the
icon within the Screen Rotation
button is green. If the icon is gray,
activate the setting by tapping
the button. Your screen should
now adjust to the orientation in
which you hold the device.

Landscape Orientation and Apps

Not every app in the Google
Play Store was developed to take
advantage of the landscape orientation of your Galaxy S6. If you
notice this issue while using an
app, close the app and then see
whether your Galaxy S6 can situ-
ate itself in landscape orientation.
If so, launch the app again and
see how it works.

Troubleshooting Wi-Fi Accessibility Problems

Your Galaxy S6 provides you the convenience and flexibility of wireless Internet access via Wi-Fi connectivity. Along with this convenience and flexibility
comes the potential for connectivity issues regarding wireless networks. If
you are unable to access a Wi-Fi network, or if your connection is sporadic,
there are some troubleshooting tips you can use to pinpoint basic accessibility options.

Make Sure Wi-Fi Is Activated

First and foremost, make sure that the Wi-Fi antenna is on. You can determine
this by looking on the right side of the status bar at the top of your Galaxy S6
screen to see whether the Wi-Fi icon is visible. If it is not on, you can open the

Quick Settings and Notification Panel by swiping down from the top of the screen and then activate Wi-Fi by tapping the Wi-Fi button.

The Wi-Fi icon in the Status bar

Check Your Range

If Wi-Fi is activated on your Galaxy S6 and you still cannot connect, take note of how far away you are from the Wi-Fi access point. In general, you can be only 150 feet from a Wi-Fi access point indoors or 300 feet from an access point outdoors before the signal becomes weak or drops altogether. Structures such as walls with lots of electronics can also impede a Wi-Fi signal.

However, the type of wireless protocol you're using in your Wi-Fi network also affects your range. For example, if your wireless network uses the 802.11n protocol, which the Galaxy S6 supports, you'll have much better range and signal coverage than with the older 802.11a/b/g protocols. If you still have trouble, check your network information for protocol and coverage data. Also, make sure you are close to the access point or turn on the access point's range booster, if it has one, to improve your connection.

Reset Your Router

The issue of Wi-Fi accessibility might not be related to your distance from the Wi-Fi access point, a signal-impeding barrier, or your Galaxy S6. As a last resort, you might need to reset the router. After you reset your router, you have to set up your network from the ground up.

Reset the Galaxy S6 Device

If all else fails and your technical problems still persist, as a last-ditch effort you might need to reset the Galaxy S6. Resetting your Galaxy S6 deletes all data stored on the device and restores your Galaxy S6 to the factory defaults, just like when you took it out of the box for the first time. Consider contacting support before you reset your Galaxy S6, but if you must, follow these directions to reset the device:

1. Tap Settings on the Apps screen as you learned to do earlier in this chapter.

2. Swipe from right to left within the tabs area in the menu bar.

3. Tap Personal.

4. Tap Backup and Reset.

5. Tap Factory Data Reset.

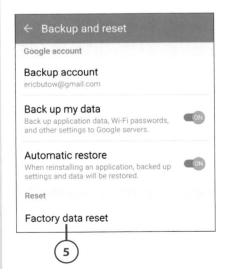

6. Tap the Reset Device button.

7. If you use a password to log in to your Galaxy S6, type the password in the Confirm Password field.

8. Tap Next.

9. Tap the Delete All button to confirm. Your Galaxy S6 is returned to its factory state.

Getting Technical Help

Many outlets are available where you can find help if you run across a Galaxy S6 technical problem that you can't seem to beat. Although limited, the user's manual is a good place to start. You can download the correct manual for your Galaxy S6 model online from the Samsung website (www.samsung.com), in the form of a PDF, and scan the table of contents or perform searches in the document for words that pertain to your problem. In most user manual PDFs, topics in the table of contents are linked to the section they pertain to within the document, so when you find what you are looking for, just click the topic to jump to the pertinent page.

Websites and Galaxy S6 forums are also a great way for you to get support for your device. Type a search phrase, such as "Galaxy S6 Google Calendar sync problem," into your favorite search engine. Chances are, plenty of other people are experiencing the same issue. Doing some online research of your own could save you a few minutes on the telephone with technical support and help you solve your problem more quickly.

Contact Your Cellular Provider or Samsung

The Samsung website is a great resource for getting help with technical issues with your Galaxy S6. The Samsung website (www.samsung.com/us/support/) offers support via Twitter, Facebook, and Google+, as well as by phone (1-800-726-7864). Before you call, you need to have your device's model number so that you can give it to the technical support representative.

Locate the Galaxy S6 Model Number

You can find the model number on the box that your Galaxy S6 shipped in, and you can also find it in the Settings menu.

1. Tap Settings on the Apps screen.

2. Swipe from right to left within the tabs area in the menu bar.

3. Tap System.

4. Tap About Device.

5. Locate your Galaxy S6 model number in the About Device list.

Swipe up to read

In this chapter, you discover how to set up your Android Wear smartwatch and use it with your Galaxy S6. Topics include the following:

→ Setting up your Android Wear watch
→ Choosing settings and installing apps
→ Navigating the Android Wear watch's interface
→ Using the Android Wear watch's apps

Using Your Galaxy S6 with an Android Wear Smartwatch

To get the most out of your Galaxy S6, you can link it to a Android Wear smartwatch. Android Wear watches are sold by vendors such as Samsung, LG, and Motorola and act as a companion for any Android smartphone, including your Galaxy S6. The Android Wear watch enables you to display essential information, make phone calls, and allow simple interactions with apps without taking your Galaxy S6 out of your pocket.

Setting Up Your Android Wear Watch

To set up the Android Wear watch, you need to use your Galaxy S6.

1. Unpack the Android Wear watch and identify its components: the Android Wear watch itself, a charging dock/clip, and the charger.

2. Fully charge your Android Wear watch.

3. Turn the Android Wear watch on by pressing and holding its button for a moment. The button is on the right side of the Android Wear watch.

4. Tap to choose your preferred language on the watch screen.

5. When you see a screen on your watch telling you to install the Android Wear app on your phone, switch to your Galaxy S6 for Steps 6–14.

6. Search the Google Play Store for the Android Wear app. When you find it, tap Install.

7. Tap Accept to accept the permissions that the Android Wear app needs to run correctly. After the app installs, run it to start setting up your watch.

8. Tap the right arrow to start setting up your watch.

9. Tap Accept to accept that the Android Wear app will synchronize data between your watch and your Galaxy S6.

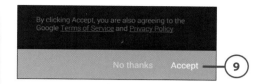

10. Tap the name of the watch you want to use. In this example, it is a Samsung Gear Live, listed as "Gear Live 10C9."

11. When prompted, accept the Bluetooth Pairing PIN on both your Galaxy S6 and your watch. The PIN should be the same on both devices.

12. When your watch and Galaxy S6 are paired over Bluetooth, you see a screen preparing you to configure Android to allow the Android Wear app to have access to notifications. Tap Notification Settings.

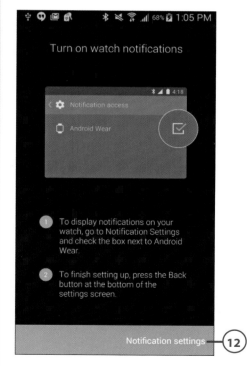

13. Check the box to allow the Android Wear app to receive access to Android notifications.

14. Tap OK to verify that you want the Android Wear app to have access to all Android notifications.

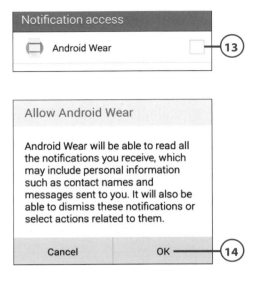

Notification access

Android Wear — 13

Allow Android Wear

Android Wear will be able to read all the notifications you receive, which may include personal information such as contact names and messages sent to you. It will also be able to dismiss these notifications or select actions related to them.

Cancel   OK — 14

Android Wear Smartwatches Explained

Android Wear is a framework that Google created to support smartwatches connecting to Android devices. This enabled different vendors to create and sell smartwatches that have their own unique look and build quality but can all be compatible with any Android device as long as the owner installs the Android Wear app. Smartwatches that use the Android Wear framework can have square or round faces. Examples of Android Wear watches that have a round face are the Motorola Moto 360 and the LG G Watch R. Examples of Android Wear watches that have a square face are the Asus ZenWatch, Sony SmartWatch 3, Samsung Gear Live, and the LG G Watch. No matter who manufactures your Android Wear–based smartwatch, and regardless of whether it has a square or round face, the instructions and guidance in this chapter are relevant.

Choosing Settings for Your Android Wear Watch

After pairing your Android Wear watch with your Galaxy S6, you probably want to spend some time customizing the Android Wear watch. You can use the Android Wear app on your Galaxy S6 to configure overall settings for the Android Wear watch, as explained in this section. To configure other settings, you use the Settings app on the Android Wear watch itself, as discussed in the following section.

Navigate the Android Wear App

The Android Wear app gives you access to features and settings for configuring and managing your Android Wear watch.

1. Tap to launch the Android Wear app from the Apps screen.

2. Tap a watch face to change it on your watch.

3. Tap to see all watch faces you have installed and find more.

4. Scroll down to see all voice actions and what apps are launched when the voice action triggers.

Set Voice Actions

Voice actions are voice commands you speak to your watch. Based on what you say, your watch either launches an app or takes an action, or it tells your Galaxy S6 to launch an app. Some voice actions can be customized to make use of third-party watch apps that you install. Voice actions that are gray are voice actions that cannot use third-party watch apps, or you have not installed a third-party watch app to make use of them.

1. Your watch shows your agenda.

2. Your watch launches the Google Maps Micro watch app and allows you to get turn-by-turn directions. The Google Maps Micro watch app also launches the Google Maps app on your Galaxy S6, which actually provides the navigation to your watch.

3. Opens the Google Play Music app on your Galaxy S6 and plays music.

4. Sets a timer on your watch.

5. Sets an alarm on your watch.

6. Shows the alarms set on your watch.

7. Shows your heart rate. Tap to choose which watch app launches to show your heart rate.

8. Scroll down for more voice actions.

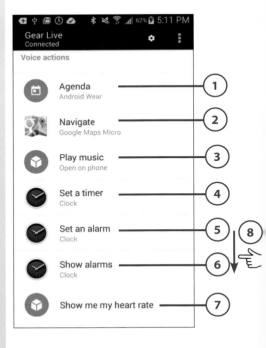

9. Shows how many steps you have walked with your watch on.

10. Starts a stopwatch on your watch. Tap to select which watch app launches to start the stopwatch.

Why Is the Icon Gray?

In the following steps, all of the voice actions shown in the figure have a gray Google Play icon next to them. That icon indicates that there is currently no app installed to handle the function provided by the voice action. After you install an appropriate app on your Galaxy S6, these actions will be available.

11. Call a car to pick you up. Install an app such as Lyft to make this voice action available. If you have two apps installed that both handle this function, tap Call a Car to choose the app you prefer to use.

12. Allows you to launch an app to start a bike ride. Install an app such as RunKeeper to make this voice action available. If you have two apps installed that both handle this function, tap Start a Bike Ride to choose the app you prefer to use.

13. Allows you to launch an app to start a run. Install an app such as RunKeeper to make this voice action available. If you have two apps installed that both handle this function, tap Start a Run to choose the app you prefer to use.

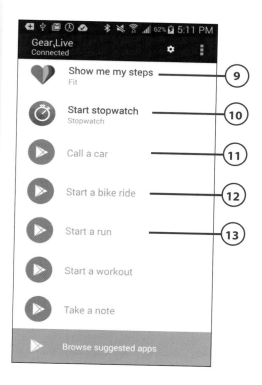

14. Allows you to launch an app to start a workout. Install an app such as RunKeeper to make this voice action available. If you have two apps installed that both handle this function, tap Start a Workout to choose the app you prefer to use.

15. Allows you to launch an app to take a note. If you do not install an app to handle this voice action, when you use this feature, the note you dictate is emailed to your Gmail address. Installing an app such as Chaos Control allows this voice action to launch your favorite note-taking app.

16. Tap to browse the Google Play Store for watch apps to handle voice actions and standalone watch apps that provide additional functionality.

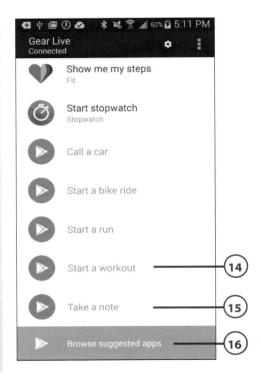

How to Handle Riding, Running, and Workouts

Start a Bike Ride, Start a Run, and Start a Workout are functions that will not work until you install an app on your Galaxy S6 to handle them. It is your choice which apps you want to install to handle these functions. The one used for writing this chapter was RunKeeper. It just so happens that RunKeeper handles all three functions, however that does not mean that you need to use just one app for all three functions. You can install three different apps to handle each of the three functions separately. Your favorite apps that you already use for tracking bike rides, for example, may already support Android Wear. If that is the case, you select that app to support the bike ride function. If you have two apps installed that handle one or more of the functions, tap the function to choose which app you want to use. For example, to change what app handles Start a Bike Ride, tap Start a Bike Ride and choose the app.

Choose a Watch Face

Your watch comes with some pre-installed watch faces, and you can use the Android Wear app to choose which one you want to use. You can also browse the Google Play Store for more. Some watch faces are free; some you must purchase.

1. From the main Android Wear app screen, tap one of the three most recent watch faces to set your watch to use it.

2. Tap More to see all watch faces you have installed.

3. Select a watch face to use.

4. Scroll down to the bottom of the screen and tap Get More Watch Faces to find more watch faces in the Google Play Store.

5. Tap to install a watch face.

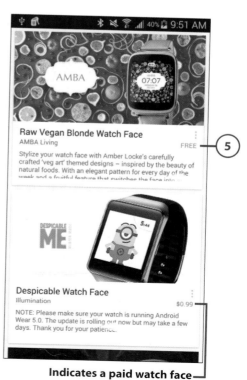

Indicates a paid watch face

6. After your new watch face has been installed, it automatically downloads to your watch and is visible in the Android Wear app. Tap the watch face to make your watch start using it.

7. Some watch faces have configuration options. If the watch face has settings that you can change that affect the way it works, the Settings icon displays over the watch face. Tap it to adjust the watch face's settings.

8. Tap to return to the main Android Wear app screen.

Adjust the Android Wear App's Settings

The Android Wear app allows for some configuration, but it also enables you to view your watch's battery life and available memory.

1. From the main Android Wear app screen, tap the gear icon to see the settings.

2. Tap to choose apps that you no longer want to receive notifications for on your watch. By default, every notification from every app is sent to your watch. Use this setting to select which ones you really care about.

3. Check the box to set your watch to keep a low-resolution monochrome version of the screen on at all times, even when it goes to sleep.

4. Check the box to set your watch to wake up when it detects you tilting your wrist.

5. Tap to see how your watch's battery is performing and how much power each app is taking. Using this screen can help you identify apps that are draining the battery.

6. Tap to see your watch's memory usage, and how much memory each app is using.

7. Check the box to allow a preview of an alert to be displayed on the bottom of the watch screen. If you uncheck this box, there will be no alert previews; however, you can still swipe up to view alerts.

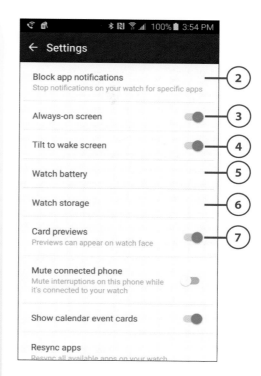

8. Check the box to mute any alerts, notifications, or any other interruptions on your Galaxy S6 while it is connected to the watch. Having this enabled helps cut down having alerts vibrate your Galaxy S6 and your watch at the same time.

9. Check the box to show calendar events on your watch in the form of a card.

10. Tap to resynchronize apps between your Galaxy S6 and your watch. You don't normally need to do this, but if you suspect that an app you recently installed on your Galaxy S6 has not installed a mini-app on your watch, you can tap here.

11. Tap to return to the previous screen.

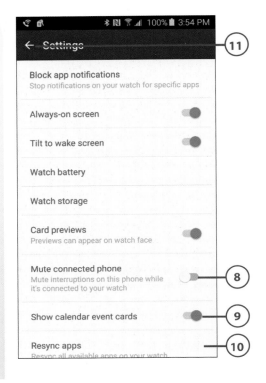

Watch Battery Usage

Viewing your watch's battery performance can help to determine how much longer your watch will last on its current charge based on current usage. You can also see which apps and watch faces are using the most battery time. Watch faces with a lot of animation can use a lot of battery charge. If you see a watch face or watch app that is using a lot of battery charge, you may choose to uninstall the app or stop using the watch face to help your watch last longer on a single charge.

Watch Memory Usage

Viewing your watch's memory usage can help you see if your watch is running out of space, and if it is, which apps and watch faces are using the most memory.

Charge already used

Estimated remaining battery life

Estimated complete power drain

Percentage battery used per app

Memory used

Memory available

Amount of memory used by each app

Install Apps on the Android Wear Watch

Some apps installed on your Galaxy S6 automatically install a watch app on your watch that helps you interact with the app from your watch. There are also dedicated watch apps that can be installed from the Google Play Store.

1. In the Android Wear app, scroll down to the bottom of the screen and tap Browse Suggested Apps.

2. Scroll down to see all of the categories of watch apps. The categories are Watch Faces, New Year, Tools, Social, Productivity, Communication, Health & Fitness, Entertainment, Travel & Local, and Games.

3. Tap More to see more apps in a specific category.

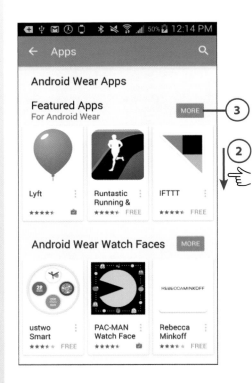

4. Tap an app you want to download. Some apps cost money. This example uses Reversi for Wear.

5. Tap Install.

6. Tap Accept to accept any device or information permission the app needs to run. In this example, the app does not need any permissions.

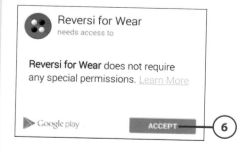

Using Your Android Wear Watch

Now that we have covered how to set up your watch via the Android Wear app, and you've installed some watch faces and apps, let's take a look at using the watch itself.

Watch Features

Your Android Wear watch actually runs on the Android operating system. As of the writing of this book, the version of Android running on Android Wear watches is Android 5.01 (Lollipop). Your watch either has a round or square face, includes an accelerometer to detect movement, a capacitive touchscreen so you can perform gestures such as tapping and swiping, and a microphone to listen for voice commands. Your watch probably also has a sensor to monitor your heart rate and a pedometer to measure your activity. Your watch relies on your Galaxy S6 for the majority of its functions, including voice commands, so you must always have your Galaxy S6 close by to use your watch. Although most Android Wear watches include a physical button, some do not.

Navigate Your Watch

Your watch responds to taps and swipes that allow you to navigate the interface, run apps, and see and respond to onscreen information.

1. While your watch is not being used, the screen becomes low resolution, monochrome, and dimmed to save energy.

2. Lift your arm to view your watch, and the screen turns to full color.

3. Swipe notifications up to read them, and in some cases take actions on them. If you have more than one notification, swipe up repeatedly to read all of them.

Notifications

Notifications

4. Tap the preview of the notification to show more of it, and scroll down to read all of it.

5. Swipe the notification to the left to see any actions that you can take on the notification. This includes an option to block the app so that you don't see notifications from it again.

6. Swipe the notification to the right to dismiss it. To dismiss most apps while using them on your watch, swipe to the right.

7. After you dismiss a notification, if you decide that you didn't want to, you can quickly swipe up from the bottom of the screen, and you see a dismiss timer. Tap the timer to undo the dismiss before it runs out.

8. Swipe down from the top of the screen to see options and settings.

9. Tap to toggle through the Interruption options. You can choose to be notified on your watch for all notifications, priority notifications only, or none.

10. Swipe left to see more options.

11. Tap to put your watch in Theater mode. When in Theater mode, the screen remains blank, you receive no notifications, and the action of lifting your arm to look at your watch is deactivated. Press the watch button to exit Theater mode.

Alternative Method of Activating Theater Mode

You can also double-press your watch's button to set it to Theater mode. Double-pressing the button makes the watch exit Theater mode.

12. Swipe left to see more options.

13. Tap to set your watch to Sunlight mode for five seconds. Sunlight mode sets the screen brightness to the maximum for five seconds to help with bright sunlight.

Alternative Method of Activating Sunlight Mode

If you triple-press your watch's button, Sunlight mode is engaged for five seconds.

14. Swipe left to see more options.

15. Tap to change your watch's settings. See the next section for a description of all settings.

Carmel Clay Public Library
www.carmel.lib.in.us
Saturday February 3 2018 01:48PM
Phone: (317) 844-3361
Telephone Renewal: (317) 814-3936

Barcode: 31690018932187
Title: My Samsung Galaxy S6
Type: BOOK
Due date: 2/24/2018,23:59

Barcode: 31690018824392
Title: Kindle Fire HD manual : the de...
Type: BOOK
Due date: 2/24/2018,23:59

Total items checked out: 2

Visit our website to view
your account details and
material due dates.

Adjust Your Watch's Settings

Use this section to adjust your watch's settings. To enter your watch's settings, you can either swipe down from the top of the screen and swipe left until you see the Settings icon, or tap your watch screen and scroll down to Settings.

1. Tap to manually adjust the brightness of your watch's screen.

2. Tap to pair your watch with Bluetooth devices such as Bluetooth speakers.

3. Scroll down for more settings.

4. Tap to toggle Always-on Screen on or off. When this is off, your watch screen no longer switches to the low-resolution mode when it goes to sleep; instead, it turns off completely.

5. Tap to toggle Airplane mode on or off. When in Airplane mode, your watch is not able to communicate using Bluetooth to your Galaxy S6.

6. Tap to power off your watch.

7. Scroll down for more settings.

8. Tap to restart your watch. All your information remains untouched; your watch just restarts.

9. Tap to reset your watch. This puts the watch back to the way it came out of the box, and all your saved information will be lost.

10. Tap to change your watch face.

11. Scroll down for more settings.

Choosing a New Watch Face

To change your watch face, swipe left and right to see all your installed watch faces and then tap the one you want to use.

12. Tap to change the size of the font used on your watch.

13. Tap to see information about your watch, as well as whether there is an update for it.

Tap to choose

Dark analog

Swipe left and right

Use Your Watch and Run Watch Apps

Your watch was designed to be used with your voice. However, you can also manually select functions and apps by tapping and swiping on the screen.

1. Wake up your watch by lifting your arm. Alternatively, you can tap your watch's screen to wake it up.

2. After your watch wakes up and the screen turns to full color, say "OK Google." Alternatively, you can tap the watch screen.

StackSocial

3. Your watch is now listening for a command. Say a command to perform an action or start an app. Use the next section to learn how to use each command and launch watch apps.

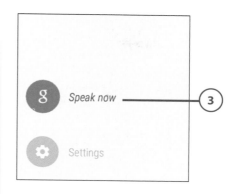

Use Watch Functions and Watch Apps

Your watch is designed for voice commands. However, if you don't speak, your watch stops listening and allows you to select functions and run apps using the touchscreen. It is your choice how you want to perform the following functions—either by speaking or by touching.

1. Say "Settings," or tap to see the Settings screen.

2. Say "Start Reversi" to start the Reversi app installed earlier in this chapter, or tap the Reversi icon to start it. Remember that Reversi is a watch app, so you must say "Start." You can also start watch apps by saying "Run." (for example, "Run Reversi").

3. Scroll down for more options.

4. Say "Start Stopwatch," or tap to start the Stopwatch watch app.

5. Say "Take a note," or tap and speak the text of the note, to take a note. For example, you can say "Take a note to drink more water" and a new note is created with the text "Drink more water." If you have previously installed an app that handles notes, the note is saved to that app. Otherwise, your note is emailed to your Gmail account.

6. Say "Remind me," or tap and speak the reminder to add. For example, you can say "Remind me to go for a run at 7 a.m." and a new reminder is created labeled "Go for a run" set for 7:00 a.m. the next day. You can also set recurring reminders. For example, you can say "Remind me to make coffee at 8 a.m. every weekday."

7. Scroll down for more options.

8. Say "Start a run," or tap to launch the app you installed to handle your runs. Start running and use the watch app you installed to monitor your run.

9. Say "Show me my steps," or tap to show how many steps you have walked. Your watch uses its built-in pedometer to keep track of your steps.

10. Say "Show me my heart rate," or tap to activate your watch's heart rate monitor. Follow the instructions to allow your watch to take your heart rate.

11. Scroll down for more options.

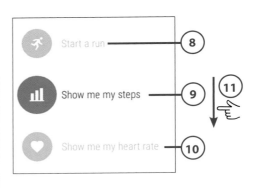

12. Say "Send text," or tap and speak the name of the recipient and the text message to send a text message to someone. For example, you can say "Send a text to Jim, see you later" and a new text message is created addressed to Jim with the text "See you later." If the contact has more than one phone number, you need to say the phone number to use, for example "Send a text to Jim mobile."

Contact Recognition

You must enable contact recognition for the "send a text" and "send an email" functions to work. To do this, on your Galaxy S6, tap Settings, Accounts, Google, Accounts & Privacy, and check the box next to Contact Recognition.

13. Say "Email," or tap and speak the name of the recipient and message. For example, you can say "Email Jim, you free on Friday?" and a new email is created addressed to Jim with the body of the message set to "You free on Friday?" If you have more than one person with the same name, and you are not specific, you are prompted to say the person's full name. If the person has more than one email address, you are prompted to say the one to use (for example, Home or Work).

14. Say "Agenda" or tap to see your agenda for today.

15. Scroll down for more options.

16. Say "Navigate," or tap and speak the desired destination to start turn-by-turn directions to your desired destination. You can say things like "to a pizza place nearby" or "home" or "work," or you can speak an address. Turn-by-turn directions start on your Galaxy S6, with a mini version of them being displayed on your watch.

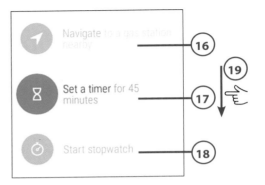

17. Say "Set a timer," or tap and speak the time the timer must use. For example, you can say "Set a timer for 45 minutes." The timer starts on your watch.

18. Say "Start stopwatch," or tap to start the stopwatch app on your watch.

19. Scroll down for more options.

20. Say "Set an alarm," or tap and speak when the alarm must be set for. For example, you can say "Set an alarm for 6 this evening." Before the alarm is finished being created, you can tap Edit to edit the alarm and even make it recurring by selecting certain days of the week when it must trigger.

21. Say "Show alarms," or tap to show the alarms that have been set on your watch. You can edit or remove individual alarms by using the touchscreen.

22. Say "Call a car," or tap to launch the car pickup service you installed on your Galaxy S6 that supports Android Wear, such as Lyft.

23. Scroll down for more options.

24. Say "Play music," or tap to start playing an "I'm feeling lucky" mix on your Galaxy S6. You can also say "Play Depeche Mode" to start playing all songs by Depeche Mode on your Galaxy S6. See the "Playing Music from Your Watch" sidebar at the end of this chapter for more information.

25. Say "Settings," or tap to see your watch's settings.

26. Say "Start," or tap and say the name of a watch app you have installed. For example, if you installed an app called Eat24, you would say "Start Eat 24."

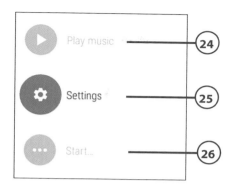

Reply to an Email Using Your Voice

When you receive a new email notification on your watch, you can reply to the email using your voice. To do this, swipe up the email notification. Swipe the notification to the left twice and tap Reply. Speak your reply. When you stop speaking, your watch sends the reply using the message you dictated.

Tap to reply

Speak your reply

>>>*Go Further*

MORE ABOUT NOTIFICATIONS

If there is more than one notification from an app (this is common for email notifications), you see a plus (+) symbol and a number indicating how many more notifications there are from this app. Tap the number, and all the notifications are shown. Tap the one you want to interact with.

Tap to see all notifications from the app

Some notifications you see come from apps that do not provide any way to interact with them. Your only choice is to have your watch tell your Galaxy S6 to open the corresponding app. You can then continue interacting with the app on your Galaxy S6. To do this, swipe the notification to the left and tap Open on Phone.

Tap to open the corresponding app on your S6

>>>Go Further

PLAYING MUSIC FROM YOUR WATCH

It's easy to command your watch to play music that is stored on your Galaxy S6; however, you can also store music on your watch. To do this, open the Google Play Music app, open Settings, and check the box next to Download to Android Wear to download a copy of any music that you choose to your Android Wear watch. To switch to playing music from your Galaxy S6 to your watch, after you say "OK Google, Play music," tap the blue X and tap Android Wear. This then allows you to play only music that is stored on your watch. To hear the music, you need to have a Bluetooth speaker paired with your watch. To switch back to playing music on your Galaxy S6, say "OK Google, Play music," tap the blue X, and tap Phone.

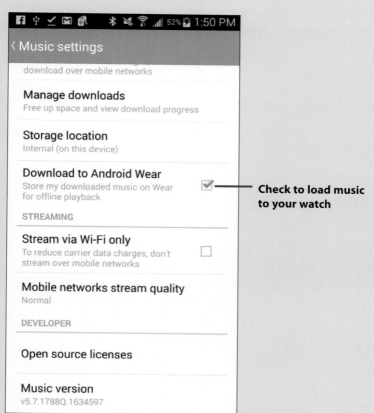

Check to load music
to your watch

Play on phone

Tap to switch to playing
music from your watch

When you choose to play music from your watch, swipe up and down to scroll
through the albums. When you find an album you want to play, swipe left to
choose to shuffle the songs on the album. Swipe left again to see the songs
on the album. Scroll through the songs and tap one to start playing it. If you
try to play music from your phone before you have paired a Bluetooth device
capable of receiving the audio, you are prompted to complete the pairing
process.

Swipe up to scroll
through your albums

Tap to shuffle

Tap a song to play it

Swipe up to scroll
through the songs

Tap to connect a
Bluetooth speaker

Track your health status
and fitness activities

This chapter covers how to use the preinstalled S Health app on your Galaxy S6 or S6
edge to track your health and fitness activities. Topics discussed in this chapter include:

→ Starting the S Health app
→ Creating activity trackers
→ Synchronizing your health data and changing
   settings
→ Tracking your physical activity and status
→ Connecting with related third-party apps and
   accessories
→ Setting activity goals and running programs

Getting Fit with S Health

As you'll probably have your Galaxy S6 or S6 edge with you as you
go places, the preinstalled S Health app makes it easy to use the
device to track your current health. If you don't like what you see
and decide to improve your health with physical activity, you can
tell S Health what activity (or activities) you want to track using your
Galaxy S6.

You can also set health goals for S Health to track over a period
of time. The S Health app contains a number of built-in goals and
programs you can set up to create a fitness plan that's right for you.
Then, over time, you can see the effects of your fitness plan on your
overall health from within the app.

Working with S Health

By default, S Health tracks the number of steps you take and your
running times and trends. You can add or remove trackers to track
as many as 16 different activities including how you walk, your caf-
feine intake, and your blood pressure.

Start S Health

Before you can use S Health, you have to start the app; accept the app terms, conditions, and privacy policy; and learn about the S Health dashboard.

1. Tap Apps on the Home screen.

2. Tap S Health.

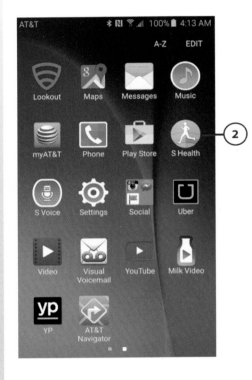

3. Tap the I Agree check boxes on the Terms, Conditions, and Privacy Policy screen. After you tap each check box, the check box turns green and includes a white check mark. Note that this screen opens only when you run the app for the first time. If you don't see this screen, proceed to Step 5.

4. Tap Next.

5. Tap Let's Go.

S Health is for fitness and wellness, not medical purposes.

Terms and conditions

☑ I agree ——

To provide aspects of its functionality, S Health may collect data on the following:

- 👤 Profile
- ▣ Sensors and usage
- ◯ Location

Privacy Policy

☑ I agree ——

③

NEXT → ④

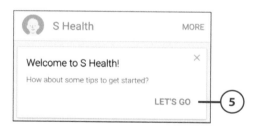

👤 S Health   MORE

Welcome to S Health!   ✕

How about some tips to get started?

LET'S GO — ⑤

6. Swipe up and down in the screen to learn how to add or delete items and customize your S Health dashboard.

7. Return to the S Health screen by tapping the Back icon; the Welcome to S Health tile disappears from the top of the S Health screen.

Add and Remove Trackers

1. In the S Health screen, tap More.

2. Tap Manage Items in the menu.

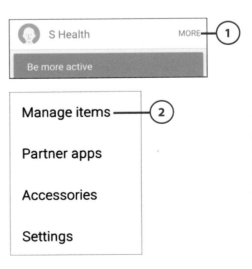

3. In the Trackers tab, the only two trackers turned on by default are the Steps and Running trackers.

4. Turn the tracker off by sliding the slider button from right (On) to left (Off).

5. Swipe up and down in the list to view all the trackers you can add.

6. Add a tracker by sliding the slider button from left (Off) to right (On).

7. When you finish adding and/or removing trackers, tap the Back icon.

Sync Your Health Data and Change Settings

After you set up your S Health account, you may see a notification from the app in the Status bar. The notification icon looks like the S Health icon you saw in the Apps screen. When you open the Quick Settings and Notification Panel, you see a reminder to synchronize your health data with your Samsung account.

If you have a Samsung account, you can synchronize your health data when you view and/or change other help settings. This example presumes that you set up a Samsung account before you launched the S Health app.

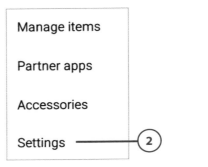

1. Tap More in the menu bar.

2. Tap Settings.

What Happens When I Reset Data?

When you erase all data, you do so both on the Galaxy S6 and in your Samsung account. After the S Health app finishes erasing your data, the app closes and you need to open it again. After you open the app, you'll see the Terms, Conditions, and Privacy screen that you learned about earlier in this chapter.

3. Tap Account to turn on synchronization with your Samsung account.

4. Tap Unit to change the units of measure for height, weight, distance, temperature, and blood glucose levels.

5. Tap Notification to turn notification of S Health events on or off, and also set the notifications to report.

6. Tap Data Permissions to allow the S Health app to share specific data with third-party apps. You find out more about third-party apps you can use with S Health later in this chapter.

7. Tap Reset Data to erase all S Health data you have accumulated since the time you either started tracking or the last time you erased your data. You need to enter your Samsung account password to erase your data.

8. Tap Help for quick information about using S Health.

9. Tap About S Health to view information about the S Health app and check for app updates.

10. Return to the S Health screen by tapping the Back icon.

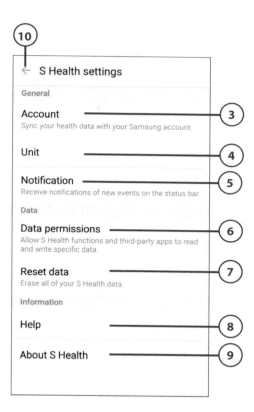

Using Activity Trackers

After you set up your activity trackers, you can begin using one or more trackers to monitor your physical activities. This example uses the Steps and Sleep trackers because those are two common physical activities.

Set Daily Step Goals and Track Your Steps

When you track your daily steps, you can see how many steps you've taken over a 24-hour period. What's more, you can see how the number of steps you've taken in a day compares with the number of steps you've taken in recent days as well as your daily activity goal.

1. Tap the Be More Active tile.

2. Tap Info to get more information about how to be more active.

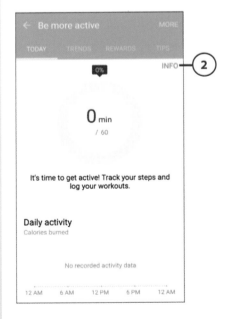

3. Swipe upward in the list to view a summary of your daily activity, number of calories burned, the distance you've traveled all day, and the longest period of active minutes.

4. Tap the Trends tab to view your recorded activities over the period of one week and see how the number of steps each day compares with other days and with your daily goals during the week-long period.

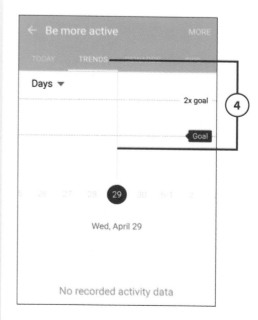

5. Tap the Rewards tab to view any rewards that S Health gives you for meeting goals. If you have no rewards, you see "No rewards" on the screen.

6. Get more tips for being more active by tapping the Tips tab.

7. Swipe up and down to view all the article summary tiles. S Health periodically adds new health articles to the Tips screen for you to read.

8. Read an article on the screen by tapping View More in the tile.

9. Tap More to open a menu with more options.

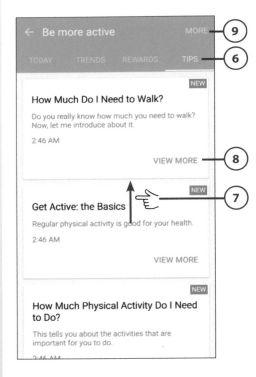

10. Tap Edit to remove one or more articles from the Tips screen. You don't see this menu option when you view the Today, Trends, and Rewards tab screens.

11. Tap View Goal Details to view information about your fitness goal.

12. Swipe within the timeline to change the number of minutes per day you want to be active. The default number of minutes is 60.

13. Tap Info to get recommendations for the number of minutes you should be active each week.

14. Tap Cancel Goal to cancel your goal of being more active and return to the S Health screen.

15. Tap the Back icon to return to the Be More Active screen.

16. In the Be More Active screen, tap the Back icon to return to the S Health screen.

17. Tap the Steps tile to view how many steps you've taken.

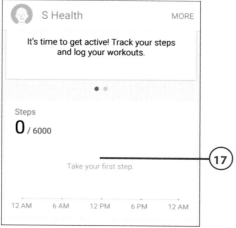

18. Tap Info to get tips about how many steps you need to take for good fitness.

19. View the number of steps you've taken today and compare them with the targeted number of steps.

20. View the number of steps you've taken over the last 24 hour period in the chart.

21. Swipe down the screen to view more Steps data.

22. View the current distance you've traveled, how many calories you've burned, and how many steps you've taken at a healthy pace (100 steps per minute for 10 minutes).

23. Tap the Trends tab to view your recorded steps over the period of one week and see how the number of steps each day compares with other days and with your daily goals during the weeklong period.

24. Tap the Rewards tab to view any rewards that S Health gives you for meeting your step goals. If you have no rewards, you see "No rewards" on the screen.

25. Tap More to open a menu with more options.

26. Tap Set Target to set your daily target for number of steps in a day.

27. Tap Pause Counting Steps to have S Health stop counting the number of steps until you tell it to resume by tapping More again as you did in Step 25 and then tapping Start Counting Steps.

28. Close the menu by tapping the Back touch button.

29. Return to the S Health screen by tapping the Back icon.

Track Your Sleep

Getting a good night's sleep is important for everyone, and if you're concerned about your sleep patterns, you can tell S Health when you go to sleep and when you wake up. After a period of time you'll be able to see your sleep pattern and determine if you need to make changes to your sleep schedule.

1. In the S Health screen, swipe down the screen until you see the Sleep tile.

2. Tap the Sleep tile.

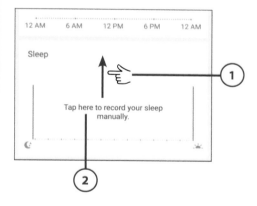

3. View sleep data for the previous or following day by tapping the left and right arrows on either side of the current date.

4. Tap the date button to change the date within the calendar window that appears at the bottom of the screen.

5. Record your sleep times by tapping the Record Manually button.

6. Tap the Bedtime date and time button to set your bedtime day and time in the date and time screen.

7. Tap Save to save the bedtime date and time.

8. When you wake up, repeat Steps 1 through 5 and then tap the Wake-Up Time button to set the wake-up day and time in the day and time screen.

9. Tap Save to save your wake-up date and time.

10. Tap Cancel to return to the Sleep screen without setting your bedtime and/or wake-up time.

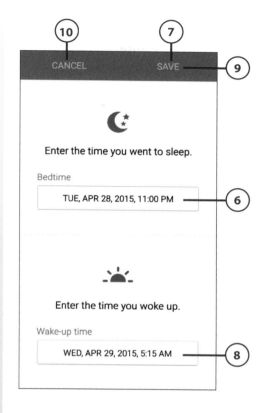

11. Tap Trends to view sleep data over the past few days.

12. Swipe left and right in the Days chart to view sleep data for previous and/or subsequent days.

13. Tap Days to change the chart monitoring period between Days, Weeks, and Months.

14. Return to the S Health screen by tapping the Back icon.

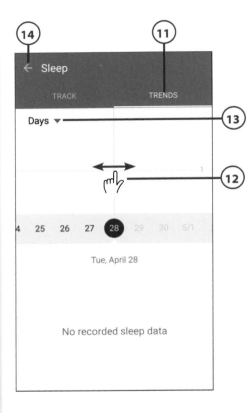

Viewing Partner Apps and Settings

Samsung has partnered with a variety of hardware and app accessories that work with S Health to enhance your monitoring experience and give you even more tools to stay active and healthy.

1. In the S Health screen, swipe up in the screen until you see the partner tiles.

2. Tap one of the partner tiles to learn more about the partnership offer in your preferred web browser app.

3. Tap More.

4. Tap Partner Apps in the menu.

What Must I Do to Register My Fitness Device?

Before you register your fitness device, you need to turn your device on so your Galaxy S6 can find your device using a wireless technology such as Bluetooth. The Galaxy Apps or the Google Play app may also open so you can install an app on your Galaxy S6 that is necessary to operate the fitness device.

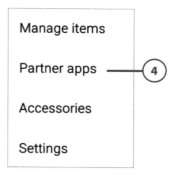

5. Swipe up and down the screen to view all the partner app tiles.

6. Each partner app tile contains the name of the app, the company that produced the app, and a brief description.

7. You can get more information about the app and download it within the Google Play Store by tapping the download icon.

8. Return to the S Health screen by tapping the Back icon.

9. Tap More as you did in Step 3 and then tap Accessories in the menu.

10. Swipe up and down the screen to view fitness hardware accessories from Samsung and partner companies.

11. Tap View More to view more accessories in the Samsung Accessories or Partner Accessories category.

12. Tap the accessory in the list to open the device screen and view the device. Within the device screen you can also get more information from the company website and also register your device on the Galaxy S6.

13. If you're in the device screen, return to the Accessories screen by tapping the Back touch button.

14. Return to the S Health screen by tapping the Back icon.

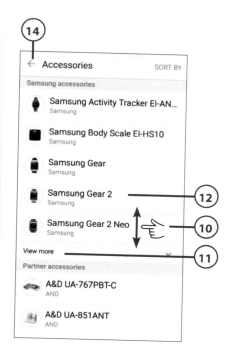

Setting Goals and Creating Running Programs

The S Health app has several preset goals, and each goal takes you step by step through setting your daily goals such as how many calories to eat in a day. If you're a runner, there are also several programs that you can initiate in S Health to prepare you to run up to 10 kilometers (10K), or 6.2 miles.

1. Tap More in the menu bar and then tap Manage Items as shown in Steps 1 and 2 of the "Add and Remove Trackers" task.

2. Tap the Goals tab.

3. Select a goal from Be More Active, Eat Healthier, or Feel More Rested. If you're already working toward a goal, the In Progress text appears underneath the goal name.

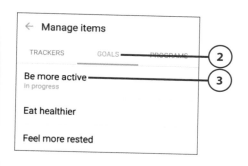

4. The screen you see next depends on the goal you selected. You can follow the step-by-step instructions on the screen to set up your goal, or you can return to the Manage Items screen by tapping the Back touch button.

5. Tap the Programs tab.

6. Select the type of run you're looking for. If you're just getting started, tap Baby Steps to 5K.

7. The next screen you see depends on the program you selected. You can follow the step-by-step instructions for creating a workout program over a period of weeks, or you can return to the Manage Items screen by tapping the Back touch button.

8. If you decide you don't want to set a goal or program, tap the Back icon to return to the S Health screen.

Index

REGISTER THIS PRODUCT

SAVE 35%*

ON YOUR NEXT PURCHASE!

How to Register Your Product

- Go to quepublishing.com/register
- Sign in or create an account
- Enter the 10- or 13-digit ISBN that appears on the back cover of your product

Benefits of Registering

- Ability to download product updates
- Access to bonus chapters and workshop files
- A 35% coupon to be used on your next purchase – valid for 30 days
  To obtain your coupon, click on "Manage Codes" in the right column of your Account page
- Receive special offers on new editions and related Que products

Please note that the benefits for registering may vary by product. Benefits will be listed on your Account page under Registered Products.

We value and respect your privacy. Your email address will not be sold to any third party company.

* 35% discount code presented after product registration is valid on most print books, eBooks, and full-course videos sold on QuePublishing.com. Discount may not be combined with any other offer and is not redeemable for cash. Discount code expires after 30 days from the time of product registration. Offer subject to change.

quepublishing.com